Thinking about Social Thinking

Thinking about
Social Thinking

The Philosophy of the Social Sciences

Antony Flew

Basil Blackwell

First published 1985

Basil Blackwell Ltd
108 Cowley Road, Oxford OX4 1JF, UK

Basil Blackwell Inc.
432 Park Avenue South, Suite 1505,
New York, NY 10016, USA

British Library Cataloguing in Publication Data

Flew, Antony
   Thinking about social thinking: the philosophy of
   the social sciences.
   1. Social Sciences—Philosophy
   I. Title
   300'.1   H61

   ISBN 0-631-14189-8
   ISBN 0-631-14191-X Pbk

Library of Congress Cataloging in Publication Data

Flew, Antony, 1923—
   Thinking about social thinking.

   Bibliography: p.
   Includes indexes.
   1. Social sciences—Philosophy.   I. Title.
   H61.F59 1985   300'.1   84-28452
   ISBN 0-631-14189-8
   ISBN 0-631-14191-X (pbk.)

Typeset by Freeman Graphic, Tonbridge, Kent
Printed in Great Britain by
Whitstable Litho Ltd., Whitstable, Kent

Contents

1   What is to be Done

Although I am mainly interested in the methods of physics ... I have also been interested for many years in the problem of the somewhat unsatisfactory state of the social sciences ... and especially of social philosophy.

Sir Karl Popper, *The Open Society and its Enemies*, vol. I, p. 2

Our treatment will be adequate if it achieves the sort of illumination appropriate to its subject-matter. For the same precision is not to be sought in all enquiries, any more than it is in all the tasks of manufacture.

Aristotle, *Nicomachean Ethics*, 1094B11–14

The present book is, in the first place, an essay in the philosophy of the social sciences. It is intended to be serviceable as a setbook for courses such as already are taken by many whose main studies are in either philosophy or sociology; and which should, surely, be required of all those who aspire to become any sort of social scientists. In this aspect the book belongs to a fairly crowded class. For instance, that class includes: first, two different works – by, respectively, Alan Ryan and Vernon Pratt – both called, simply and straightforwardly, *The Philosophy of the Social Sciences*; second, Michael Lessnoff's *The Structure of Social Science*; and, third, David Papineau's more aggressively titled *For Science in the Social Sciences*. All these four, however, as well as all those others in the same genre which we have been able to examine, have a scope narrower than that of *Thinking about Social Thinking*.

The most succinct way of indicating the nature of the extra is by saying that the present book also does, and has to do, some things of the sort done in exemplars of two other kinds. The first of these other kinds is concerned to bring out that and why so much of what is both offered and accepted as social science is so bad: Stanislav Andreski, *Social Sciences as Sorcery,* for example, or Digby Anderson, *The Ignorance of Social Intervention.* The second is that of coaching guides to a general intellectual self-improvement: such as *Straight and Crooked Thinking* by R. H. Thouless – a minor masterpiece in its day but now, inevitably, dated – or my own *Thinking about Thinking.*

It is with the needs of students in mind that the present book is furnished with both an Index of Names and an Index of Notions, the hope being that the latter will serve as a checklist for purposes of revision. Partly but only partly for the same reason it makes far more references to the classical philosophers than are to be found in most works dealing with the philosophy of the social sciences: such references should, by displaying connections, help those whose chief interests lie in other areas.

But the main reason is, as we shall see, that certain of these classical philosophers said, and said well, things which remain very much to the point. They also contributed various concepts which are, for better or for worse, still employed in what it has been suggested that we call "*developing* subjects" – a mischievous allusion to the established euphemisms under which formerly backward countries are now described as underdeveloped or, better, as developing (Anderson, 1980, p. 55: here, as always later, except where due notice is given, the emphasis in quotations is that of the original text). Some, including one who was a classical philosopher in both the narrower (upper case) as well as the broader (lower case) sense of the adjective, must be allowed to rate as themselves creative social scientists.

One wry yet formidably important example of such a conceptual contribution is what Sir Karl Popper christened Method-ological Essentialism. This ultimately derives, by way of Aristotle, Hegel and Marx, from Plato's Theory of Forms (or Ideas, or Essences). These etherial, timeless, unchanging Platonic Ideas, laid up in a heaven accessible only to the pure vision of the intellect, are together supposed to constitute the immaterial infrastructure of our everyday world of common sense and common experience. All such banausic, changing, merely sensible, material realities are in truth – Plato would have us concede – unrealities. Hence, the Methodological Essentialist argues, the truly scientific student of social institutions must seek to discover their essential natures. Thus the essence of the state, once discovered, will be both what the state originally was and what it is bound to remain. No doubt it could be destroyed; it might (or it might not!) simply 'wither away'; but what cannot happen is any progressive transformation into something substantially different. (Popper, 1956, vol. I, pp. 32, 109 and 220–1; and vol. II, pp. 5ff. and 291–2; Popper, 1957, ch. I, sec. 10; and compare Engels, 1878 and 1884 and Lenin, 1917.)

If we were to accept these misguiding and – any genuinely critical Marxist ought to object – entirely undialectical principles, then we should have to conclude that, because Greek and all other drama originated in religious rites, therefore every current Broadway or West End production must be – essentially, and the misleading appearances notwithstanding – a religious rite.

As for those classical philosophers with claims to be accounted something else as well, the least contestable case is, surely, that of the creator of the discipline of political science? For besides his *Politics,* with its extensive and always astringent critique of utopian proposals made by Plato in *The Republic* and *The Laws,* Aristotle both wrote his own study of *The Constitution of Athens* and inspired or cajoled pupils and associates to produce similar studies of the constitutions of over one hundred and fifty other Greek city states. Nor should we forget the great Smith, whose two Scottish chairs were both in philosophy rather than in economics. (The first holder of the first chair of Political Economy to be established in the United Kingdom was in fact Thomas Robert Malthus. This was at the college set up by the old East India Company for the training of its future executives, a college later to become the independent school which educated the Prime Minister of Britain's first parliamentary majority Labour government.)

1 Some neglected essentials, for our attention

Many, perhaps most, of the introductions to the philosophy of the social sciences which are at this time available in print either deliberately disown or fail adequately to treat several topics which certainly are fundamental, and which ought to be central.

All the four listed in the first paragraph of the present chapter, for instance, discuss laws of nature. Yet none of them raises the direct question whether statements of laws of nature carry implications of practical necessity and practical impossibility. On the contrary, one goes so far as to insist that they are statements only of regular succession or regular accompaniment: "A *causal law* states a relation of regular succession between *events* (i.e. changes of state) of specified types, for example, 'When an object is heated, it expands.' Alternatively, one might say: 'Heating an object *causes* it to expand'" (Lessnoff, 1974, pp. 13–14).

This analysis cannot suffice. For it leaves us at a loss to distinguish: on the one hand, statements that regular succession or accompaniment is, just as it happens, a brute fact; and, on the other hand, statements of laws of nature or of causal connection – two different sorts of statements embraced within the single class of nomological propositions. In order to appreciate what the difference is we need to contemplate a celebrated example, the example of the Two Ideal Clocks. This illustration was introduced by the Flemish Occasionalist philosopher Arnold Geulincx (1625–69). He invented it precisely and only in order to bring out that and why such statements of mere 'just as it happens' regularities cannot be equivalent to authentically nomological propositions.

Imagine two ideal clocks, equipped with mechanically independent, perpetual-motion movements; and suppose that no one ever is going to interfere with either movement. Then we shall certainly have, in the tellings of given o'clocks by one clock and the other, perfect series of regular accompaniments. Or – suppose we choose to stipulate that one starts a split second fast on the other – we shall have perfect series of regular successions. Nevertheless no one will want to say: either that a law of nature links these two regularly related series of events; or that members of the earlier cause members of the later. This is, surely, because we all recognize that there are no practically unbreakable connections here. No one could bring about or prevent changes in the readings of one clock by tampering with the readings of the other. Connoisseurs of paradox in the history of ideas may now relish the reflection that the account of what causation involves, indeed of all that it can involve, given by David Hume (1711–76), thus fits perfectly what everyone has always been ready to admit to be a paradigm case of regularity *without causal connection* (Flew, 1982a).

A second equally fundamental topic, and again one nowadays normally either neglected or botched, is that of choice. One of our four listed competitors does at least start his work by asserting, as in Book VI of his *Logic* did John Stuart Mill (1806–73), that "The way we study people will reflect what we take them to be; so that at the outset of social study we have to make up our minds on the question ... what is the nature of the human being ..." (Pratt, 1978, p. 1). Pratt is nevertheless unwilling to insist and expatiate upon the crucial and differentiating realities of choice. These inexpugnable facts need to be stated, loud and clear, from the beginning: we are, and we know that we are, creatures which make, and which cannot but make, choices; and hence, in that very high proportion of all our behaviours which are actions, whatever we do do, we could have done otherwise.

These facts must be for all the social sciences of the last importance. If once they are granted – and given too, what unreconstructed Humeans will not of course concede, that the concept of a law of nature does include notions of physical necessity and physical impossibility – then many of what are vouchsafed to us as findings of social science will have to be dismissed as plain false: a conclusion applying especially to some of the supposed findings most often urged as guides to social policy.

In one excellent recent review of criminological studies the author, level-headed and conscientiously well-informed, complains of those for whom "the individual who is confronted with a choice among kinds of opportunities, does not *choose,* he 'learns deviant values' from the 'social structure of the slum'" (J. Q. Wilson, 1977, p. 63). For, as the same author argues earlier, "if causal theories explain why a criminal acts as he does, they also explain why he *must* act as he does ..." (p. 58). The crucial points – points which we hope to establish more fully in chapter 4, below – are that there neither are nor can be either laws of nature, or necessitating causes, determining that we must act in one sense and no other. If persons truly are acting, then they cannot but be able to act in two or more different and alternative senses. They cannot, qua agents, be inexorably and inescapably necessitated to behave thus and thus, and not otherwise.

A third properly central topic which in most works appears to be almost wholly neglected is that of unintended consequences of intended actions. For, if surely not the only, then certainly still "the main task of the social sciences . . . is the task of analysing the unintended social repercussions of intentional human actions . . . An action which proceeds precisely according to intention does not create a problem for social science . . ." (Popper, 1956, vol. II, p. 96).

A fourth fault in the competition is that it is inclined to imitate those who have given the title *The Philosophy of Science* to what has in reality covered only the philosophy of physics (Toulmin). As Lord Rutherford used to say in the Cambridge of the thirties: "In science there is only physics; and stamp-collecting!" This inclination to imitate has two manifestations. One consists in behaving as if the actual conditions of the social sciences and the natural were comparably sound. Most emphatically they are not; and no one with even a modest acquaintance with what is and is not going on in the social sciences would be willing to make outright the claim that they are. That is why, to be halfway adequate, any introductory book here needs to contain some material of kinds to be found in greater abundance in Andreski, *Social Sciences as Sorcery* and Anderson, *The Ignorance of Social Intervention*.

The other unfortunate piece of imitation is concentration on not one but two model social sciences, anthropology and sociology. If we concentrate in this way we neglect not only economics – an established discipline years before Auguste Comte and other Saint-Simonians, more or less simultaneously, coined both the word 'sociology' and the word 'socialism' (Hayek, 1979, pt 2). We also neglect all work directed towards the discovery of the effects and effectiveness of actual or possible social policies. To neglect either is unwarrantably narrow-minded, while the findings or supposed findings of both are in fact all the time being misunderstood by practitioners and misrepresented to the laity. That is why an introductory work aspiring to even minimal adequacy has to include at least some materials of sorts to be mined more richly in such general books as Thouless, *Straight and Crooked Thinking* and Flew, *Thinking about Thinking*. It is the same well-nigh universal relevance of the social sciences to our practical life, combined with besetting confusions about the nature and directions of that relevance, which ought to endow the result with some appeal to a public much wider than that of the students for whom it may be prescribed as a setbook.

2 The way things often are, but should not be

Before proceeding in subsequent chapters to tackle particular major topics of the philosophy of social science, it will be useful, because in a salutary way disturbing, to review a miscellany of falsehoods and fallacies, muddles and misconceptions. Although what follows is indeed a miscellany rather than a systematic collection, all the faults to be pilloried have been drawn from publications by persons enjoying high standing and respect as social scientists. In every case it would have been easy to cite similar gross defects in the output of other workers in the same fields; in every case the bad thinking refers to matters of substantial and obvious human importance; and in every case the issues raised indicate something more widely significant about the too often sorry state of social investigations.

Since it has, however, obliquely, been suggested that, while the rest may be mere "stamp-collecting", anthropology and sociology together constitute the standard-setting physics of the social sciences, it is appropriate to begin with the case of Derek Freeman's *Margaret Mead and Samoa* (Freeman, 1983a). Margaret Mead, who was later to become a doyenne of her subject in North America, published her all-time anthropological bestseller *Coming of Age in Samoa* in 1928. Fifty-five years were to pass before Freeman of the Australian National University was able to follow this with his entirely decisive demonstrations: that every one of Mead's major general claims about the Samoans was not just false but diametrically wrong; and, what is much more significant, that they could have been known to be so on the basis of sources available at the time, but not used.

For instance: whereas Mead assures us that "Samoans never hate enough to want to kill anybody", and that "The idea of forceful rape or any sexual act to which both partners do not give themselves freely is completely foreign to the Samoan mind", the criminal records of the then colonial powers show that, on the appropriate international comparisons, both murder and rape were exceptionally common (Freeman, 1983a, pp. 162 and 244). Verily, to quote the famous nineteenth-century preacher Charles Haddon Spurgeon, "A lie travels round the world while truth is putting on her boots"!

Mead's false findings were derived from misinformation supplied by presumably mischievous adolescent informants, misinformation comfortably fitting into a matrix of extreme environmentalist preconceptions contributed by her own supervisor-guru Franz Boas. (An extreme environmentalist, in this context, is someone maintaining that we are in all things completely creatures of our several environments.) These twenty-five misinformants visited her in the house where she roomed with an American missionary family: she was unwilling to endure the hubbub, and the un-American diet, of a Samoan home.

When confronted long afterwards by indignant Samoans telling her how wrong she had been, or by the contradictory findings of fieldworkers who had thrown themselves more generously into the life of the people they were supposed to be studying, she resolutely refused to correct or to withdraw anything, much less to make an effort to undeceive some of the innumerable readers whom she had unwittingly deceived. Instead, in Prefaces to the 1949, 1961 and 1973 editions of *Coming of Age in Samoa,* she insisted, in a characteristic outburst of obscurantist relativism, that it "must remain, as all anthropological works must remain, exactly as it was written, true to what I saw in Samoa and what I was able to convey of what I saw, true to the state of our knowledge of human behaviour as it was in the mid-1920s; true to our hopes and fears for the future of the world". (Quoted Freeman 1983a, pp. 113–14; and compare p. 327 and passim.)

It appears that Mead felt no pressure from her professional

colleagues to try to put things right. No doubt they were reluctant to be accounted pedants; not even according to Bertrand Russell's definition of that term—"A person who prefers his statements to be true."

Another case of the apparent absence of proper professional peer-group pressures is the failure of the American Anthropological Association to demand the withdrawal of the doctorate awarded by the University of California at Los Angeles to Carlos Castaneda. This was given for what seems to have been a work of strictly stay-at-home fiction, *Journey to Ixtlan: The Lessons of Don Juan*. In its guise as a doctoral thesis this was submitted to the Department of Anthropology under the staider title *Sorcery: A Description of the World* (de Mille, 1976 and 1980). This recent case is made the more scandalous, as well as the more like that of *Coming of Age in Somoa*, by two further facts: that Castaneda's books also are bestsellers; and that he too deploys what are supposed to be anthropological facts in advocacy of what has proved to be a popular world-outlook. (We learn from *The Chronicle of Higher Education* for April 15, 1974 that *Journey to Ixtlan* was Number 4 on the 1973 list of campus bestsellers, immediately behind von Daniken's *Chariots of the Gods?* and in front of two other Castaneda books, *The Teachings of Don Juan* and *A Separate Reality*!).

Contrast these stories of the anthropological scandals with the affair of the bogus N-rays. These were supposedly detected by René Blondlot, a French physicist who had previously achieved distinction by determining the speed of electricity travelling through a conductor. When in 1903 he believed that he had discovered a new kind of radiation, he invented the label 'N-rays'. (This was in honour of his home town of Nancy.) Soon many of his French colleagues also believed that they had succeeded in producing and observing N-rays. So more than one hundred papers dealing with the putative N-ray phenomenon were published by the French Academy. But then Robert Wood, an Englishman, having failed to replicate any of this French work in his laboratory, visited Blondlot in Nancy. He was able at once to demonstrate to everyone's satisfaction or, alternatively, dissatisfaction that all those who had thought they were observing N-rays had been deceiving themselves. Once his report had been published in *Nature*, and reprinted with supplementary material in *La Revue Scientifique*, there were no more credulous papers. And, although the French Academy went ahead with plans to honour Blondlot, it now took care to give a clear hint that this was for all and only his previous good work. So, it may be urged, even the physicists are not infallible? Of course not, but what separates the scientific men from the pseudo-scientific boys is the sincere concern of the former to uncover, and to learn from, the mistakes which it is only human to make (Randi, 1982, pp. 196–9).

From falsehoods about *Coming of Age in Samoa* we move next to a fallacy. A fallacy is, strictly, a mistake in argument, arguments being either valid or invalid; whereas propositions, which may appear as either premises or conclusions in arguments, can, in a similarly strict usage, be only true or false rather than valid or invalid (Flew, 1975, sec. 1.1–1.53). Our particular fallacy now consists in arguing that, because members of one social set are not represented in some occupation or organization in the same proportion as in the population as a whole, therefore members of that social set must be being, whether intentionally or unintentionally, discriminated against, and cannot have enjoyed equal opportunities to pursue that occupation or to enter that organization. We employ the expression 'social set', rather than 'social class' or 'social group', in order to disown any undesired implications that the social sets in question must be either social classes or else other social or racial groups which may either be seen by others, or see themselves, or be organized, as such. By Cantor's Axiom for Sets the sole essential feature of a set is that its members have at least one common characteristic, any kind of characteristic.

Once this currently popular argument is thus clearly spelt out, it becomes obvious that it can go through only on the assumption that abilities, inclinations and the senses of actual choices fall into exactly the same distribution pattern in the social set in question as in the population as a whole. In fact, as one might expect, there is abundant evidence that, for most of the sorts of social sets in which there is most interest, this assumption is wildly wrong (Sowell, 1981a and 1983). So, while it may be reasonable enough to construe very wide differences in outcome as indicating places where it might be worth looking for evidence either of inequalities of opportunity or of hostile discrimination, it is methodologically monstrous to present evidence of differences in outcome as itself and by itself demonstrating either such inequalities or such discrimination.

Yet exactly this fallacious move has been made by many leading sociologists in Britain, in France, and in the USA (Flew, 1981, pp. 49–52); that false assumption was employed as the main prop to support their decision in *Regents of the University of California* v. *Bakke* by four judges of the Supreme Court (438 US 265, pp. 365–6); while both the fallacy and the falsehood are now entrenched in the theory and practice of most organizations charged or charging themselves with the tasks of promoting equalities of opportunity and/or combating racist or sexist discrimination.

Such entrenchment can be seen, for instance, in the use of a factitious concept of structural or institutionalized racism. This is defined as anything whatever the end result of which is any inter-racial inequality of outcome. So this sort of 'racism' may very well include ideally colour-blind procedures in selection or admission (Flew, 1983b). In a book called *Poverty and Discrimination* Lester Thurrow, one of America's best-known younger economists, who has served as an adviser to Senator McGovern and other Democratic leaders, simply defines 'discrimination' as the cause of all actual differences in life-prospects (Thurrow, 1969, p. 9).

The same entrenchment of fallacy and falsehood is manifested also in the ambiguous misemployment of the word 'access'. The fact that you are in certainly proves that you were able to get in. *Ab esse ad posse valet consequentia,* as the Scholastics loved to say: the argument from actuality to possibility is valid. But the fact that you are not in does not prove that you could not have got in; much less that you were 'denied access'.

A suitable textbook example of these faults, found in the report of a major sociological survey, is provided by Raymond Boudon, who previously wrote the Penguin Books guide to *The Logic of Sociological Explanation.* His own later study of *Education, Opportunity and Social Inequality* is introduced in the USA by Seymour Martin Lipset as the work of "France's leading sociological theoretician and methodologist"; who, fittingly, "holds the

chair at Paris once occupied by Durkheim" (Boudon, 1974, pp. vi
and vii). On the first page of his own Preface Boudon defines
'inequality of educational *opportunity* (IEO)' as "differences in the
level of educational *attainment* according to social background".
From this definition he immediately infers that "a society is
characterized by a certain amount of IEO if, for instance, the
probability of going to college is smaller for a worker's son than
for a lawyer's son" (1974, p. xi: emphasis added). Next 'Inequality of social opportunity (ISO)' is defined similarly. The
parallel immediate consequence is that "a society is characterized
by a certain amount of ISO if the probability of reaching a high
social status is smaller for the former child than for the latter"
(1974, p. xi).

Boudon thus from the beginning collapses not just one but two
crucial distinctions. For he is not only confounding outcome with
opportunity. He is also failing to distinguish: on the one hand, the
question whether contestants were treated fairly – whether, that is,
they were all accorded the chance to compete on equal terms; and,
on the other hand, the question of who, even given such ideally
fair competitive conditions, was in fact most likely to win. The
actual chances of success will be equal for all contestants only if
and where those contestants all happen to be in all relevant
respects equally well endowed and equally well disposed.

It is, sadly, as unsurprising as it is significant that Alan Little,
chosen to review Boudon's book for *New Society,* a weekly
journal seen by everyone in Britain engaged in either social work
or social science, completely missed these points. Having faithfully
quoted both of Boudon's disastrous definitions, Little ended
almost on his knees before such "originality in approach, a
mixture of creative imagination and intellectual vigour, a con-
tinual juxtaposition of logic and fact, statistical sophistication,
theoretical acumen and wide reading" (23 May 1974).

The significance of the whole incident is underlined by the
further fact that it was not a social scientist, but rather the
experimental psychologist H. J. Eysenck, who two weeks later
intervened in the correspondence columns to remark: "Boudon
constructs a whole model of education and social opportunity . . .
very much as if every child . . . were an identical twin to every
other child" (6 June 1974). Had Eysenck been willing to incur still

greater unpopularity among professing social scientists, he might have added a mention of a ruling made, at a time when the customer could have any colour he liked just so long as black was his beautiful, in the *Encyclopaedia of the Social Sciences*: "... at birth human infants, regardless of heredity, are as equal as Fords" (quoted in Hayek, 1978, p. 290).

In one of the innumerable books of Radical this or Radical that which started to pour from prestigious presses during the sixties and the seventies one contributor asserted, typically, that "Applied social science assumes the prevailing ideology of 'piecemeal social engineering'. Racialism, poverty, labour 'unrest' or underdevelopment are not seen as the expressions of basic social contradictions but as problems which can be solved by appropriate reforms" (Pateman, 1972, p. 26: the use of inverted commas here, as always later, is that of the original).

A piquant falsification of this statement is provided by David Donnison, at that time Director of the Centre for Environmental Studies, in his Foreword to *From Birth to Seven,* a report on the National Child Development Study (Davie and others, 1972). Although he would then, I think, unlike many of the others employed in the Centre, still have claimed to be himself a piecemeal reformist rather than a wholesale revolutionary, he nevertheless writes: "The patterns glimpsed ... are so deeply embedded in this country's economic and social structure that they cannot be greatly changed by anything short of equally far-reaching changes in that structure." (Here and later, by the way, falsifications are showings to be false; the opposite of verifications.)

In a manner in fact altogether typical of educational sociologists, the authors themselves remark: "Poor housing is often mentioned as one of the contributory causes of school failure" (Davie and others, 1972, p. xvi); and they then proceed to quote the here rather Radical R. M. Titmuss, maintaining that it is impossible to do much good in the schools "while millions of children live in slums without baths, decent lavatories, leisure facilities, room to explore and space to dream" (p. 54). So committed are they to these pessimistic preconceptions that, without for one moment allowing themselves to reflect on educational achievement in any of the places or periods in which all but the most tiny minorities have suffered housing worse than the most deplorable in contemporary Britain, they proceed to calculate how much retardation in reading age is to be put down to overcrowding and how much to the lack of basic amenities. They thus contrive not to grasp the refutatory significance of certain items in their own tables of data.

If their Titmussian assumptions were correct, then, presumably, areas with a lot of overcrowding would also have to have a deal of poor reading. So what do we find, when we take our own critical look at their data? Far and away the worst region in the United Kingdom for overcrowding is Scotland, where 39 per cent of children live in conditions rated 'overcrowded'. In none of the other regions distinguished did the figure go above 20 per cent, and four were below 10 per cent. Now what about the percentages of those accounted 'good readers' and 'poor readers'? Still without apparently noticing its relevance, they give the decisive answer: "In reading attainment the most striking feature to emerge from the results (Fig. 34) is that the proportion of good readers (Southgate reading test score 29–30) in Scotland is markedly higher than in any other region of Britain. The difference is even more marked for poor readers (score 0–20). For example, for every eighteen poor readers in Scotland there were, proportionately, twenty nine poor readers in England and thirty in Wales" (pp. 107–8).

From Birth to Seven has not been the only report on the NCDS in which well-publicized conclusions have not in fact been sustained by the data deployed in their support (Cox and Marks, 1980 and 1982). The worst feature of this present case, however, is not so much the invalid derivation of support for a false preconception. It is, rather, the consequent failure to press the question of how we are to account for the apparent superiority, at least in the teaching of reading, of Scottish schools. For if only we could discover the correct answer it could, presumably, be put to use helping teachers in England and Wales to do better.

Nor should such concern to improve education this side of total social revolution be mistaken either to imply or to warrant any lack of concern about wretched housing. This diversionary and false suggestion might perhaps be most appropriately seen off by pointing out that a housing policy precariously erected upon similarly blinkered and prejudiced research would be unlikely to achieve the best possible outcomes for its putative beneficiaries.

We arrive next at two common modes of misrepresentation, through which comparatively modest and maybe true contentions become discredited. These misrepresentations make it seem that something manifestly false or otherwise unacceptable is being claimed, when in fact it is not. The first involves a failure to employ the indispensable distinction between necessary and sufficient conditions. This is a necessary condition of that, iff you cannot have that without this; whereas this is a sufficient condition of that, iff you are bound to have that wherever you have this (Flew, 1975, sections 2.15–2.19 and 2.23–2.26: the abbreviation 'iff' should be read as 'if and only if').

To any controversialist it is always tempting to pretend that the opponent who is in fact maintaining only that some condition is necessary has instead rashly asserted that it is sufficient. The second, more comprehensive contention is, of course, much easier to refute. That first employment of the word 'refute' must not, in a book such as this, be allowed to pass without occasioning a warning that it ought never to be abused as a synonym for 'deny'. If I say that she refuted the proposition p, then I am associating myself with her claim, not merely to have said, but also to have shown, that p is indeed false. Perhaps it should further be remarked here that, in the vocabulary of philosophers and logicians, as opposed to that of businesspersons and playboys, a proposition is whatever can significantly be said to be either true or false.

This constant temptation is one to which controversialists do continually succumb. Thus, for example, there are very strong reasons for holding that a pluralist, 'vote the scoundrels out' political democracy can be maintained only on the basis of a pluralist and largely private economy. This important contention is frequently dismissed with snide references to Chile, where the military government has yet to follow the example of those several fellows in Latin America and Southern Europe which have already handed power over to civilian politicians popularly chosen in a freely contested election. That institution, as the protagonists of this contention insist upon emphasizing, is not to be found in any country of the Socialist Commonwealth (Hayek, 1944 and 1979; and contrast, for instance, *New Society* for 13 November 1980, p. 307).

Again, suppose someone makes so bold as to suggest that genetics has some part to play in explaining the differences between human individuals or human sets and that not every infant or every set of infants is, even given the most ideal environment, able to reach the topmost levels of achievement. Then such dissidents may expect to be met, or rather not met, with the true but irrelevant counter-contention that genetics cannot hope to explain all or even most of those differences. Thus in the Penguin Education collection *Race, Culture and Intelligence* (Richardson and Spears, 1972) we can find two contributors, one from a School of Education and the other from a Division of Behavioural Sciences, proudly presenting what they see as a knock-down refutation: ". . . if 80 per cent of adult performance is directly dependent on genetic inheritance, how have the styles of our lives and the patterns of our thinking changed to the extent that they have?" A little later they repeat their failure to distinguish sufficient from necessary conditions in a different context: "It is hard to see how the grading system can be retained when a guarantee of job opportunity can no longer be given" (pp. 74 and 78). So, if ever there were more qualified surgeons than surgical jobs, one would no longer care whether the surgeons who operated on us were or were not qualified?

The second mode of misrepresentation is to urge that anyone who points some similarity between this and that thereby identifies the two terms of the analogy: they must be asserting or implying that this *is* that, and nothing else; or that this is *merely* that. Perhaps because of the high degree of abstraction involved in economic analysis, this mode seems to be a favourite with those hostile either to economics in general or to particular economic writings. Thus a correspondent to *The Times,* provoked by a leading article which "compared the labour of a human being with a commodity such as butter", immediately, yet quite invalidly, infers: that the leader-writer was by this committed to maintaining that the analogy obtains in all respects; and that he "has accepted that human lives can be evaluated *simply* as 'goods' to be bought in the marketplace with the bananas and the butter" (5 July 1977: emphasis added).

One doubts whether the correspondent from whose letter these passages are drawn was aware that she had been anticipated in this kind of objection by such eminent Victorians as Carlyle and Marx, Engels and Ruskin. Thus Marx, attacking Ricardo in *The Poverty of Philosophy,* writes: "To put the cost of manufacture of hats and the cost of maintenance of men on the same plane *is to turn men into hats*" (Marx, 1847, p. 44: emphasis added).

In an article in *New Society* on 'A radical strategy to help the poor?' (29 October 1981) David Donnison, whom we earlier saw introducing *From Birth to Seven,* commends *Poverty in the United Kingdom* (Townsend, 1979). A tribute to some of his professional colleagues is followed by a put-down for the benighted vulgar: "From Charles Booth to Peter Townsend some of Britain's ablest social scientists have devoted the best years of their lives to studying poverty and policies for the poor. The academic quality of their work may explain why their ideas take so long to make any impact on the thinking of ordinary people, and fail to generate any broadly based movement to eliminate poverty."

But, if we undertake the unappealing task of probing Townsend's enormous tome, an alternative explanation forces itself forward. Maybe it was wrong in the third quarter of our century to hope for anything comparable with the fascinating vignettes in the works of Henry Mayhew and Charles Booth. But three faults in this successor are vitiating. First, Townsend is, as he confesses, concerned as much about equality as about poverty: indeed he is far and away more concerned. Second, and consequently, he insists on devising factitious criteria which enable him, to his own satisfaction, to demonstrate the unbelievable conclusion that fifteen million people, or more than a quarter of the population, live in poverty or "on the margins of poverty" – or, rather, they did in 1968–9 when his data were first put on file (1979, p. 275). Third, and again consequently, he has no concrete and practical suggestions for immediate policies to deal with whatever remains of what the despised populace would recognize as real poverty. Instead he confines himself to ritual calls for a total, all-purpose, socialist "transformation of work organization and social relations".

Nor is there any sign that this one "of Britain's ablest social scientists" has ever devoted much critical attention to his proposed ultimate panacea. Had he done so he scarcely could have suggested "extending public ownership" as a means to a "wider distribution of land, property and other [unspecified] assets" (1979, p. 925). For in what way is any individual citizen personally advantaged by the establishment of yet another state monopoly, even when that monopoly is not drawing vast direct and indirect subsidies from (that same individual as) the exploited taxpayer–consumer? Certainly, in making calculations of income and wealth distribution, here and elsewhere, Townsend himself is no more inclined than anyone else to add in estimates for the value of every citizen's notional shares in the various nationalized industries.

The only halfway relevant reason for adding an appeal for more nationalization is the same as for intruding a chapter on 'The Rich' into what is supposed to be a study of poverty. It is that Townsend seems to be stirred more by a craving for (relative) equality rather than by any longing to improve the (absolute) condition of the worst off. Necessarily, however, equalization is advanced as much by grinding down the rich as by elevating the poor.

We have to regret that Townsend did not put the Rowntree Trust's original grant to rather different and more practically constructive use. An excellent – and most appropriate – example for him to have followed would have been that of Seebohm Rowntree, whose discoveries about the prevalence in York at the turn of the century of genuine, absolute, hardship-producing poverty did a lot to prepare politicians and public for the attacks on that evil launched by the great reforming Liberal administration of 1906. Indeed the time which elapsed between the publication of *Poverty, a Study of Town Life* and the election of that administration was exactly half that between the collection of Townsend's interview data and the appearance of that most obese of Penguins, *Poverty in the United Kingdom*.

Donnison, of course, will have no truck with any such unsophisticated, plebeian talk of relieving hardship. Instead he asks, disdainfully: "What do the British mean by poverty?" He notices that in the answers given to Townsend's interviewers "scarcely anyone gave poverty the egalitarian, relative meaning ('It's when you can't have the things which everyone else has') which Town-send himself uses." Yet Donnison seems not to see any of the theoretical implications of this not very surprising finding. For, in so far as Townsend is concerned with inequality rather than with poverty, as ordinarily understood, this must distance his work from that of Booth or Rowntree. And, given that this is true about Townsend, Donnison's rebuke to the benighted laity is like nothing so much as that of an egregiously insolent Marxist-Leninist reproaching plain old-fashioned democrats for refusing to support Communist policies; while explaining this refusal by referring to the obtuse inability of the democrats to appreciate "The academic quality" of that similar persuasive redefinition which allows him to describe Soviet Germany as the German Democratic Republic.

Both Townsend's work and Donnison's commendation of that work show how social research and social policy can be and often are vitiated by a failure to make, sometimes perhaps by a deliberate determination to collapse, the distinction between two utterly different policy objectives. One is that of establishing a welfare floor or safety net such that no one needs to fall below some specific absolute level. Another is to make the relative condition of all – or perhaps only of all but the elite of equalizers – as near as may be equal. The first of these two different possible objectives could be labelled Good Samaritan, the second Pro-crustean (Flew, 1983a).

2 Our Reasons for Acting

I say the following about the Whole ... Man is that which we all know.

> Democritus of Abdera: Fragment 165,
> in H. Diels, *Fragmente der Vorsokratiker*

Perhaps the simplest and most psychologically satisfying explanation of any observed phenomenon is that it happened that way because someone wanted it to happen that way.

> Thomas Sowell, *Knowledge and Decisions*, p. 97

Scientists or would-be scientists approaching a fresh subject area are like emigrants about to set foot upon an unknown continent. If that continent happens to be uninhabited, then – as Milton said of Adam and Eve after the expulsion from Eden – "The world [is] all before them, where to choose." But suppose that already there are indigenous settlers and settlements. Then our immigrants will have, either to search out vacant lots in the interstices of existing habitation, or else to find means to dispossess some of the previous occupants. In this respect the investigatory fields of the social sciences resemble the already partly settled continent. For, unlike the stars above, people offer and have every right to offer both descriptions and explanations of at least some of their own movements. The aspiring social scientist has, therefore, either to show that some or all of these prior descriptions and explanations are illegitimate, or else to excogitate new questions which no one before has thought to ask or been able to answer.

1   How we explain ourselves

The sort of self-explanations offered by those peculiar creatures which we are is explanation of conduct in terms of the agent's reasons for doing what is done, or for deliberately not doing what is deliberately not done. These reasons, as we all know, will, in so far as they are the true reasons, be the wishes, purposes and intentions of the agent; and they will refer to that same agent's not necessarily correct beliefs about the situations in which the actions are performed. It is to this sort of explanation that, in deference to Max Weber (1864–1920), the label 'verstehen' is applied; 'verstehen' being the German word for 'understand'. As the motto quotations of the present chapter indicate, it is, where it is available, "the simplest and most psychologically satisfying explanation". For indeed, since people are what we all are, "Man is that which we all know."

With most phenomena, of course, explanations of this peculiarly satisfying sort are not available. The fact is that most phenomena do not happen "because someone wanted it to happen that way". The progress of the natural sciences and of cosmological thought has, therefore, required the expulsion of all such anthropomorphic notions from innumerable areas where neither human agency nor anything like it in fact occurs. Later, in chapter 3 below, we shall be going on to argue that no one has any claim to be an initiated social scientist until they have become almost obsessively aware how many of the consequences of human action, including many consequences which we are overwhelmingly tempted to put down to design, were not themselves intended.

The first presupposition, therefore, of the provision of explanations of this sort is that the behaviour to be explained did indeed constitute intended action. Action is rated social when it takes account of the actions of other people. If we remember that Weber preferred to speak of meaning rather than of motives, purposes or intentions, then we can fix this point in mind with a single, short, classical quotation: "Action is social in so far as, by virtue of the subjective meaning attached to it by the acting individual (or individuals), it takes account of the behaviour of others" (Weber, 1904, p. 88).

Conduct to be explained in this way has to be, always given the beliefs of the agents about their situations, intelligibly related and appropriate to the claims made in the explanation offered. (Perhaps it will be useful to introduce two dog-Latin terms here: 'explanans' for what is vouchsafed by way of explanation; and 'explanandum' for what it is which is to be explained.) It is these requirements of intelligibility and appropriateness which alone give purchase to accusations of hypocrisy. For if intentions were like causes, and if any intention in any circumstances could conceivably give rise to any kind of conduct, just as – as Hume maintained – anything could conceivably be the cause of anything; then we should never be able to conclude that someone's actual conduct proved that their real motives must have been both other, and far less creditable, than those they professed so fervently.

Whereas hypocrites are supposed to be aware of their real motives, those subject to unconscious motivation are not: precisely this is half of what is meant by describing motives as unconscious. (The other half, which perhaps applies only in the primary psychoanalytic context, consists in so extending the notion of a motive that what is not under the agent's control may nevertheless be said to be motivated; albeit unconsciously – Flew, 1978, ch. 8.) It has, for instance, been suggested that in sentencing, which is certainly an activity subject to the will, Norwegian judges unconsciously discriminate against working-class offenders (Aubert, 1964).

A second unavoidable limitation upon this sort of explanation is that it cannot employ any concepts not available to the agents themselves. Sociologists, anthropologists, and indeed any other third parties whom anyone cares to mention may, of course, be able and inclined to subsume particular actions under their own several preferred concepts; and, in so doing, they may succeed in indicating some significance in those actions additional to that which the actions had for the agents themselves at the time of acting. Those agents, however, cannot actually have acted for any reasons which they were not equipped to understand.

The obverse of this observation is that, if they are to achieve the peculiar understanding which agents are able to have of their own actions, then the sociologists, anthropologists and A. N. Others have got first to master the concepts employed by those agents. Only those who have mastered the rules, and thus the concepts of chess are able to understand what chess players are doing. Only when he is fluent in the language of his adopted tribe can the anthropologist be sure that he understands what the tribespersons know themselves to be doing, and what their reasons are for doing those things. Suppose that some Unidentified Flying Object (UFO) were, for once, actually to identify itself as a spaceship from a planet in another galaxy, discharging a platoon of Bug-Eyed Monsters (BEMs). If, however superior their intelligence, these were too different from us to be able to acquire our concepts, then, notwithstanding any possible strong powers to predict our behaviours, they still could not achieve this special *verstehen* understanding of our conduct.

It is nevertheless altogether familiar to us all, even to those who have never been exposed to anything deserving the name of science, whether natural or social. So it was entirely fair for Andreski to use one of the big books of Talcott Parsons as an example of what Andreski ridicules as "Rediscovering America". For, after much fretting over *The Structure of Social Action*, Parsons does rediscover something which everyone else already knew. He finally dignifies his rediscovery with the pretentious label, "the voluntaristic theory of action" (Parsons, 1968; and compare Andreski, 1972, ch. 6).

A third fundamental point, related to the second, is that agents respond to their predicaments as they themselves believe these to be. They respond, that is to say, to their perceived situations rather than to their actual situations. The latter may be vitally different. Some writers, taking this important point, have gone on to argue that investigators should attend only to perceived and never to actual situations: to do the latter, they say, would be to fall into the new deadly sin of ethnocentrism (Sumner, 1940).

Because it requires us to conceal interesting and potentially revealing problems arising from the subsistence of (often glaring) gaps between what people contrive to believe and (what might seem to be the inescapably obvious) facts of their actual situations, this is a serious mistake. The philosopher anthropologist Ernest Gellner makes much here, and rightly, of two findings from his own fieldwork among the Moroccan Berbers. Igurramen (singular, agurram) are in Morocco highly respected. They perform important functions as arbitrators, and so forth. There is no manifest procedure for selecting igurramen, who are believed to be chosen by God. They are also believed to be: both abundantly, even fecklessly generous; and yet eternally prosperous (B. Wilson, 1970, pp. 43–5).

The ethnocentric scientific observer is bound to raise two questions. First, allowing that the ultimate explanation of everything must lie in the inscrutable will of the First Cause, still what are the humbler secondary causes through which God operates in order to make his secret selections publicly effective? Second, since no one could for long be both so generous and so prosperous, how is it that at least those Berbers who are not themselves igurramen manage to maintain two such, in the short run and practically, incompatible beliefs?

Writing as I am in the thirtieth week of a miners' strike, it might seem that our sociologists would be hard put to go on not pressing several similar but much more domestic questions. How is it that a large part of the British public persuades itself that the demands of unions in and on the nationalized industries are not at the same time demands on themselves as taxpaying citizens? Certainly all of us in fact are, through our very high taxes and in other ways, already contributing heavily to support the British coal industry: both by supplying various large subsidies, direct and indirect; and by paying for enormous investments, investments which almost no one would judge to be prudent on any strictly commercial basis. So why does the common call, 'Support the miners!' never meet the rude response, 'We already do; and far, far too abundantly!' Such a response might well be considered rather ungenerous or wholly deplorable. But here that is not the point. There are many other appeals to which many people respond in ways which are ungenerous or deplorable. Why not to the demands of strikers in nationalized industries, especially when these industries are already massively subsidized?

The fourth fundamental is that there is an enormously large number of kinds of behaviours – including, surely, all those which are peculiarly and distinctively human? – in which the possession of certain concepts is a presupposition of the performance: these concepts are thus integral to performances of these kinds. It is this which makes the by now often quoted methodological manifesto of B. F. Skinner, a leading American behaviourist psychologist, egregiously grotesque: "We can neither assert nor deny discontinuity between the human and subhuman fields so long as we know so little about either. If, nevertheless, the author of a book of this sort is expected to hazard a guess publicly, I may say that the only differences I expect to see revealed between the behaviour of a rat and a man (aside from enormous differences of complexity) lie in the field of verbal behaviour" (Skinner, 1938, p. 442).

No doubt experiments upon rats must be, somewhere, as essential as they are convenient. Yet to write 'only' here is like excusing the omission of the Prince of Denmark on the ground that he is only one character in *Hamlet*. That it is possible to concentrate on the behaviour of rats and pigeons without attending to any verbal behaviour is a clear sign that experimental psychology, so pursued, is not a human, much less a social science. The French anthropological writer Lévi-Strauss, in *Tristes Tropiques,* uttered one lucid, succinct and true proposition: "Qui dit homme, dit language, et qui dit langage dit société" (Lévi-Strauss, 1955, p. 421; and compare Leach, 1970).

In deference to Emile Durkheim (1858–1917), another Frenchman with a German name, consider suicide. To suicide it is necessary: not only to do something which you expect will result in your own death, and consequently to die; but also to do it with that intention, and consequently to die. It is thus possible, appealing to the principle of double effect, to argue that, when Oates walked out into an Antarctic blizzard, his sacrificial death was not a suicide. Here and later, readers may find *A Dictionary of Philosophy* useful, both to learn more about people mentioned, and to fill vocabulary gaps (Speake, 1984).

Again, it may be too much, with La Rochefoucauld, to claim: "Few men would fall in love if they had not heard about it." Yet it is the unexaggerated truth to insist that embarking on or continuing a married life, as opposed to mating and cohabiting as do the birds, is impossible for creatures not possessed of the notion of a long-term union, and hence incapable of intending any such union. Nor is this truth to be escaped by cynical references to duplicity. For even to pretend to intend, or falsely to promise, such permanent fidelity requires an understanding of what it would be to fulfil that promise.

Besides activities which cannot be understood by others without possessing notions with which the agents explain themselves, and activities in which it is impossible oneself to engage without having the relevant constitutive and directive concepts, there are also, as the Cambridge philosopher Elizabeth Anscombe has indicated, those which cannot be properly understood by an observer altogether unable to perform the activities in question. Her point applies, for example, to mathematics but not to acrobatics. None of this, however, has any tendency to show that there is something viciously subjective or projective about verstehen explanations.

Certainly that is hinted by talk of this understanding as involving a "rediscovery of the I in the Thou" (Dilthey, 1961, p. 67). It becomes more explicit in the assertion: "It appears to be a basic assumption of *verstehende Soziologie* ... that what we know within our minds is somehow more intelligible than what is outwardly observed. But that is to confuse the familiar with the intelligible" (Ginsberg, 1956, p. 155).

My knowledge of your reasons for doing what you did is, like all my other knowledge, my knowledge; and that I know facts about you is a fact about me. But this does not make it any the less of an objective fact that you did it, and did it for those reasons; an objective fact, that is, in the sense of a fact altogether independent of any whims or wishes of mine. Contemplate, and cleave to, the true and unsubjective tale of Willie Sutton – the least sociologically corrupted of bank-robbers. Asked why he robbed banks, Sutton replied, with utter integrity: "Because that is where the money is."

A more elaborate, incorrigibly perverse doctrine of subjectivity and projection is among those taught as sociology of education in the University of London Institute of Education, as well as preached from the radio pulpits of the Open University (Young, 1971; and compare Flew, 1976a, chs. 2 and 3, and Dawson, 1981). In what must be the most bizarre contribution to a preposterous setbook, Alan Blum, now of York University in Toronto, gives his answer to his own curiously Kantian question:

'How is sociology possible?' It is, he concludes, "easy to see that the methodical character of marriage, war and suicide is only seen, recognized and made possible through the organized practices of sociology. These regularities do not exist 'out there' in [a] pristine form to which sociologists functionally respond, but rather, they acquire their character of regularities and their features as describable objects only through the grace of sociological imputation. Thus, it is not an objectively discernible purely existing external world which accounts for sociology; it is the methods and procedures of sociology which create and sustain that world" (Young, 1971, p. 131).

Blum himself appears to think it unnecessary to produce here any warrant for drawing these professionally megalomaniac conclusions. But other evidence suggests that, in so far as they have any basis at all, they are based upon misunderstandings of some of the fundamentals discussed in the present section 1. None of these, however, provides any good reason for asserting – what is manifestly false – that "the methodical character of marriage, war and suicide is only ... made possible through the organized practices of sociology." Nor is the consequential fact that certain things can be truly said only of people who possess some relevant concepts a good reason for maintaining that these things cannot even be true of anyone until someone else turns up actually to make the appropriate assertions – that indispensable someone else being, of course, a sociologist equipped with those same essential organizing concepts.

As for Blum's own answer to his Kantian question, it must in truth be an absolute presupposition of the existence of sociology as a science that there are people – or, as Blum prefers to say, "societal members" – capable of doing their own social things, without benefit of sociologists and their imputations. It must be: just as much as it is an absolute presupposition of the existence of the science of the heavens that the stars in their courses exist and revolve in their own right, and are not mere creatures or fictions of the Astronomer-Royal. The truth is flat contrary to what Blum asserts. There has to be, as there is, "an objectively discernible, purely existing external world which accounts for sociology". It cannot be, and it is not, "the methods and procedures of sociology which create and sustain that world". If it were, then that would constitute the decisive reason: both for dismissing its pretensions to be any sort of science; and hence for closing down all schools, departments, and institutes of sociology.

2 Dispossessing such explanations: (i) by reform

There are two quite different ways in which aspiring social scientists may hope to challenge explanations of the familiar kind discussed in section 1. The first maintains that some sets of such explanations are in fact partly or wholly false. The second urges, much more radically, that in some way all must be inadequate or bogus.

The first sentence of the Preface to *The German Ideology* reads: "Hitherto men have constantly made up for themselves false conceptions about themselves, about what they are and ought to be" (Marx and Engels, 1846, p. 23). Such false notions are forthwith, and very forthrightly, contrasted with the intractabilities of objective truth.

The authors then proceed to develop their own distinctive and potentially fruitful conception of ideology. All ideas, it is said, have material causes: "The production of ideas, of conceptions, of consciousness, is at first directly interwoven with the material activity and the material intercourse of men, the language of real life" (1846, p. 37). But now systematically erroneous notions, usually linked together into some sort of system, are contrasted with correct appreciations of how things actually are. In this understanding ideology is essentially erroneous. A system of ideas is ideological to precisely the extent that it is wrong, and in as much as the error is the work of concealed interests and more or less unconscious motivations: "If in all ideology men and their circumstances appear upside-down as in a *camera obscura*, this phenomenon arises just as much from their historical life-process as the inversion of objects on the retina does from their physical life-process" (1846, p. 32).

When the word 'ideology' is employed in this way the interest is epistemological, concerned with what and how we can know. The opposition is between, on the one hand, falsehood and distortion, and, on the other hand, a clearly focused true picture. Realism requires that we labour to expose false consciousness for what it is: "Whilst in ordinary life every shopkeeper is very well able to distinguish between what somebody professes to be and what he is, our historians ... take every epoch at its word and believe that everything it says and imagines about itself is true" (1846, p. 64). Such wretched, Brand X, pseudo-historians thus share – in a memorable phrase – "*the illusion of that epoch*" (p. 51).

The word 'ideology' is, however, also employed, from the beginning, in a quite different sense. Especially when the interest is metaphysical, and when Marx and Engels therefore want to affirm the ontological primacy of the material over the ideal, everything in the second of these two great fundamental categories counts as ideological, or as an element in ideology: "Conceiving, thinking, the mental intercourse of men, appear at this stage as the direct efflux of their material behaviour. The same applies to mental production as expressed in the language of politics, laws, morality, religion, metaphysics ..." (1846, p. 37). So in this second sense the term 'ideology' embraces, neutrally and non-committally: not only everything which is ideological in the first interpretation; but also all sound ideas involved in truly reporting the plain facts. (These first two different senses need nowadays to be distinguished from a third, in which a person's ideology consists in their particular values and general world-outlook.)

Always when any key term is ambiguous or of otherwise indeterminate meaning it becomes imperative that all those introducing that term begin by indicating which sense or what sense they favour; and equally imperative that they remain constant in their fidelity to that choice. For the sociologist, as the Marquis de Vauvenargues insisted it was for the philosopher, "clarity is a matter of good faith".

Nevertheless, in many recently popular works, sound practice would appear to be an exception rather than the rule. Consider, for instance, *Ideology in Social Science: Readings in Critical Social Theory,* a paperback collection which certainly sold well in the seventies. Although the Editor eschews any unequivocal ruling, both the fact that 'Critical' is here a code-word for 'Marxist' and the contrast drawn in his first sentence suggest that he is at least starting from the first of the three interpretations just now distinguished: "The essays in this collection seek to challenge the prevailing ideologies in the social sciences and to indicate scientific alternatives to these ideologies" (Blackburn, 1972, p. 9; and compare Flew, 1976b).

Then in the second paragraph there is a reference to an "essay by Gareth Stedman Jones entitled 'History: the Poverty of Empiricism'". In this paragraph we hear tell of ideology "in an entirely different sense". The nearest we get to an explanation of this proposed sense is, however, in the next sentence but two: "The choice of a particular field of investigation, the choice of a given range of concepts with which to investigate that field, all express assumptions about the nature of society and about what is theoretically significant and what is not." We are thus, within the space of a single short paragraph: both shown how, in the proposed new sense, ideology is for the scientist unavoidable; and assured that this is a sense which still permits us to "counterpose science to ideology" (1972, pp. 9, 9–10 and again 9). In the ordinary exoteric senses of the word such work scarcely merits the diploma self-description 'critical'.

Again, in this and too many similar books, terms such as 'Positivism' and 'Empiricist' – terms ending with the suffixes 'ism' or 'ist' – are employed, or misemployed, in violation of the most basic principles of clear thinking. Take a recent book by the professor in what was formerly the most fashionable of 'the Shakespearian Seven' new universities. Without attempting to explain what, if anything, he himself proposes to mean by the key term, this sociologist considers whether Durkheim and Weber were positivists; speaks of critical theory "in its assault on positivism"; tells us that among "the principal features ... of recent paradigms" are "an attack on positivism"; and draws attention to Marcuse's contrast between "critical reason" and "positivist sociology" (Bottomore, 1984, pp. 3, 20, 26 and 52). Finally, without noticing the self-destructive significance of this belated addition, he adds a note to his first employment of the word: "The question is further complicated by the variety of meanings attached to the term 'positivism'" (p. 10)!

Something must also be said to throw light on the contentions that "Conceiving, thinking, the mental intercourse of men, appear as the direct efflux of their material behaviour"; and that, in terms of two other favourite images, the ideological superstructure is some sort of reflection of the material foundations. Again, and more perplexing, "Legislation, whether political or civil, never does more than proclaim, express in words, the will of economic relations" (Marx, 1847, p. 70).

Such contentions recall the thesis of Epiphenomenalism. This, like Occasionalism or Two-way Interactionism, is one of the rival answers to the problem of mind and matter as set by Descartes (1596–1650). In that Cartesian formulation the question is: 'What are the relations between consciousness and stuff?' The Epiphenomenalist maintains that consciousness is always an effect and never a cause. With mind and body it is, it is suggested, as with phosphorescence on water and the water below or – with one mischievous American philosopher – the halo over the saint and the saint beneath. The effects are produced by ongoings in the water – or the saint – but these effects never react back upon their causes (Flew, 1964).

Epiphenomenalism, like several similar doctrines, makes a strong, immediate appeal to all who think of ourselves as tough-minded and down-to-earth. For how, after all, could anything so etherial and insubstantial as a moment of consciousness or an idea bring about any effects in the real world of matter in motion? "The general conclusion", according to the classic Preface to the *Critique of Political Economy*, "can be summarized as follows. In the social production of their existence, men inevitably enter into relations ... The totality of these relations ... constitutes the economic structure of society, the real foundation on which arises a legal and political superstructure, and to which correspond definite forms of social consciousness ... It is not the consciousness of men that determines their existence, but their social existence that determines their consciousness" (Marx, 1859, pp. 20–1).

The compelling straightforwardness and seeming inevitability of such doctrines disappears just so soon as we begin to probe their content. How bold and how comprehensive are the claims which they are actually making? Or, better – for it is impossible to exaggerate the importance of putting our test questions this way round – what would have had to have happened, or to be happening, or to be going to happen, in order to prove that the doctrine is not, after all, true (Popper, 1934, and 1963, ch. 1)? Certainly, at first blush, an idea or a moment of consciousness must appear too elusive and too etherial to succeed in either effecting or affecting anything. But now, before we can determine the direction of causal relations, we have to identify their terms. And, of course, once that question has been raised, it becomes obvious why our putative entities appeared doomed to ineffective impotence. For thoughts and pains can be identified only by reference to the flesh-and-blood creatures who have them: it simply makes no sense to speak of thoughts or pains subsisting in detachment from any persons to think the ones or suffer the others. The dependence of consciousness upon the organism which it characterizes is thus as total as Epiphenomenalist heart could desire.

In the Introduction to his 'Contribution to the Critique of Hegel's Philosophy of Law' Marx insists that "Material force can only be overthrown by material force ..." Yet he concedes immediately that "theory itself becomes a material force when it has seized the masses" (Marx, 1843, p. 182). It is no less material a force, though weaker, when it is guiding or misguiding a single individual. For persons inspired by even the most elevated ideas and ideals are just as much ordinarily flesh-and-blood human agents as more sordid persons striving merely to maintain or increase their incomes. Once this is appreciated, do we any longer have any sufficient reason for holding that causal transactions between economic foundations and ideological superstructure can go only one way?

That ostensibly bold and strong general hypothesis was, from the beginning, all set to suffer the death by a thousand qualifications. So we should not be surprised to find Engels, in a very late letter to Bloch (21–2 September 1890), conceding that, while of course it remains absolutely and incontestably true, nevertheless it applies not to the appearances but to the substance, not immediately and superficially but ultimately and in the last analysis: "According to the materialist conception of history, the *ultimately* determining element ... is production and reproduction in real life ... The economic situation is the basis, but the various elements of the superstructure ... political, juristic, philosophical theories, religious views and their further development into systems of dogmas, also exercise their influence upon the course of historical struggles and in many cases preponderate in determining their *form*."

Later still Lenin, without for one moment admitting even to himself what he was doing, went on to abandon, first in the practice of his October coup and then in his theoretical justifications of *Our Revolution*, not only the present hypothesis but also the entire materialist conception of history, of which it is an essential part. In this as in so many other ways Stalin went even further in the direction in which Lenin had led (Hook, 1975, ch. 8; and compare Hook, 1943 and Conquest, 1967, ch. 1).

Consider, for instance, how it is laid down in the Preface to the *Critique of Political Economy* that "No social order is ever destroyed before all the productive forces for which it is sufficient have been developed, and new superior relations of production never replace older ones before the material conditions for their existence have matured within the framework of the old society" (Marx, 1859, p. 21). Then contrast this with Lenin, accepting and indeed underlining the objection that "Russia has not attained the level of development of productive forces that makes socialism possible"; but countering it by asking: "If a definite level of culture is required for the building of socialism ... why cannot we begin by first creating the prerequisites for that definite level of culture in a revolutionary way, and *then* ... proceed to overtake the other nations?" (Lenin, 1922, vol. II, p. 837). No reason, perhaps, no reason at all – except that by making your revolution in one of the least advanced capitalist countries and thereafter building socialism you are bound to falsify (to show to be false, that is) the scientific pretensions of your own so-called scientific socialism.

"And as in private life one differentiates between what a man thinks and says of himself and what he really is and does, so in historical struggles one must distinguish still more the phrases and fancies of parties from their real organism and their real interests, their conception of themselves from their reality" (Marx, 1852, p. 38). Indeed we must. And, furthermore, the categorical imperative of both academic and practical good faith is to exercise the same suspicion – although not, surely, an invincible suspicion? – against every social group and every social institution. Notwithstanding that it is all too often done, it will not do to confine our critical attention to opposing parties and disfavoured institutions. The more sincere we become in our scientific and other stated purposes, the more scrupulous we shall be to recognize and to counter our own inclinations to wishful thinking and self-deception. Not without reason did someone – was it Nietzsche? – describe social study as "the art of mistrust".

In the main Marx and his followers have been interested in what they have perceived as social classes, rather than the actual workings of smaller organizations. Indeed, it has been left largely to people trained in economics, and of an opposite political persuasion, to notice the ideological significance of the fact that people employed in both private firms and public institutions, including those employed at the highest levels, are, just as much as the rest of the human race, apt to strive to maximize their own utilities. A gap thus opens between the official story about the aims of the organization and the true facts of its operation. So that official story necessarily becomes, in the primary and seminal Marxist sense, an ideology.

The story is that all privately owned corporations have a single-minded commitment to profit maximization. But, except in those rare cases in which the pay and perquisites of all employees are very directly linked with the rate of return on capital employed, this is less than perfectly true. And, even in those cases, any individual's share in the profit increase dependent on any particular action or decision may well not outweigh the sum of his or her other, possibly competing, individual utilities. The same is just as true, or even more true, of organizations supposedly dedicated to the fulfilment of some public purpose. The employees will all have – being, along with the rest of us, human – their own private purposes. The pursuit of these may well conflict with the perceived public interest in the purpose of the organization. Indeed the conflicts here are likely to be more important and more extensive. For it is extremely uncommon, and may often be impossible, to link the rewards of individual employees directly, or even at all, with the most economical fulfilment of such public purposes

(Seldon, 1978 and Sowell, 1980, ch. 5; and compare, mischievously, Parkinson, 1981).

The reality of such conflicts, and hence the ideological character of the official stories, came out sharp and cruel in Britain recently when all the public sector labour unions declared their total opposition to putting any of the services at present provided by local or national government out to competitive tender. Under the slogan 'Public service not private profit', they argued that government could always provide the best and cheapest services 'because it did not have to make a profit'. Maybe it could; maybe, maybe. But the union leaders, who were in a good position to know, made it obvious that they did not themselves believe that their members in fact were, always or even most often, providing the best and cheapest possible. For they became, and remain, committed to opposing any testing of the question by putting anything out to tender anywhere. In any such fair and open competition the public sector alternative is, apparently, bound to lose. The outcome of the competition would be – in a giveaway phrase – 'the hole in the dyke'; to be indefinitely expanded by a torrential surge of privatization.

It is unfortunate that in Marx acuteness and a zeal to unmask ideological distortions in the thinking of the class enemy is not paralleled by any anxious awareness of the possibility, indeed the overwhelming likelihood, of similar infections in his own theorizing. This is unfortunate because only by being constantly alert to the danger can anyone hope to avoid or to correct the distortions. Although his prophecies of proletarian revolution and of the wholly happy consequences thereof were based originally upon a high-flying Hegelian philosophical analysis rather than any pedestrian investigations in the Reading Room of the British Museum, Marx appears never to have wondered whether he too might not have succumbed to the temptations of wishful thinking (Marx, 1844, and compare Flew, 1985).

Again, very unlike Darwin, to whom Engels would have had us compare him, Marx never committed himself to any full, clearcut and unequivocal statement of what in their correspondence is referred to as "our view", nor to any review of difficulties seen in squaring that view with the facts. So they always found it easy, after an event, to satisfy themselves that "our view" had not been falsified by that occurrence; however little either of them might have anticipated anything of the sort. Nor could Freud have found in the Marx papers anything to match Darwin's private resolution to make an immediate note of any fact seemingly hard to reconcile with his cherished theory (Flew, 1984, ch. III, sec. 3). Experience had shown Darwin how easily such intellectual inconveniences will be forgotten!

3   *Dispossessing such explanations: (ii) by revolution*

Explanations of actions in terms of desires, beliefs and decisions of the agent may be challenged in two very different ways, one fundamental and the other not. So far we have considered that other; where an explanation of this kind is acceptable, but where the particular specimen previously established is thought to be wrong. But the more fundamental challenge, urging that no such explanation is acceptable at all, comes from behaviourist psychologists and from others under their influence. Thus B. F. Skinner of Harvard, the doyen of them all in the USA, in a popular book under the sinister and threatening title *Beyond Freedom and Dignity,* makes what the dustjacket calls his "definitive statement about man and society".

Skinner's most catastrophic misguiding principle is that, to be scientific, any study of man must eschew all anthropomorphic notions. He begins: "We have used the instruments of science; we have counted and measured and compared; but something essential to scientific practice is missing in almost all current discussions of human behaviour" (Skinner, 1971, p. 7; and compare Flew, 1978, ch. VII). What seems to be missing is, awkwardly, the absence of certain notions which, he wants to insist, can have no place in scientific discourse: "Although physics soon stopped personifying things . . . it continued for a long time to speak as if they had wills, impulses, feelings, purposes and other fragmentary attributes of an indwelling agent . . . All this was eventually abandoned, and to good effect . . ." Nevertheless, deplorably, what should be "the behavioural sciences still appeal to comparable internal states ..." (1971, p. 8). We are, therefore, supposed to regret that "Almost everyone who is concerned with human affairs – as political scientist, philosopher, man of letters, economist, psychologist, linguist, sociologist, theologian, educator, or psychotherapist – continues to talk about human behaviour in this prescientific way" (p. 9).

Certainly such discourse is prescientific, in the obvious but purely temporal sense that it was going on long before there was anything deserving the diploma description 'science'. But Skinner is mistaken in implying that it is not merely, in this innocuous sense, prescientific but also, damagingly, unscientific. He misconstrues the disowning of anthropomorphic notions by physicists as being: not a rejection of misapplications of ideas in themselves entirely proper and indispensable; but a repudiation of notions, or pseudo-notions, which are essentially and irredeemably non-scientific.

Skinner puts his first objection to all these everyday explanatory notions in an awkward way: "... we do not feel the things that have been invented to explain behaviour. The possessed man does not feel the possessing demon and may even deny that he exists ... The intelligent man does not feel his intelligence or the introvert his introversion" (1971, pp. 15–16). Certainly, if we confine ourselves to these examples, there is something in what Skinner says. But this something does not destroy the obvious truth. The man, for instance, who confesses, 'I am determined to make it with Cyn', very obviously does have, and knows without inference that he has, a will, impulses, feelings, and – definitely – a purpose in life. Yet it is "wills, impulses, feelings, purposes", not the higher-order notions of intelligence and introversion, which Skinner wants to dismiss as prescientific fictions.

In order the better to appsreciate what Skinner's first objection really is, we have to turn to certain gurus of social science who have demanded a behaviourist approach. This they have often preferred to label 'positivist' or 'empiricist'. In his *Cours de philosophie positive* Auguste Comte (1798–1857) appears to have been ambivalent. He there wanted to maintain: not only that positive science can admit nothing but behaviour, having no truck with thoughts or desires or anything else supposedly somehow behind and guiding that sole human observable; but also that, because we are ourselves people, we do have what amounts to or is as good as observational experience of such things. They therefore can, after all, be admitted into the solid realm of positive science (Hayek, 1979, pp. 321–32).

In *A Scientific Theory of Culture* the anthropologist Bronislaw Malinowski (1884–1942), without equivocation or hesitation, takes his stand as a defining, paradigm-case Behaviourist: thoughts, beliefs, ideas, desires, and so on can be admitted iff "fully defined in terms of overt, observable, physically ascertainable behaviour" (Malinowski, 1944, p. 23).

Durkheim too, in *The Rules of Sociological Method,* is equally emphatic and categorical: "Social phenomena are things and ought to be treated as things ..."; and "All that is subject to observation has thereby the character of a thing." Ideas, however, "cannot be perceived or known directly, but only through the phenomenal reality expressing them" (Durkheim, 1895, pp. 27–8). Again, "Since objects are perceived only through sense perception ... Science, to be objective, ought to borrow the material for its initial definitions directly from perceptual data" (p. 43). So, finally, to be thus scientifically objective the definition of social facts must "characterize them by elements external enough to be immediately perceived" (p. 35).

To be able to decide whether "wills, impulses, feelings, purposes" are "immediately perceived" or in some other way directly experienced, or whether they are, as has sometimes been asserted, "the phlogiston of the social sciences" (Lundberg, 1963, pp. 53–4), we need to distinguish two radically different senses of 'experience', and hence two correspondingly different senses of 'empiricism'.

In the ordinary workaday interpretation of the word, to claim to have had experience of cows or of political subversion or of anything else is a claim to have had perceptual or other cognitive dealings with various public realities; realities wholly independent of the mind of the claimant. In the second and highly artificial interpretation, an interpretation much favoured by philosophers since Descartes, verbally identical claims would not entail the objective existence of anything. Such a claim would be sufficiently warranted, in the cows case, by the fact that the claimant had had a dream or a waking hallucination featuring cows pasturing in lush meadows. Dreams, however, and hallucinations are mind-dependent and purely private, in the sense that it is simply absurd to speak of dreams and hallucinations existing apart from, and other than as affections of, their subjects (Flew, 1971, ch. VI, sec. 6).

Given the first or public sense of 'experience', then empiricism becomes the surely unexceptionable contention that all claims to knowledge of the Universe around us ought to be somehow based upon, referred back and accountable to, our actual or possible experience. But if we insist on construing the word 'experience' in the second or private sense, then empiricism becomes a most unappealing doctrine. The philosophical constructions of George Berkeley (1685–1743) and David Hume suggest that the empiricist in this second understanding will be hard put to vindicate claims to knowledge of any mind-independent realities. Yet, having discerned these ruinous implications, on no account must we permit anyone to take them as discrediting empiricism in the scientifically fundamental first sense.

But now, given again that familiar first or public sense of 'experience', we have, surely, every one of us had plenty of experience of "wills, impulses, feelings, purposes", and of all the other items so frequently and so confidently mentioned in our explanations both of our own conduct and of that of other people? None of these, of course, are "material things", those "moderate-sized specimens of dry goods" which are often though falsely believed to be the only objects revealed by "direct perception" and found among our hard "perceptual data" (Austin, 1962, p. 8). They are, none the less and undeniably, objects of our everyday experience. As such they are neither to be denied nor ignored by anyone aspiring to develop a science of human beings, as we actually are. Nor, as has been stressed before, is there anything relevantly unobjective or observer-dependent about the facts of people's beliefs, desires, feelings, or what have you. These things are all, if you like, subjective; in the sense of being facts about subjects. But that does not make it any the less a matter of objective fact that some particular subject either wanted this or hated that.

Skinner's second objection to prescientific explanations of conduct arises because he wants to ask and to answer questions other than those to which such prescientific explanations are relevant; and because he believes that different explanations must always and necessarily be competing for the same logical space. Thus he writes: "If we ask someone, 'Why did you go to the theatre?', and he says, 'Because I felt like going', we are apt to take this reply as a kind of explanation" (Skinner, 1971, pp. 12–13).

We are indeed. For that 'I wanted to go to the theatre', or that 'I am determined to make it with Cyn', may fully explain conduct previously found puzzling. What these responses will not do is answer as well the further questions: why I have a taste, and this particular taste, for the theatre; and why I find girls, and in particular Cynthia, so powerfully attractive. But these are the kind of questions which Skinner wants to press: "It would be much more to the point to know what has happened when he has gone to the theatre in the past, what he has heard or read about the play he went to see, and what other things in his past or present environments induced him to go . . ." (1971, p. 13).

There are two general lessons to be learnt here. The first is that explanations are answers to questions, and hence that explanations answering different questions are not necessarily rivals. The second concerns the suggestion that a truly scientific explanation of conduct must refer to some sort of environmental determination.

The first lesson can be taught somewhat frivolously, yet none the less effectively, with the help of an Andy Capp comic strip. The tried and suffering Flo is shown, protesting: "There was twelve light ales in the pantry this mornin' – now there's only ONE! 'ow d'yer explain THAT?" To which her incorrigible husband responds, with deadly predictability: "It was that dark in there, I didn't see it." The cartoonist Smythe felt no call to spell out the ways in which the question intended – about the eleven – differed from the question answered – about the one. Any such superfluous and heavy-footed spelling out ought to have taken notice also of the fractionally less obvious truth that the original challenge was to justify the doubtfully proper rather than to explain the perplexing.

The first moral, therefore, is that there is not just one single, *the* explanation for anything which we may wish to have explained. There may instead be as many, not necessarily exclusive, alternative explanations as there are legitimate explanation-demanding questions to be asked. Before moving on from the present thesis, notice how it can be set to work to resolve some tough interdisciplinary conflicts.

Commenting on 'Is the Brain a Physical System?', a paper by a physiologically oriented experimental psychologist, a philosopher wrote: "It is a matter of fact, indisputable for all that our knowledge of it is pre-scientific, that much of our behaviour is done because we want to act in the way we do, because we have purposes, motives, wants and intentions, and not because some physiological causal sequence, of which we know nothing, produces some movement such as flinching or starting at a sudden loud noise." To this the experimental psychologist replied: "We can already assign physiological causes to certain wants and actions." He went on to say, "A hypothalamic tumour may turn a woman into a nymphomaniac . . ." – a complaint, like satyriasis, about which the loudest complaints tend to come from those not themselves directly afflicted (Borger and Cioffi, p. 135; and compare Flew, 1973).

More, much more, will have to be said later about possible necessitating causes of behaviour (chapter 4, below). But here and now it is both necessary and sufficient to point out that an explanation of why she did what she did, in terms of her beliefs and desires, is by no means necessarily a rival to an explanation, in physiological terms, of why she happens to be subject to the various desires to which she is subject.

The second lesson to be drawn from Skinner's second objection attaches to his reason for preferring to ask only his own favourite kind of question: "A scientific analysis shifts both the responsibility and the achievement to the environment" (Skinner, 1971, p. 25). It is, therefore, according to Skinner, unscientific to claim that anyone ever effected anything. Hence certain unnamed Freudians are rebuked for recklessly "assuring their patients that they are free to choose among different courses of action and are in the long run architects of their own destinies" (pp. 20–1).

Skinner's curious yet common contention is actually inconsistent with the presupposition of universal causality, from which by many it is thought to follow. For, if everything which has a cause is by that fact disqualified from being in its turn a cause, then there can be no causal chains. Every discovery of the cause of what before had seemed to be itself a cause must be sufficient to show that that original seeming cause was not, after all, truly a cause. For all true causes must be themselves uncaused.

Perhaps the main reason why Skinner holds that explanations of human behaviour must be sought always and only in the environment is that he sees any alternative as involving the black beast notion of "autonomous man". This he believes to be the foundation of the to him equally repugnant concepts of human freedom and dignity. Let Skinner explain himself: "Two features of autonomous man are particularly troublesome. In the traditional view, a person is free. He is autonomous in the sense that his behaviour is uncaused. He can therefore be held responsible for what he does, and justly punished if he offends" (1971, p. 19).

Two but only two comments can and need to be made at this stage. The first is that all those who hope to develop human sciences, and in particular social sciences, should without preconceptions study people as we actually are. No one has any business to insist that we cannot be in any way autonomous, and that every bit of our behaviour must be inexorably necessitated; just because it would, supposedly, be so inconvenient and so uncomfortable if we cannot and it were not. The second is that it would be narrow-minded and gratuitously defeatist to despair of erecting a science, in the sense of an orderly and growing structure of authentic knowledge, if ever and wherever we cannot assume such total necessitation. For both in the life of the laity and in the writings of historians we encounter innumerable perfectly satisfactory explanations of human conduct; explanations provided in terms of the new-named yet in fact immemorially ancient "voluntaristic theory of action". And it is, after all, history which is by prescriptive right Queen of the Social Sciences.

4   Action explanation as forever fundamental

Whatever further kinds of questions social scientists may think to ask, and however much extra light answers to these questions may throw upon the institutions and activities studied, explanations of this most familiar kind will remain always both essential and fundamental. This cannot but be so, since all social collectives are composed of individuals, and can act only through the actions of their components. Whatever is said about any mass movement, organized collectivity, or other supposed social whole, must at some stage be related and in some way reduced to discourse about the doings, beliefs, attitudes and dispositions of its components. Who actually did and thought what; and what led them to act and to think as in fact they did, and not otherwise?

All this, once it has been sharply stated, will appear obvious and beyond dispute. Yet it is often forgotten; and sometimes, if only by indirection, denied. Take for example a recent work by a Lecturer in Sociology of Education in Goldsmith's College. In the course of disquisitions on the scurvy doings of such hypostatized abstractions as imperialism, racism and monopoly capitalism, the author finds no occasions, either to mention any particular case of someone advantaged or disadvantaged for no other or better reason than the colour of their skin, or to name as much as one single private corporation even alleged to be enjoying a monopoly position. (It would, of course, have been too much to hope that a man offering *A Marxist Perspective*, and uncritically preaching Lenin as gospel truth, would see imperialism in the maintenance and expansion of the Soviet Empire!) Instead he prefers to write: "It may be useful at this point to indicate how capitalism has grown into a world system of colonial oppression, and how in its economic essence imperialism *is* monopoly capitalism" (Sarup, 1982, p. 94; and compare O'Neill, 1973, pp. 3–26). For him, it seems, these are the real and ultimate historical agents; with mere flesh-and-blood human beings their almost never mentioned creatures. He is even prepared outright to denounce "The assumption that the individual is more important than the group or class ..." (1982, p. 9).

The contrary truth can scarcely be better or more appropriately enforced than with a quotation from *The Holy Family*: "*History* does *nothing*; it 'does *not* possess immense riches', it 'does *not* fight battles'. It is *men*, real living men, who do all this, who possess things and fight battles. It is not 'history' which uses men as a means of achieving – as if it were an individual person – *its own* ends. History is nothing but the activity of men in pursuit of their ends" (Marx and Engels, 1845, p. 93).

The dispute between Methodological Holism or Methodological Collectivism, and Methodological Individualism, is best seen in the perspective provided by the previous three paragraphs. For those denouncing the former and espousing the latter there is no need: either to deny any sort of reality to social wholes, or to maintain that all statements embracing social notions are by logical analysis reducible to statements referring only to single individuals. No such rash commitment is required by their determination to defend the simple truth of the first three paragraphs, and the important consequences to be derived therefrom.

Certainly the Methodological Individualist both can and should concede that, in a way, "The social group is *more* than the mere sum total of its members, and it is *more* than the mere sum total of the merely personal relationships existing at any moment between any of its members." And it is not merely "even conceivable" but a familiar fact "that a group may keep much of its original character even if *all* its original members are replaced by others" (Popper, 1957, p. 17). For this is all true of a nation, or of a club, or of a social class.

But these admissions are not in the least inconsistent with the truth that, in the end and at bottom – as Marx put it in a letter to Annenkov – "the social history of men is never anything but the history of their individual development" (28 December 1846). This is the truth because everything done or suffered by the nation, or club, or class can be done or suffered only in the persons of its members; and because, if and when they and their successors are all dead, nothing will remain of that nation, or that club or that class – nothing, that is, save perhaps documents and memories in the possession of others.

Again, the Methodological Individualist can afford to concede the logical irreducibility of social facts and social concepts. And, as Thomas Carlyle said of the lady who announced her acceptance of the Universe, "Gad, she'd better!" For 'social behaviour' was in section 1 of the present chapter, following Weber, defined as behaviour in which the agent "takes account of the behaviour of others". So there can be precious little if any social behaviour which we are able either to describe or to explain without the employment of concepts referring in some way to social institutions.

Take, for example, what two writers on *Rational Economic Man* offered as the nearest possible approach to a brute and atomic economic fact; an unexplained economic fact, that is, and one not susceptible of further analysis. Contending that "All facts are theory-laden and economic facts are 'visible' only to a man with the right economic concepts", they conclude: "Even if 'Raven no. 1 is black' can claim to be theory-free, 'George paid £1 for string' cannot" (Hollis and Nell, 1975, pp. 96 and 108). Certainly no one could have access to either of these two facts without first mastering the relevant concepts. But this applies equally to both. Nor does it make the second either more theory-laden or less objective than the first. What is peculiar to that second specimen is its employment of the essentially and irreducibly social notion of money. For what is, in general, money and, in particular, one pound sterling is whatever the relevant social set is prepared to admit and to use as such.

The sort of thing which money is is central to most if not all the studies customarily rated social sciences. These have thus been "called the Appearance sciences – those concerned with the phenomena whose very essence it is that they 'mean' something to participants" (Gellner, 1973, p. 152). As John Watkins puts it, pointing the Methodological Individualist moral, "Whereas physical things can exist unperceived, social 'things' like laws, prices, prime ministers and ration-books, are created by personal attitudes. (Remove the attitudes of food officials, shopkeepers, housewives, etc., towards ration-books and they shrivel into bits of cardboard.) But if social objects are formed by individual attitudes, an explanation of their formation must be an individualistic explanation" (O'Neill, 1973, p. 150; and compare Hayek, 1949, ch. III and Hayek, 1979, ch. 3).

Such explanation will not and cannot exclude references to social groups or the use of social concepts. Nor does it have to be only of the sort which the individuals concerned might offer for their own actions. But what is imperatively required is that everyone should recognize, and never forget, that all social activities, and the operations of all social institutions, are and cannot but be the actions of individual human beings. Therefore, whatever else may be added by way of further explanation in answer to further questions, all those actions must be explicable, and at least in principle explained, in terms available to, and understandable by the agents at the time of their acting.

Consider, for instance the "general and obvious statement" that "no superior knowledge the observer may possess about the object, but which is not possessed by the acting person, can help us in understanding the motives of their actions" (Hayek, 1948, p. 60). To this May Brodbeck responds with a rhetorical question: "... can anyone, at this stage of the game, really believe that to explain people's actions we need to know no more than they do, not only about the external world, but about themselves?" (O'Neill, 1973, p. 95).

Suppose now that the announcer whso read out the sentence, which in fact signalled the revolt of the four insurgent generals and the beginning of the 1936–9 Spanish Civil War, was not himself party to the plot. Then no explanation of why he performed the speech act of announcing, "There is a clear sky over Spain", could correctly refer to his intentions to signal a military coup. For, by the hypothesis, he could have had no such intention. The historian, however, trying to piece together his account of how the coup was organized and launched, does need to know what the announcer at the time did not; and also how the plotters contrived to get that sentence inserted into his script.

A more sociological and hence more piquant example is provided by Durkheim. Reviewing, in the December 1897 issue of the *Revue Philosophique,* Labriola's *Essays on the Materialist Conception of History,* Durkheim wrote: "I consider extremely fruitful this idea that social life should be explained, not by the notions of those who participate in it, but by more profound causes which are unperceived by consciousness, and I think also that these causes are to be sought mainly in the manner according to which the associated individuals are grouped."

But earlier, in *The Rules of Sociological Method,* when trying to decide whether either or both of two recorded correlations manifested any causal connection, he tackled the task in a different and more methodologically individualist way. The correlation between secularization and suicide, rather than that between education and suicide, has to be causal if either is. Why? Because Durkheim cannot think of any psychological process through which the acquisition of secular knowledge could weaken the instinct for self-preservation, whereas the loss of the traditional belief that God punishes suicides by tormenting them for ever is, obviously, the removal of a powerful inhibition (Durkheim, 1895, pp. 131ff.).

5　Society as the supposed universal agent

The previous section 4 dealt with two untenable positions which Methodological Individualists are not required to occupy. What they do have to do – resolutely, systematically and persistently – is to refuse to treat any of the most numerous outcomes of various social arrangements, those outcomes which were not in fact planned and intended, as if they were, what by the hypothesis they are not, the planned and intended consequences of the actions of some super-agent, or of some committee of such super-agents. The expression 'the conspiracy theory of society' was introduced, some forty years ago, as a label for the assumption that all outcomes, or at any rate all disagreeable outcomes, are in fact planned and intended (Popper, 1945, vol. II, pp. 94–5). It has turned out to be a rather unfortunate coinage, commonly misused to warrant unargued and contemptuous dismissals of evidence for the existence of conspiracies which undoubtedly do exist (Flew, 1975, sections 4.22–3).

The point which it was originally coined to illuminate is, nevertheless, hugely important. For all of us and, it sometimes seems, not least those with claims to have enjoyed a training in, or pretensions to be actually pursuing, social science, are inclined to detect intention and planning where no intention or planning is, or was. As a first, piquant though antique example consider a passage from *The Condition of The Working Class in England*. Here the revolutionary denounces, as the calculated consummation of capitalist conspiracy, what the social scientist cannot but recognize to have been an unintended consequence of intended action: "To such an extent has the convenience of the rich been considered in the planning of Manchester that the plutocrats can travel . . . by the shortest routes, without even realizing how close they are to the misery and filth which lie on both sides of the road." But then, having denounced "this hypocritical town-planning device",

Engels concedes "that, owing to the nature of their business, shopkeepers inevitably seek premises in main thoroughfares . . . and . . . the value of land is higher on or near a main thoroughfare than in the back streets." So that was how this "hypocritical" result came about, without direct intention, and in "the very town in which building has taken place with little or no planning or interference from the authorities" (Engels, 1845, pp. 55–6).

Again, among those studying or discussing who ends up holding what capitals and enjoying what incomes, it is the almost universal practice to speak of showing how *Society* distributes *its* wealth and *its* income. But in most of the countries to which such studies and discussions refer there is in fact no such centralized, active and controlled distribution. No super-person and no committee decides what everyone is to have and to hold.

The usual response to this objection when, very rarely, it is heard at all is to try to dismiss it as a mere matter of words. The tactic is to suggest that any proposed alternative is substantially synonymous. Therefore, we are asked to believe, the present objection is on all fours with that of the purist protesting at the introduction of the expression 'societal members' as a jargon substitute for 'people', or preferring 'car' and 'lift' to those terse Americanisms 'automobile' and 'elevator'. But the truth is, rather, that it is that usual response which itself parallels the performance of someone saying that the argument among the jury as to whether their Foreman is to say 'Guilty' or 'Not Guilty' is an argument about a mere matter of words. For there the alternatives are not synonymous but actually incompatible, and their alternative implications make a difference – possibly even a life-or-death difference.

The importance of this misemployment of the active word 'distribution' comes out very clearly when we examine what has perhaps been the most influential work of social philosophy published since World War II. For in what he miscalls *A Theory of Justice* John Rawls from the beginning implicitly assumes: both that the distribution of all goods of every kind is or ought to be an activity consciously and deliberately performed by central authority; and that all such goods, whether already produced or in the future to be produced, are available for such distribution or redistribution free of all prior claims of possession or entitlement. It remains for him simply, or not so simply, to work out the principles which ideally ought to guide all such distributions.

Those enormous and unargued assumptions are entrenched in his very definition (not of 'justice' but) of 'social justice'. This is, he says, concerned with "the basic structure of society, or more exactly, the way in which *the major social institutions distribute fundamental rights and duties and determine the division of advantages from social cooperation* ... The justice of a social scheme depends on how fundamental rights and duties are *assigned*" (Rawls, 1971, p. 7: italics supplied). As he begins, so he continues: "For simplicity, assume that the chief primary goods *at the disposition of society* are rights and liberties, powers and opportunities, income and wealth ... All social values – liberty and opportunity, income and wealth, and the bases of self respect – *are to be distributed* equally unless an unequal distribution is to everyone's advantage" (p. 62: italics again supplied).

This is not the place for any examination of the principles proposed, although I have myself had some say elsewhere (Flew, 1981, chs. III and IV). But we do have to emphasize once more how enormous are the two assumptions to which Rawls has, apparently all unwitting, helped himself; and how formidable is the task of justification to which he would be committed had he not tacitly taken it for granted that such universal active distributions are everywhere occurring, accepted, and acceptable. For there are or will be prior claimants on all the various goods so far produced and in the future to be produced. So Rawls needs to show that all these claims ought to be of no account compared with those of his would-be all-providing state.

Certainly too there are many – to put it mildly – opposed to such a vast extension of the role of the state. Otto von Bismarck is not often seen as an opponent of centralized, state power. But he said to the Imperial Reichstag (17 September 1878): "If every man has to have his share allotted to him from above, we arrive at a kind of prison existence where everyone is at the mercy of the warders. And in our modern prisons the warder is at any rate a recognized official, against whom one can lodge a complaint. But who will be the warders in the general socialist prison? There will be no question of lodging complaints against them, they will be the most merciless tyrants ever seen, and the rest will be the slaves of the tyrants" (quoted Schwartzschild, 1948, p. 364).

To speak of Society distributing wealth and income where there is no active, central distribution is lamentably careless; and can be, as we have just seen, very seriously misleading. But the next pair of cases calls for a much stronger condemnation. For here we have two notions introduced and strenuously propagated in the name of social scientific enlightenment. These notions suggest, and are surely intended to suggest, that many things which are not in fact the intended results of intended action, on the contrary in fact are. And, furthermore, these notions are being widely and energetically employed – especially in programmes for Women's Studies, Peace Studies, Black Studies, and the like – in order to incite the victims of the suggested sinister intentions to react in ways which all would agree to be appropriate if their supposed victimization was indeed actual and intended (Flew, 1983b; and compare Cox and Scruton).

Both the provenance and the prevalence of these two factitious concepts constitute excellent reasons for reiterating one of the chief contentions of chapter 1. Many things in the social science and social policy worlds are not as they ought to be. So a philosophical introduction needs to contain materials of kinds neither found nor required in introductions to the philosophy of the physical sciences or of biology.

The first member of the present pair is the concept of structural or institutionalized racism. Now racism, in the only proper sense of that properly abusive word, is an essentially intentional as well as an utterly deplorable business. It is a matter of advantaging or disadvantaging people for no other or better reason than they are members of some particular favoured or disfavoured racial group (Flew, 1976, pt I, ch. 5 and Flew, 1983b). But the new sin of institutionalized racism is discovered wherever in any occupation, grade, social class, social club or what have you, any racial group is not represented in as near as makes no odds the same proportion as in the population as a whole. It is not necessary to show that anyone actually has exercised any racial preference, or that anyone actually has gained or suffered by reason of the mere fact of their racial group membership.

Edmund Burke once declared – in his speech on conciliation with America (27 March 1775) – "I do not know the method of drawing up an indictment against a whole people." But we can now do better, or worse. A whole society, a whole people can be condemned – as the British and the Americans today constantly are – for pervasive, endemic, institutionalized racism. Given what is known, or what can be known, about the huge differences, both in inclination and performance, which there may be and have been as between different immigrant groups of the same or different race but with different cultural backgrounds, the only escape from this charge would seem to be the introduction of some universal and comprehensive system of racial quotas (Sowell, 1975, 1981a and 1983). That, however, is something which ought to be, and is, utterly unacceptable and repugnant to every authentic opponent of (old sense) racism.

The second member of the pair is structural or institutionalized violence. Once again, violence in the original and proper sense is essentially intentional. A paradigm case of your doing violence to me would be your striking me in a way calculated to cause grievous bodily harm. The reason, furthermore, why people react to injuries caused by violence in ways different from those in which they react to injuries not so caused precisely is that they do, correctly, perceive the injuries caused by violence as intended. This perception is clearly relevant to questions about the relevance of their various reactions since, whereas intenders may possibly be constrained, deterred or punished, neither constraint, not deterrence, nor punishment can be applied without an intending agent.

It is a remarkable index of the bemusing and diversionary power of prejudice that many students in recent years have contrived to overlook both this defining characteristic and its decisive importance. Thus an academic lawyer, of all people, writes in a BBC publication *The Lawbreakers*: "Why then is violent behaviour perceived as so socially problematic? The answer may seen obvious: because it injures people. However, upon closer examination, such an answer turns out to be inadequate. Other forms of behaviour which are not legally or commonly defined as violence turn out to be much more injurious."

But what is supposed to be the full, true and sociologically sophisticated answer comes from the man who was to become

Professor of Sociology in the Open University, writing to assist the Department of Health and Social Security with his social scientific wisdom: "... to understand why we fear certain behaviour of young people we must explain how that behaviour comes to be classified as violent behaviour." It seems that it becomes so classified by the fiat of the press or of TV, which "gives it a certain meaning". Events which are, presumably, in themselves unobjectionable are thus made to frighten people. A "moral panic" ensues (quoted, Morgan, 1978, ch. 3).

It is, therefore, not surprising that those subject to such indoctrinated scotoma, capable of this degree of perversity in hypothesis, should be receptive to a concept of institutionalized or structural violence; a concept which permits them to include as the effects of violence every variety of injury and misfortune, including, indeed including especially, injuries and misfortunes not in fact intentionally inflicted. And, even though they may themselves not have noticed either that true violence is essentially intentional or that it is this logical fact which supports the disturbing and affronting overtones of the word, they are nevertheless bound to think, because ingrained speech habits are just as hard to break as any other ingrained habits that all these things must be, as the effects of violence, intended. Any society, or usually it is only any society not yet fully socialist, thus becomes one in which all the ills to which flesh is heir are inflicted intentionally. It is manifest that such a society can be redeemed, if at all, only by the most total revolutionary transformation.

Finally, as the satyr play of the tetralogy, the light relief after a trilogy of tragedies, consider how after the second General Election of 1974 *New Society* interpreted the verdict of that strange, single but many-headed beast the British Electorate. Other journals, of course, lapsed in similar ways. But the charade performed in *New Society* is the most significant, since that journal pretends to do for the social sciences what *New Scientist* does do for the rest.

The first leader in *New Society* began: " 'Now go back and get on with governing the country' – this sounds like the main message from the electorate to their (mainly) reelected MPs" (31 October 1974). It went on, with its attention concentrated exclusively upon the House of Commons, to consider two possible dangers: "the oppression of the majority by a coalition of minorities"; and "the oppression of a bare minority by a bare majority."

But, of course, it is not the case that either British Society in general or those millions of individuals who turned out and voted constitute a single organism with a perhaps enigmatic will, which chose a Parliament with a particular party constitution. In fact every voter voted for one or other of an always fairly short list of candidates: voters had no other choice. When we look at these choices, which were that leader-writer's only evidence for determining the will of the electorate, we see that it was not a bare majority of the electorate, but fractionally less than 40 per cent, which put its individual crosses against the name of the local candidate of the party which achieved a parliamentary majority.

The scandalous fact, concealed by this leader-writer's mystificatory personification of the British Electorate, is that the result of that election, as of every other General Election for the last fifty years, has been the oppression of the majority by a minority. No party since 1935, not even Labour in 1945, has won an absolute majority of all votes cast; and there has always been a large proportion even of individual constituencies in which a majority of voters voted against the candidate elected. Such are the effects of a monstrously unfair, unrepresentative and undemocratic electoral system. But the moral for us now is that what social science is wanted and needed for is, not to conceal and to mystify, but to reveal and to clarify, the actual workings of our social institutions.

3 Making Visible the Invisible Hands

> But it is only for the sake of profit that any man employs a capital in the support of industry ... As every individual, therefore, endeavours as much as he can ... to employ his capital ... that its produce may be of the greatest value; every individual necessarily labours to render the annual revenue of the society as great as he can. He generally, indeed, neither intends to promote the public interest, nor knows how much he is promoting it ... By directing ... industry in such a manner as its produce may be of the greatest value, he intends only his own gain, and he is in this as in many other cases, led by an invisible hand to promote an end which was no part of his intentions. Nor is it always the worse for the society that it was no part of it. By pursuing his own interest he frequently promotes that of the society more effectually than when he really intends to promote it.
>
> Adam Smith, *An Inquiry into the Nature and Causes of the Wealth of Nations,* bk IV, ch. II

This motto passage must be in all *The Wealth of Nations* the one to which reference is most often made. It can well bear all, indeed rather more than all, the attention which it does in fact get. For very few even of those who have actually read it seem to become seized of its full significance. I myself met it first nearly forty years ago, as an undergraduate in the University of Oxford. It was cited then in a popular series of lectures given by G. D. H. Cole, the then Chichele Professor of Political and Social Theory. Like most of us in his audience, Cole could see nothing more here than the occasion for a swift passing sneer. This was, after all, merely a piece of apologetics for those obviously outmoded and altogether indefensible arrangements called by Cole laissez-faire capitalism; the arrangements which Smith himself knew only as "the natural system of perfect liberty and justice", or "the obvious and simple system of natural liberty" (A. Smith, 1776, bk IV, ch. vii, pt 3 and bk IV, ch. ix). To such principled secularists as Cole this particular defence was made the more repugnant by what we misinterpreted as the suggestion that these ongoings are benevolently guided by the Invisible Hand of an All-wise Providence.

Certainly Cole and the rest of us were right to see in this passage some defence of pluralistic and competitive capitalism. For it does indeed offer, for that and against monopoly socialist alternatives, an argument far more powerful than anything which Cole was able to recognize; or, I will now add, to meet. But where we were utterly wrong was in suspecting Smith of making some sort of anti-scientific appeal to supernatural intervention. On the contrary: this text is a landmark in the history of the growth of the social sciences. For – almost a century before Darwin's *Origin* – Smith was uncovering a mechanism by which something strongly suggesting design might, indeed must, come about quite spontaneously and without direction.

Like so much else in Smith, the argument here begins from an uncynical yet coolly realistic appreciation of our human nature. Any political economy for this world must treat people as we are, not as we might become, yet will not. As George Stigler said in a volume of bicentennial essays: "*The Wealth of Nations* is a stupendous palace erected on the granite of self-interest" (Skinner and Wilson, 1976, p. 237). It is indeed; Scottish granite, and erected also on Scottish self-reliance: "It is not from the benevolence of the butcher, the brewer or the baker that we expect our dinner, but from their regard to their own interest. We address ourselves, not to their humanity but to their self-love, and never talk to them of our own necessities but of their advantages. Nobody but a beggar chooses to depend chiefly upon the benevolence of his fellow-citizens" (A. Smith, 1776, bk I, ch. ii).

Put in marginally more modern terms, the nub of Smith's argument is that the most productive, the most wealth-creating, the most economically efficient investment decisions are likely to be made by persons who have some large and direct personal interest in achieving the most satisfactory combination of the maximum security of, and the maximum return on, the capital employed. Of course there is no guarantee that all such persons will get all their decisions right. Even those who do turn out usually to have spotted winners will sometimes pick losers. It is indeed precisely because things are so difficult, and so apt to come unstuck, that anyone concerned to increase the wealth of nations has such an excellent reason for wanting to have the crucial initiatives made, the crucial initiatives taken, always and only by directly and appropriately interested parties.

Also, where and in so far as people are – as Smith nicely has it – "investing their own capitals", the unsuccessful will, to the extent that they have made bad investments, necessarily be deprived of opportunity to make further costly mistakes; while the successful will, by a parallel necessity, be enabled to proceed to further and hopefully greater successes. Smith himself appears not to have seized this further point about feedback, although it must be of the last importance in any consideration of alternative ways of providing for the taking of economic initiatives.

Our interest here is in the general nature of social mechanisms, rather than the particular merits and demerits of rival economic arrangements. Yet even from that present point of view it is perhaps worth devoting a paragraph or three to the contrast, and to some similarities between, the way described by Smith and the way actually followed in the making of some of the biggest investment and disinvestment decisions in Britain during recent decades. For these decisions – the decisions on the public investments which have constituted a very high proportion of total investment – have not been made by persons harbouring direct individual interests in the security of the capital and the maximization of the returns. Rather they have been made by, or have somehow emerged from the interactions of, various persons and groups not having, and often required not to have, any individual stake in the achieving of the maximum, or indeed any, return on the capital employed.

Being human – like the definitionally grasping capitalists of socialist demonology, and like the rest of us as well – all such persons are inclined to strive to maximize their own utilities; or, for those who prefer the jargon of a lost Broadway world to that of the economists, to do the best they can for themselves and for their families (Runyon, 1950). The trouble has been that the utilities of these public decision-makers have been very little connected with, and sometimes more or less directly opposed to, the direction of tax-moneys into what will turn out to have been maximally wealth-creating investments. Overgrown unions in declining smokestack industries have, inevitably, more political clout than their perhaps still unformed sunrise successors; politicians who make politically profitable but economically ruinous investment decisions actually increase their chances of making similar even larger decisions later; and so on.

This is no place for detailed documentation. It should be sufficient, before referring to other sources, to mention two specially flagrant British examples: first, the building of the longest single-span bridge in the world, undertaken to buy victory in an especially crucial parliamentary bye-election; and, second, successive decisions to invest still more in various loss-making nationalized industries, decisions reached under pressure from the relevant labour unions, and made always without unbreakable guarantees that those unions would then permit the working practices and manning levels which might enable these investments to become profitable. Would any of the various civil servants, politicians, and union barons involved in these decisions have been so imprudent, or so irresponsible, as to subscribe to the equity from their own private pockets, or even from any trust funds for which they were individually accountable?

Perhaps as taxpayers we ought to require, from this day forward, that all politicians involved in the actual making of such public investment decisions should be compelled to back their judgement with an investment of their own money in some sum which they could not afford to lose! (On the general issues of investment in and by the British nationalized industries see G. and P. Polanyi, 1976, Redwood, 1980, and Pryke, 1981; and, on several more particular decisions, compare Broadway, 1976, Jones, 1977, Bruce-Gardyne, 1978, and Burton, 1979.)

1   Smith and the other Scottish Founding Fathers

So far we have been giving general consideration to Smith's argument that a free capital market, with all the individual owners of capital seeking the best possible return on any investment made, must tend to maximize the gross national product. It is time to concentrate upon one particular sentence: ". . . he intends only his own gain and he is, in this as in many other cases, led by an invisible hand to promote an end which was no part of his intentions". It is on his attention, "in this as in many other cases", to such unintended consequences of intended action that Smith's claim to have been one of the Founding Fathers of the social sciences must rest.

To understand that claim is to realize how totally wrong it must be to construe Smith's invisible hand as an instrument of super-natural direction. To do this would be as preposterous as to interpret Darwin's natural selection as being really supernatural selection. For Smith's invisible hand is no more a hand directed by a rational owner than Darwin's natural selection is selection by supernatural intelligence. As was suggested earlier, both Smith and Darwin were showing how something which one might be very tempted to put down to design could and indeed must come about: in the one case without direction, in that direction; and in the other without any direction at all. By uncovering the mechanisms operative in the two cases they both made supernatural intervention as an explanation superfluous.

Adam Smith's invisible hand is not a hand, any more than Darwin's natural selection is selection. Or, putting the point in a somewhat more forced and technical way, 'invisible' and 'natural' are in these two cases just as much alienans adjectives as are 'imaginary' or 'positive' in the expressions 'imaginary apples' or 'positive freedom'. Alienans adjectives – this technical expression is part of our Scholastic inheritance – do not pick out a sub-class of that wider class to which their noun refers. Instead they indicate that it is not a sub-sort of that sort which is to be discussed. Imaginary apples are not, like Golden Delicious, a variety of apples; while positive freedom is not freedom at all, but being able but also required to act in ways approved by those who commend it.

Nor, continuing, would it be fair to accuse Smith, as he so often is accused, of assuming or asserting that the unintended results of the operations of all such social mechanisms are always, if only in the long run, Providentially happy. (In the long run, as Lord

Keynes famously remarked, we are all dead.)

The most elegant refutation of this charge against Smith can be drawn from his treatment of the division of labour. Certainly, he writes, this "is not originally the effect of any human wisdom, which foresees and intends the general opulence to which it gives occasion. It is the necessary though very slow and gradual consequence of a certain propensity in human nature which has in view no such extensive utility: the propensity to truck, barter, and exchange one thing with another" (A. Smith, 1776, bk I, ch. ii). But Smith himself goes on to describe and lament the dehumanizing consequences of the more extreme developments of this occasion of opulence. It is precisely these purple passages which find a place in *Capital*, colourfully adorning this part of the author's polemic against what he calls capitalism (Marx, 1867, vol. I, pp. 362 and 459–60). It should nevertheless be noted, partly because it so infrequently is, that Marx himself has precious little to say about how socialism as centralized ownership and control is supposed to be going to achieve abundance without both the division of labour and, hence, the ills consequent thereon.

Another example of a social mechanism producing results not merely other than but even flat contrary to both the intentions and the best interests of the participants is 'The Tragedy of the Commons' (Hardin, 1977). Where, without restrictions of private property, access to some resource is common to several, those sharing that access will all, and quite rationally, be inclined to make the most use they can of that resource. It will, therefore, tend to be wastefully and rapidly exhausted or destroyed; a result universally unintended and unwanted. In our contemporary world one appalling token of this type is the ruin of the Sahel. There, as the then UN Secretary-General Kurt Waldheim warned, "the encroachment of the desert threatens to wipe four or five African countries from the map". Certainly other causes have exacerbated the problem. But the basic trouble is that on unenclosed land no one has an individual interest in doing what stops, or not doing what starts, desertification (Burton, 1978, pp. 69–91). Notoriously, as philosophers and others ought to have learnt first from the critique of Plato's *Republic* in Aristotle's *Politics,* everyone's business tends to be no one's. By contrast, as one of Smith's own younger contemporaries used to say: "Give a man the secure possession of a bleak rock and he will turn it into a garden: give him a nine years lease on a garden, and he will convert it into a desert." (That younger contemporary was Arthur Young, the first great agricultural journalist.)

Nor was it only Smith who, "in this as in many other cases", was systematically developing this sort of approach to social phenomena. He was in fact one of a small group, a main part of "the Edinburgh Enlightenment". This group also included, among others, the sometime Chaplain to the Black Watch and later Edinburgh professor Adam Ferguson, William Robertson, and – slightly older and starting to publish much earlier – David Hume.

It is to the point here to recall that Hume presented his own first published work not as an essay in conceptual analysis but as *A Treatise of Human Nature*; "an attempt to introduce the experimental Method of Reasoning into Moral Subjects". The word 'moral' in this subtitle is roughly equivalent to 'human'; as in the fossil phrase 'moral sciences', only very recently – and regrettably – abandoned by the University of Cambridge. The word 'experimental', as Hume's Introduction eventually makes clear, should have been replaced by 'experiential'. His list here of his major recent predecessors excludes Berkeley, but, most significantly, includes Bernard de Mandeville (1670–1733). This Anglo-Dutch doctor with a French name published in 1723 the final and fullest version of *The Fable of the Bees, or Private Vices, Public Benefits*. This mischievously provocative yet profoundly unfrivolous work is increasingly recognized as another landmark in the history of the development of the social sciences. (Anyone who appreciates Mandeville will get similar pleasure and profit from Walter Block's equally mischievous yet perhaps even more seriously purposed *Defending the Undefendable*.)

Hume's characteristic contentions, even where he is dealing with what is in the narrowest sense most strictly philosophical, clear the way for the open-minded discovery of causes which are altogether unlike their effects: "If we reason apriori", he argues in *An Enquiry concerning Human Understanding*, "anything may appear able to produce anything" (Hume, 1748, p. 64); whereas the contrary assumption "is the bane of all reasoning and free inquiry" (1748, p. 26). Indeed it is; and, above all, this is true in the areas of social science and social policy. For, especially but not only when partisan passions are running high, we are all tempted to argue from (sometimes falsely) attributed intentions to actual outcomes; without labouring to investigate whether what has in fact resulted falls short of, exceeds, or simply differs from what those attributed intentions might have led us to expect. The burden of Hume's great negative thesis about causality is, in our present context, that the unintended consequences of intended actions may be altogether surprising, and are certainly not to be determined apriori. ('Apriori' – which, since it has been a landed immigrant for over a quarter of a millenium, I insist on rendering as a single unitalicized word – means without or prior to investigation.)

Two examples of this fallacious form of argument may help to put us all on our guard. Since 1979 it has been repeatedly asserted, and is, surely, widely believed, that the Prime Minister has her heart set on dismantling the National Health Service. By invalid inference it is concluded that the NHS is now being deliberately and systematically run down. But, whatever the truth-value of the premise, this conclusion is certainly false. For the fact is that the resource input has increased, in real terms, every year; although never, of course, enough to satisfy those charged with the allocation of these inputs.

Again, it has been customary in Britain for Education Ministers of both main parties to boast of increases in the number of teachers, improvements in the teacher/pupil ratios, and so on; and then to infer from this, directly, that, because the stated intention has been to ensure that more pupils learn more, and better, therefore the educational results must have been exactly proportionate to the educationally intended expenditure (Anderson, 1981b, pp. 11–17).

In spokespersons for the teachers' unions this argument, and the assumption upon which it is based, are, no doubt, unsurprising. But we may reasonably react with both surprise and shock when we find one of the most academically able of all post-war Ministers arguing as follows, in calm and considered print: "... expenditure on education rose from 4.8 per cent of GNP in 1964 to 6.1 per cent in 1970. As a result, all classes of the community enjoyed significantly more education than before." The second proposition would thus appear to be asserted as an immediate inference from the first. Certainly only one further reason is offered to sustain that conclusion: "The huge expansion in the supply of teachers produced a steady reduction in the pupil/ teacher ratio" (Crosland, 1976, p. 20).

The undogmatic and open-minded approach thus advocated by Hume became characteristic of all the leading members of "the Edinburgh Enlightenment". Robertson, for instance, in a long methodological note to the Proofs and Illustrations of his *History of Scotland,* first published in 1759, compares the institutions and customs of the Germans, as seen by Caesar and Tacitus, with those of the North American Indians, as studied by Father Charlevoix and Monsieur Lafitour: "A philosopher", Robertson concludes, "will satisfy himself with observing, that the characters of nations depend on the state of society in which they live, and on the political institutions established among them; and that the human mind, whenever it is placed in the same situation, will in ages the most distant and in countries the most remote, assume the same form, and be distinguished by the same manners" (Robertson, 1890, vol. I, p. 372).

Later, in his *History of America,* first published in 1777, one year after *The Wealth of Nations,* Robertson unwittingly staked a claim to have anticipated Marx in formulating what came to be called (not A but) *The* Materialist Conception of History: "In every inquiry concerning the operations of men when united together in society, the first object of attention should be their mode of subsistence. Accordingly, as that varies, their laws and policy must be different (vol. II, p. 104: since Marx certainly knew the works of Robertson and Ferguson as well as Smith, Marx could have been borrowing).

In the same eighteenth century, but with no other connection with these Edinburgh social scientists, we find John Wesley analyzing an unwelcome yet apparently inevitable development in the movement which he founded: "I fear, wherever riches have increased, the essence of religion has decreased in the same proportion. Therefore I do not see how it is possible, in the nature of things, for any revival of true religion to continue long. For religion must necessarily produce both industry and frugality, and these cannot but produce riches. But as riches increase, so will pride, anger and love of the world in all its branches. How then is it possible that Methodism, a religion of the heart, though it flourishes now as a green bay tree, should continue in this state? For the Methodists in every place grow diligent and frugal; consequently they increase in goods. Hence they proportionately increase in pride, in anger, in the desire of the flesh, the desire of the eyes, and the pride of life. So, although the form of religion remains, the spirit is swiftly vanishing away" (Runciman, 1978, p. 165: a British colleague drew Weber's attention to this passage, which Weber quotes in his famous article on 'The Protestant Ethic and the "Spirit" of Capitalism').

What in the first place Smith is pointing to in our motto paragraph is a mechanism by which a certain sort of intended action produces unintended consequences. And, even if not the whole, it is certainly a main part of the truth about the social sciences that "They are concerned with man's actions, and their aim is to explain the unintended or undesigned results of the actions of many men" (Hayek, 1979, p. 41). A second point to emphasize is that what Smith and the others were offered was evolutionary as opposed to creationist.

A sophisticated capital market is not put together overnight, to open on a statutorily determined Vesting Day; and the division of labour "is not originally the effect of any human wisdom . . . It is the necessary consequence of a certain propensity in human nature . . ." Nine years earlier Adam Ferguson had made the same point quite generally: "Mankind in following the present sense of their minds, in striving to remove inconveniences, or to gain apparent and contiguous advantages, arrive at ends which even their imagination could not anticipate . . . Every step and every movement of the multitude, even in what are called enlightened ages, are made with equal blindness to the future; and nations stumble upon establishments, which are indeed the result of human action but not the execution of human design" (Ferguson, 1767, pp. 122–3).

The same seminal passage at once proceeds to enforce the point that – at any rate in default of sufficient independent evidence of their particular existence – there is no longer any call to postulate great creative culture heroes to explain the origin of such "establishments". For, "If we listen to the testimony of modern history, and to that of the most authentic parts of the ancient; if we attend to the practice of nations in every quarter of the world, and in every condition, whether that of the barbarian or the polished, we shall find very little reason to retract this assertion ... We are therefore to receive, with caution, the traditionary histories of ancient legislators, and founders of states. Their names have long been celebrated; their supposed plans have been admired; and what were probably the consequences of an early situation is, in every instance, considered as an effect of design ... If men, during ages of extensive reflection, and employed in the search of improvement, are wedded to their institutions, and, labouring under many inconveniences, cannot break loose from the trammels of custom; what shall we suppose their humour to have been in the times of Romulus and Lycurgus?" (1767, p. 123).

Durkheim once said in this connection, in his lectures on *Montesquieu and Rousseau, Precursors of Sociology,* that the myth of the inspired and revolutionary legislator, had, more than anything else, been the hindrance to the development of his subject. Notice too that there are parallel, indeed still more forceful objections to the hypothesizing of creation not by an individual but by a collective. Already in the *Treatise* Hume had deployed many of these objections to dispose of suggestions that the actual origins of all governments must have been in historical contracts: "philosophers may, if they please, extend their reasoning to the suppos'd *state of nature*; provided that they allow it to be a mere philosophical fiction which never had, and never cou'd have any reality" (Hume, 1739–40, p. 493). Later Hume speaks in precisely parallel terms about the legend of historical social contracts made to end that "*state of nature*" (1739–40, bk III, pt ii, sec. 8). Since the justificatory employment of one of these "mere historical fictions" has been revived by Rawls, it is well to emphasize that in this at least Rawls is operating with Hume's consent).

Hume's insight is that not only government but also other fundamental social institutions neither in fact arose nor could have arisen through a contract from a pre-social state of nature; if only because promising itself already essentially presupposes the social institution of language.

Hume's own solution to this problem of actual origins is subtle, hard-headed, and profound; notwithstanding that some of the terms in which he states that solution must, unfortunately, suggest the sociologically unsophisticated crudities which he himself is striving to reject. Where his less enlightened opponents tell tales referring back to deliberate foresight and contractual agreement, Hume argues that the fundamental social institutions could not have originated from this sort of planning. What *is* possible is that recognitions of common interest will lead to the regulation of conduct in ways which are not, and often could not be derived from prior contracts: "Two men, who pull the oars of a boat, do it by an agreement or convention, tho' they have never given promises to each other. Nor is the rule concerning the stability of possession the less deriv'd from human conventions, that it arises gradually, and acquired force by a slow progression ... In like manner are languages gradually establish'd by human conventions without any promise. In like manner do gold and silver become the common measures of exchange ..." (1739–40, p. 490).

To the philosopher, or at any rate to the philosopher who has been to school with Austin, that penultimate illustration is the most impressive of all. To think that the natural languages, formations whose richness and subtleties it is so hard even faithfully to delineate, not merely may but must be in the main evolved, and not planned, by-products of the actions and inter-actions of people who were themselves, whether individually or collectively, incapable of designing anything of comparable complexity. In what language, after all, would the Select Committee charged with the task of designing the first natural language have conducted its deliberations?

Anyone not so impressed, as well as all those who have learnt everything they think they know about 'Linguistic Philosophy' from Gellner's *Words and Things,* should treat themselves to a study of Austin's witty masterpiece 'A Plea for Excuses'. From this they may learn: both that the vocabulary already available here in colloquial English is vastly rich and subtle; and that – contrary to what has been so often said – Austin himself always insisted that even these rich and too often unexploited resources might some-times need supplementation or correction. (See Austin, 1961: compare Bottomore, 1984, p. 25, Pateman, 1972, p. 115, and

Rubinstein and Stoneman, 1972, pp. 36–7; and contrast Flew, 1976a, pp. 126–7.)

It is no wonder that, in considering the magnificent structures of the more highly developed natural languages, Ferguson becomes lyrical: "This amazing fabric . . . which, when raised to its height, appears so much above what could be ascribed to any simultaneous effort of the most sublime and comprehensive abilities." Indeed, he goes on, "The speculative mind is apt to look back with amazement from the height it has gained; as a traveller might do, who, rising insensibly on the slope of a hill, should come to look from a precipice of almost unfathomable depth, to the summit of which he could scarcely believe himself to have ascended without supernatural aid" (Ferguson, 1972, vol. I, p. 43).

The eccentric and studiously old-fashioned Lord Monboddo, who surely knew as much about linguistics as any of his contemporaries, but who was not so fully seized of the evolutionary possibilities, takes up Ferguson's hint of some supernatural aid. He "can hardly believe but that in the first discovery of so artificial a method of communication, men had supernatural assistance". So he is "much inclined to listen to what Egyptians tell us of a God, as they call him, that is an intelligence superior to man, having first told them the use of language" (Burnet, 1774, vol. IV, p. 484).

The third main point which needs to be made about these insights into social mechanisms consists in underlining a distinction which seems not to have been developed either by any of these Scottish Founding Fathers themselves or by their most sympathetic modern interpreter, F. A. Hayek. In a posthumous masterpiece published a year or so later than *The Wealth of Nations,* Hume recognized that something which had not been designed either by one individual nor even by a committee might nevertheless be the ultimate product of innumerable more-or-less intelligent initiatives. In part V of the *Dialogues concerning Natural Religion* Philo is scripted to say: "If we survey a ship, what an exalted idea we must form of the ingenuity of the carpenter, who framed so complicated, useful and beautiful a machine? And what surprise must we entertain, when we find him a stupid mechanic, who imitated others, and copied an art, which, through a long succession of ages, after multiplied trials, mistakes, corrections, deliberations, and controversies, had been gradually improving?" (Hume, 1779, p. 167).

The distinction needed is: between, on the one hand, social mechanisms producing results unintended by, and even contrary to the wishes of, those whose actions constitute the operations of these mechanisms; and, on the other hand, the generation of what may suggest brilliant individual or collective design through the not intentionally and collectively coordinated initiatives and responses of various persons or groups of persons, most of whom cannot have been directly acquainted with one another.

It is often said – by people who have, apparently, forgotten the King James Bible – that no great work of art ever emerged from a series of committee meetings. Yet it is, surely, true to say that at least some of the greatest – the *Iliad* and the *Odyssey,* for instance – were the ultimate achievements of successive generations, with many individual bards making their several anonymous contributions piecemeal. Certainly the natural languages themselves must be products of still continuing processes of this kind. It has been well said that the history of every language is a history of corruptions; in the sense that every change must involve some deviation from what was previously established as correct usage. Presumably it was ever so. Presumably the whole growth of language has, from the beginning, been a series of unplanned lapses and intended initiatives; some of which have, through the effluxion of time, become accepted usages. This was indeed one of Darwin's models for his account of evolution by natural selection in biology (Flew, 1984, ch. III, sec. 2 (iii)).

The contemplation of either of the two kinds of phenomena just distinguished should teach us how fallacious it is to argue that, if something is the product or result of conscious human agency, then it must always be in practice possible radically to redesign and reshape that product or that result in such a way that it shall the better accommodate the wishes of the persons concerned. It may be, or then again it may not. Every single case needs to be examined separately, and argued on its individual and particular merits.

Descartes was, therefore, quite simply wrong when in part 2 of the *Discourse on the Method* he made his characteristic claim that there is, typically, "less perfection in works composed of several portions, and carried out by the hands of various masters." So too, and consequently, is the entire tradition of what has been christened 'constructivistic rationalism' (Hayek 1967 and 1978). This tradition resonates to the cry of that early French socialist Etienne Cabet: "Nothing is impossible for a government which really wills the good of its people." But nowhere and by no Providence is it guaranteed that good intentions will produce all and only their intended good effects. To the disappointed it should nevertheless be some consolation to contemplate the other side of the coin. For intentions less than perfectly disinterested and universally benevolent are perhaps the more common; and these too, in this Universe, are equally liable to produce consequences additional and even contrary to those intended.

2   Social functions and social needs

Closely associated with the idea of social mechanisms are the notions of social functions and social structures. To say that this is a function of that is to say that this is something, presumably and typically something useful, which results from the availability and operation of that; and which, all other things being equal, would not come about if that were removed or its operation prevented. The function for instance, of the heart, is to circulate the blood; and this is indisputably useful to the organism since without a properly functioning heart it will die.

The choice of this familiar biological illustration should remind us that, especially when we are discussing human affairs and human institutions, it is always tempting to argue that anything said to have and to fulfil a function must therefore: both have been originally designed to fulfil that function; and now be deliberately maintained precisely and only for that purpose. But, of course, the argument is not valid: neither of these conclusions follows. Those succumbing to the temptation to argue in this way will also be inclined to think that to have established that a social institution does in fact fulfil such and such a function is at one and the same time to have explained: both how that institution first came into existence; and how and why it continues. It was, they will assume, first created by people who had and who saw that they had some interests here; and it is maintained still by persons having, perceiving and pursuing those interests. They may furthermore assume, if they are gripped by Methodological Essentialism, that that institution essentially has been, is now, and ever will be nothing but an instrument for fulfilling its consciously intended purpose; whatever that may be.

To say that this or any other form of argument is invalid, and that the assumptions based thereon are not warranted, is not to deny that propositions thus invalidly deduced may happen to be true, and even, on other grounds, be known (Flew, 1975, ch. 1). In *The Republic,* for example, Plato takes it that the social function of beliefs about both the gods and a future life is to assist in sustaining good order and discipline. It is reminiscent of the legendary 1948 Italian election poster where, under a picture of a wavering voter in the privacy of the polling booth, the caption read: "Stalin can't see you. But God can. Vote Christian Democrat!"

It was in order that this function might be more adequately fulfilled in his allegedly ideal state that Plato recommended a literary purge: the home life of the Olympians, as recorded by Homer and other literary authorities, was so unlike that of Plato's golden Guardians, or, for that matter, that expected of their subjects! But his mother's cousin Critias, later leader of the notoriously murderous Thirty Tyrants, expressed in verse the conjecture that religious doctrines had been originally invented and introduced by some anonymous culture hero: "And lawlessness turned into law and order" (Popper, 1945, vol. I, p. 142: Fragment 25 in Diels). While there is no good reason to believe that the conjecture of Critias is correct, we do have abundant evidence of the exploitation of religious beliefs for purposes of political control in the Ancient World (Farrington, 1965); and in more recent times too.

This same fallacy is often mediated through the notion of need. If the fulfilment of some function can be seen as answering to a need in some social set, then, it is invalidly inferred, this discovery of the function and of the corresponding need is at the same time a discovery of two explanations: it explains who originally created the institution which has that function, and for what end; and it explains who are those who are sustaining it, and why. But the argument is no more valid in this elaborated form. For there are several possible slips between a need and its satisfaction. First, the persons whose need it is may not recognize that they have this need: while each one of us may be the best expert on our own wants, someone else can point to needs which we never appreciated (Flew, 1981, ch. V). Second, even when the need is recognized we may decide that, in our present circumstances, as we see them, other things are more important to us than trying to satisfy that particular need. Third, we may not see what it is that we ourselves could do in order to satisfy that need: there may not even be any courses of action open to us which would in fact do the trick.

Once these various points about functions and needs have been clearly stated, and once the fallacious form of argument involving these two notions has been starkly displayed, it all begins to look too obvious to have been worth doing. Yet obviousness, of course, really is, what so many other things are nowadays falsely said to be, essentially relative: what is obvious to us now might not have been obvious to us or to anyone else at another time, or in another place. Failure to take account of what are now to us obvious considerations has greased the slipways for launching many a grotesquely unseaworthy assertion.

Anyone who served on a university Senate throughout "the recent expansion of sociology" must be only too able and eager to sink the suggestion, brashly made by a newly appointed Lecturer in Sociology, that this was a response to "capitalism's need" (Blackburn, 1972, p. 33). But, for a less narrowly academic example, let us go to a book on *The Culture of Inequality*; a book described in its Foreword and by rave reviewers as a "milestone study" by "a skilled, judicious social scientist", presenting a "brilliantly reasoned argument", in a "daring attempt to unravel the ideological knots".

The thesis of the author is: "Because of its peculiar history American society has given rise to a ... culture of inequality", such that "many Americans make of their commonplace successes praiseworthy achievements by viewing disadvantage as the just desert for insufficient effort ..."; and hence that "the maintenance of poverty is ... a function of the collective need to sustain a visible population of pariahs ..." (Lewis, 1980, pp. 87–8 and 184).

He takes it for granted, presumably on the strength of unsound arguments of the kinds previously exposed, that to point to a supposed need, which some institution would satisfy, just is to show both why and how that institution is maintained. Consistently with his chief contention he too, like so many others, prefers to speak of deprivation or of low pay rather than of poverty or of low earnings. This is a difference which makes a difference. For the preferred terms suggest: not only that the people in question are intended victims; but also that there is little or nothing of a non-political kind which they could do, or be helped to do, in order to raise themselves. On the opposite side, the author sees a collective of those who "invest in the perpetuation of an underclass of objectionables" (1980, p. 28). Yet he never even tries to tell us what the individual members of this supposed collective are from day to day actually doing or not doing with intent to satisfy their supposed collective need.

Whatever, if anything, they have in truth been and are so doing, certainly they have not succeeded in preventing the Congress from continuing to vote enormous funds for various anti-poverty programmes. Maybe it is they, or some of them, who have somehow contrived to ensure that this expenditure has not been fully effective? So maybe this is where the research effort should have been directed? But to contribute thus to the eradication of poverty the researchers would have to be Methodological Individualists; and also to be willing masters, and Lewis is not, of all the several distinctions explained here and in chapter 1, above. Certainly, "If these funds were all going to the poor, there would be no poor left – they would be among the comfortably well-off at least" (Friedman, 1980, p. 108).

A second example, immeasurably more important on a world scale, shows the invalid argument moving in the opposite direction: from the disappearance of the (original) function to the disappearance of the institution. In a chapter of *Anti-Dühring* later to form part of *Socialism: Utopian and Scientific,* perhaps the most widely read of all Marxist works, and in a passage quoted and expounded by Lenin in *State and Revolution,* Engels wrote: "Former society, moving in class antagonisms, had need of the state, that is, an organization of the exploiting class ... for the forcible holding down of the exploited class ..." But, come the Revolution, "*The proletariat seizes the state power, and trans-*

forms the means of production into state property ... The interference of the state power in social relations becomes super-fluous in one sphere after another, and then ceases of itself ... The state is not 'abolished', *it withers away*" (Engels, 1878, pp. 308 and 309: quoted Lenin, 1917, p. 15).

There is no doubt but that the proposed transformation of the means of production into state property is, by definition, social-ism. But, if anything ever has been utopian rather than scientific, it is the assertion that organizations with monopolies on military and police power are bound, once they are fulfilling no functions useful to outsiders, to *wither away*. It would be easy, yet it is scarcely necessary, to bring forward long lists of organizations and institutions much less powerful, and therefore much less attractive to their own members, which seem all set to survive indefinitely, notwithstanding that they are doing no good and some harm to the rest of us.

It is, however, more constructive to point out that in Marx and Engels this cherished conclusion about the withering away of the state is not based solely upon invalid arguments about social functions and social needs. It is sustained also by their more fundamental but surely false doctrine of the priority of economics; a doctrine which is part if not the whole of The Materialist Conception of History. Consider, for instance, two characteristic claims from the *Communist Manifesto*: first, that "The executive of the modern state is merely a committee for managing the common affairs of the whole bourgeoisie ..."; and, second, that "Political power, properly so called, is merely the organized power of one class for oppressing the other" (Marx and Engels, 1848, pp. 82 and 105).

But now, when we are told that those who seem to be the rulers, the men of power, really are the independently powerless creatures of various outside interests, then we have to demand, not only as social scientists but also as practical people, accounts of the effective checks and pressures by which those external collec-tivities contrive always to keep these merely seeming rulers subordinate to their own actual control.

Had Marx and Engels ever tried to provide such detailed, Methodological Individualist accounts, then they could scarcely have failed to discover that it is not by any means true that the immediate exercisers of military and political power are always and everywhere the subservient creatures of outside class interests. No doubt cabinets in Britain, from the Glorious Revolution until the great Reform Bill, were devoted to the welfare of – indeed they very largely consisted in members of – the landowning class. But elsewhere, and in other periods, it is all too easy to find examples of civilian rulers or military commanders pursuing ends of their own, ends quite independent of and even flat contrary to any interests attributable to economic classes outside the state machine. After all – to put things at what is at the same time not only the simplest but also the most fundamental level – it is only in so far as, and to the extent that, there are men with guns, able and willing to maintain and defend property rights, that rich people can possess that access to political power, which, allegedly, riches always offer. Those major industrialists, for instance, who financed the rise of Hitler's National Socialists, soon discovered, once he was secure in office, that they were the suppliants now.

This Marxist failure – indeed, more truly, this Marxist refusal – to investigate actual and possible social mechanisms through which rulers may be made accountable to those whom they rule has, among the faithful, continued to this day; and this despite the ever-accumulating evidence of how totally parties of the new Leninist type can exercise autonomous and arbitrary rule over a whole society – not least over the class of which they profess to be the devotedly representative leading cadres. Consider, for instance, Poland; and how Solidarity, the ten-million-strong union of the Polish workers, was destroyed almost overnight by the state machine of army, police and party. Again, it must have been at least in part because that appeared to falsify the doctrine of the priority of economics that Marx was so reluctant to come to terms with the phenomenon of *Oriental Despotism* (Wittfogel, 1981; and compare Seligman, 1907).

Functionalism as a doctrine for social scientists was formulated in its most extreme form by Malinowski, and the first major report on his own fieldwork in Melanesia was published in 1922 as *Argonauts of the Western Pacific*. "The functional view", Malinowski wrote "insists . . . upon the principle that in every type of civilization, every custom, material object, idea and belief fulfils some vital function, has some task to accomplish, represents an indispensable part within a working whole." This doctrine was extremely influential, not only on the work of such other anthropologists as A. R. Radcliffe-Brown and E. E. Evans-Pritchard, but also on sociologists such as Talcott Parsons (who studied with Malinowski in 1924) and R. K. Merton. But it was, almost from the beginning, strongly attacked. It has since been "virtually criticized to death" (Pratt, 1978, pp. 117ff. and compare Jarvie, 1973).

The first point for us to stress is that Functionalism takes very seriously the analogy so often drawn between human societies and individual organisms. Just as (most) organs serve some function useful to the organism, so, it is asserted, every social institution "fulfils some vital functions, has some task to accomplish, represents an indispensable part within a working whole." Again, just as organisms are integrated, with their several organs mutually adapted for cooperation, so the Functionalist will look for ways in which the various apparently disparate institutions of any particular society are integrated, and adapted one to another. Again, they will discern the phenomena of homeostasis not only in organisms but also in societies: just as organisms have mechanisms for maintaining internal equilibrium through changing external conditions so too, they will insist, do societies.

The second and subsequent point is that Functionalism would be better presented: not as a rashly universal doctrine about what is always in fact there to be found; but rather as an heuristic maxim, telling us what it is always worth looking for, even if in the end we shall have to concede that it is sometimes not there. Indeed careful contemplation even of the biological model teaches caution. For, surely, we have all been told that the vermiform appendix is a vestigial organ, which no longer performs any function useful to the human organism? And human societies are in any case not often under the strong selective pressures of a state of nature.

The third thing to notice is more complicated but no less important. It is that the analogy between societies and organisms breaks down in several often crucial respects. For a start, organisms are composed of cells, all of which will die fairly soon after the death of the whole. But the individuals or families composing a human society are capable of surviving separately or as members of another society. So, as the anthropologist Edmund Leach has wittily remarked, when a culture dies out or a society decomposes it may mean no more than that "Cowboys and Indians have learned to drive Cadillacs"; a development to be regretted, perhaps, but not in anyone's book a fate worse than death.

Next, because societies unlike organisms are composed of individual human beings, it is entirely possible that some institution which meets some need and has some function for some set of members of some society, and which may even yield some general collective benefit, simultaneously and necessarily imposes severe costs upon some other set. Again, some institutions, perhaps even those same institutions, may be essential to the preservation of a particular society in approximately its present form without being by any means essential to the preservation of any society at all. All this would seem to be true of, for instance, human sacrifice among the Aztecs at the time of the Spanish conquest, suttee among traditional Hindus in nineteenth-century India, and female circumcision among the Kikuyu of contemporary Kenya.

Functionalism has frequently turned out to be a very conservative doctrine, at least with regard to the institutions of the sort of peoples studied by anthropologists. (Many believing and practising Functionalists have been incongruously reluctant to apply their doctrine to their own societies, and to draw equally conservative conclusions there; or, as the case may be, here.) Repudiating whatever they saw as ethnocentric, and therefore believing themselves to be committed to maintaining the absolute wrongness of trying to impose our alien and always relative or subjective valuations, such Functionalists have proved ready to support the conservation of many practices which in their hearts they knew ought not to be conserved. Yet none of this is to deny: either the heuristic value of Functionalism, in leading researchers to ask and answer questions about the functions of those institutions which do happen to have functions; or the more practical value in application of pointing out either likely but unwelcome knock-on consequences of abolishing some particular and especially obnoxious practice, or possible alternative institutions for fulfilling necessary or desirable functions at lower cost. (For one altogether delightful example of the latter, see Grimble (1952) on how cricket was itself transformed when introduced to replace more lethal inter-village contests in his islands.)

3 Social structures and Structuralism

"A spectre is haunting the intellectual scene – structuralism, or better, *le structuralisme*. It is important, it is fashionable, but what the devil is it?" (Gellner, 1973, p. 150). The temptation is to call a halt on reaching the third interrogative response offered to this excusably exasperated question: "Is it just the latest Left Bank fashion, filling a gap left by the exhaustion of Existentialism?" (p. 150). For that seems to be just about it. Nor is enthusiasm stirred in reading a judgement by a most sympathetic interpreter of the Modern Master of Structuralism, Lévi-Strauss: "The outstanding characteristic of his writing ... is that it is difficult to understand; his sociological theories combine baffling complexity with overwhelming erudition" (Leach, 1970, p. 8). Yet one or two things can perhaps usefully be said.

One expositor invokes as his motto the claim: "Science would be superfluous if there were no difference between the appearance of things and their essence." In saying this Marx was going to suggest that under socialism – where, it is alleged, social relations will always be exactly what they appear to be – there will be no room for social science (G. A. Cohen, 1972). But a Structuralist will want to contrast underlying and surface structures, rather as Robert Merton in the first chapter of *Social Theory and Social Structure* contrasted 'Manifest and Latent Functions'. Both the Structuralist and the Functionalist will, naturally, be more eager to discover the underlying and the latent than to record the surface and the manifest: the former is more of an achievement, and more like science.

These underlying and surface social structures also seem to have something in common with the underlying and surface structures of Linguistics. For the elements from which the structures are formed are in both cases typical objects of what have been described as "the Appearance sciences – those concerned with phenomena whose very essence is that they 'mean' something to participants" (Gellner, 1973, p. 152).

So far, perhaps, so good. Nevertheless we should begin to feel uneasy when we are told that social structures composed of such seemingly insubstantial elements do something so apparently physical as *generate* the surface social phenomena. What is the cash value of all this in terms of "societal members" – real flesh-and-blood people – doing this and suffering that? It cannot be emphasized too often or too heavily that a social structure is no more capable of producing real effects, without the involvement of people, than is a social movement, or a social class, or any other social force.

That such emphatic reiteration is necessary can be brought out best by referring yet again to Marx and Engels. For both produced most eloquent statements of the fundamental thesis of what would today be called Methodological Individualism. Yet both, especially in their more prophetic moods, remained apt to appeal to social forces operating somehow behind and beyond, rather than in and through, their component individuals. Under the continuing influence of Hegel (1770–1831), albeit a Hegel whom they had long since stood back upon material feet, they were unable to accept, always and consistently, that the subject of the social sciences must be the intended and unintended consequences of intended, individual, human actions. Instead they both hankered after materialist analogues of the activities of the Hegelian Cunning of Reason, directing people to achieve collective ends other than and independent of whatever their own individual purposes might happen to be. These were postulated as transcendent and offstage prods, rather than immanent and onstage transactions.

It is significant that this comes out most clearly in the retrospective review, *Ludwig Feuerbach and the End of Classical German Philosophy*. Engels there contrasts pre-human biological evolution with "the history of human society". In the latter "the actors are all endowed with consciousness, are men acting with deliberation or passion, working towards definite goals; nothing happens without a conscious purpose, without an intended aim". Nevertheless, Engels insists, "the course of history" is governed by necessitating laws: "where on the surface accident holds sway, there actually it is always governed by inner, hidden laws . . ."

"Men make their own history", the following paragraph begins, boldly. Yet there is a but: "But, on the other hand, we have seen that the many individual wills active in history for the most part produce results quite other than those intended – often quite the opposite ..." So far so good. The moral which Engels draws, however, is not that the social scientist needs to study the mechanisms through which particular intentions produce alien or even contrary results. In his view the proper objects of investigation are hidden, transcendent causes, rather than anything immanent in the activities themselves. So for Engels "the further question arises: What driving forces ... stand behind these motives? What are the historical causes which transform themselves into these motives in the brains of the actors?" (Engels, 1888, pp. 58–9).

Soon it emerges that history is not, after all, really made by innumerable individual men acting and interacting. The ultimate historical causes are instead largely unconscious and collective: "it is a question of investigating the driving powers which – consciously or unconsciously – lie behind the motives of men in their historical actions, and which constitute the real ultimate driving forces in history". These are, of course, "classes" (1888, p. 60). Where the metaphysical idealist Hegel had discerned direction by the invisible and cunning hand of presumably conscious Reason, the still Hegelian materialist Engels now sees individual men as the for the most part unwitting creatures of direction and control exercised by the necessarily unconscious collective intentions of hypostatized classes.

Quite apart from discussions of Structuralism, much is said nowadays about social structures and, in particular, power structures. It is, therefore, worth making two simple conceptual points: one about the meaning of 'power'; and the other about an ambiguity of 'structure'.

Roughly speaking: to say that one person is exercising power over another is to say that the first person is getting the second to do or to undergo something which the first wants the second to do or to undergo, but which the second would not himself or herself independently wish to do or to undergo; while to say that the first person possesses power, but is not exercising it, is to say that he or she could exercise it iff he or she chose. It is, surely, beyond dispute that the definitions sketched in the previous sentence are, if not perfectly polished, then at any rate substantially faithful to the ordinary meaning of the word 'power' as applied to persons.

There is, however, good reason to spell out this ordinary meaning here. For some social scientists have presented and adopted very different definitions: apparently without realizing how drastically they were innovating; and, hence, without providing any justification for introducing a new and inevitably confusing technical sense for a familiar colloquial term.

In the *International Encyclopaedia of the Social Sciences*, for instance, Robert Dahl asserts that 'C has power over R' means that 'C's behaviour causes R's behaviour'. This might be acceptable as a first attempt at a definition of the other sense of the word, in which it is applied to things as opposed to persons. (See chapter 4, below). But as an account of the power of persons, by confounding power with the exercise of power, it gets off on the wrong foot. Also it would require us to say that I was exercising power over you if, by my abominable rudeness, I caused you to punch me on the nose (Lessnoff, 1974, p. 46).

Again, many contemporary political scientists apparently want to define 'power' in such a way that to exercise power over someone necessarily involves some sacrifice of that subordinate person's interests. This perverse redefinition has been soundly criticized for making the term partly evaluative rather than purely descriptive (Lukes, 1974). But the truly overwhelming objection is that it would make all exercises of power which were allowed to be in the interests of the persons over whom the power was exercised not exercises of power at all. A truly benevolent despot must thus become a conceptual rather than a practical impossibility.

The necessary distinction is between two senses of 'order', and hence two senses of 'structure'. Here the Greeks really did have not a word but two words. One of these, 'Kosmos', from which we derive our 'cosmic' and 'cosmology', describes an order or a structure which exists or forms itself independent of any human will directed to its formation or maintenance. The other sort of order or structure is that produced and maintained by deliberate and purposive human ordering and control. This the Greeks called a taxis (pronounced to rhyme with praxis), and, significantly, this was also their word for a military formation.

Clearly a power structure will be a taxis, and power structures in the plural become taxeis. The order of nature, on the other hand, is a Kosmos. The economic order of a market economy is, paradigmatically, also a Kosmos; while that of a command economy is, equally paradigmatically, a taxis. Engels, to whom this distinction was not available, persistently describes the former as or as resulting in "the anarchy of production"; which can, he thinks, be reduced to order only by the introduction of a fully centralized command economy. (See, for instance, Engels, 1878, pp. 23, 299, 301 and 311). Whatever our personal preferences for or against socialism, it is for aspiring social scientists of the last importance to recognize that there is within their field application for the concept of Kosmos as well as of taxis.

Certainly the absence of taxis does not always and necessarily result in anarchy; if, that is, anarchy is construed as meaning, not just no commands being given or obeyed, but resulting chaos and confusion. In one brilliant recent study of various social mechanisms both fortunate and unfortunate, the economist author suggests that we draw from comparisons with "the way ant colonies work" a moral opposite to the one that is usual: "No ant designed the system. Each ant has certain things that it does, in coordinated association with other ants, but there is nobody minding the whole store" (Schelling, 1978, p. 21).

4 Natural or Human Science, Necessity or Choice?

> ... all animals, according to the known laws by which they are produced, must have a capacity of increasing in a geometrical progression ... Elevated as man is above all other animals by his intellectual faculties, it is not to be supposed that the physical laws to which he is subjected should be essentially different from those which are observed to prevail in order parts of animated nature.
>
> Thomas Robert Malthus, *A Summary View of the Principle of Population*, pp. 123 and 121–2

> A struggle for existence inevitably follows from the high rate at which all organic beings tend to increase ... This is the doctrine of Malthus applied with manifold force to the whole animal and vegetable kingdom; for in this case there can be no artificial increase of food and no prudential restraint from marriage.
>
> Charles Darwin, *The Origin of Species*, pp. 116–17

Thomas Robert Malthus (1766–1834) published a long, polemical pamphlet on *The Principle of Population* in 1798. Both this *First Essay* and his later two-volume treatise, now known as the *Second Essay*, were in the first half of the nineteenth century enormously influential. After declining in the interval this influence has been felt again since World War II, not so much directly as by contra-suggestion. For Marx and Engels abominated "Parson Malthus". In consequence their followers, even when in power, are very reluctant to admit and to tackle problems of overpopulation (Meek, 1953). Had the Communists been ready to recognize the nature and the seriousness of these problems from the beginning of their rule in China, then the Chinese people might have been spared some of the most drastic measures to which, their rulers now argue, there is no longer any more tolerable alternative.

Our present concern with Malthus is, however, different. It is with a conceptual scheme modelled on classical mechanics. By examining that scheme, and the amendments necessary to take account of the realities of choice, we shall bring out how an acceptance of this reality, and an appreciation of its implications, is fundamental and essential to the progress of any human science. One main implication is that there neither are nor can be any laws of nature necessitating human action. This conclusion raises the question of what weaker and more restricted sorts of regularity and predictability social scientists may reasonably hope to dis-cover. It also carries the corollary that it must be wholly mis-guided: either to insist that any human science has to assume that all human behaviour is determined by an absolute environmental necessitation; or to accept that the actual findings of such sciences are already showing that this is indeed the case.

1 *A conceptual scheme for population studies*

Malthus, like Comte, was soundly grounded in physics and applied mathematics. But Comte, after performing brilliantly in his first years at the *Ecole Polytechnique* was, just before his final examinations, sent down for ringleading insubordination. By contrast Malthus, who was "remarked in college for talking of what actually exists in nature or may be put to real practical use", concluded his undergraduate career with the achievement of first honours in the schools.

In taking classical mechanics as his model for social theorizing Malthus put himself into a long and distinguished tradition, extending back at least as far as the Hume of the *Treatise,* and on well into the nineteenth century, and after. There is a comprehen-sive account of this hardy perennial aspiration to become "the Newton of the moral sciences" in the chapter 1 of Halévy's study of *The Growth of Philosophical Radicalism.* Malthus himself, even in his first polemical pamphlet, goes out of his way to express his admiration for "the grand and consistent theory" and "the immortal mind" of Newton. Much more to the point, the theoretical scheme which guided and structured all his work on human populations does bear a very close resemblance to that of classical mechanics; which is perhaps rather more than can truthfully be said of the products of many other "bold attempts" to construct a physics of some sort of human action.

The basic theoretical scheme of Malthus is, except for one practically important innovation in the *Second Essay* and after, always presented as being, with only the most minor refinements, substantially the same. But for us it is crucial to bring out that neither Malthus nor his critics came anywhere near appreciating the full theoretical significance of that one practically important innovation. He just slipped it in, and they accepted it, as a fortunate second thought; happily enabling him "to soften some of the harshest conclusions of the *First Essay*", while leaving the rest of the theoretical framework unaffected.

The foundation of the whole structure, the very Principle of Population, is perhaps best stated in our motto passage from the *Summary View*; which was a separately published version of an article for the *Encyclopaedia Britannica*. The key clause is: ". . .all animals, according to the known laws by which they are produced, must have the capacity of increasing in a geometrical progression".

The next stage, again the same in every successive treatment, is: first to assert that "population, *when unchecked,* increases in geometrical progression . . ." (italics supplied); and then to argue that "the means of subsistence, under circumstances the most favourable to human industry, could not possibly be made to increase faster than in an arithmetical ratio". It is from a comparison between these misleadingly precise, yet by the same token powerfully persuasive, supposed ratios that Malthus then proceeds to derive his first conclusion. This does indeed become more cautious with the passage of the years. In the final *Summary View* he claims to have proved only that "it follows necessarily that the average rate of the *actual* increase of population over the greatest part of the globe . . . must be totally of a different character from the rate at which it would increase, if *unchecked*" (Malthus, 1824, p. 242).

Having to his own satisfaction thus established that powerful checks must always or almost always be operating to offset the mighty power of population: "The great question, which remains to be considered, is the manner in which this constant and necessary check on population practically operates." But, of course, like almost every social scientist, Malthus always had, in addition to this speculative and academic interest in how things are, a practical concern with how they ought to be. This duality of interest led him to mix two entirely different systems of classification.

The neutral one divides all recognized possibilities into positive and preventive: "foresight of the difficulties attending the rearing of a family acts as a preventive check; and the actual distress of some of the lower classes, by which they are disabled from giving the proper food and attention to their children, acts as a positive check". But then in addition to this neutral system there is another, which is from the first offered as comprising exhaustive though surely not in every context exclusive categories. This cuts right across the neutral system. It is itself not neutral but belligerent. Thus he concludes in the *First Essay*: "In short it is difficult to conceive any check to population which does not come under the description of some species of misery or vice."

In his Preface to the *Second Essay*, however, Malthus announces the admission of a third category: "... another check to population which does not come under the head of either vice or misery; ... I have endeavoured to soften some of the harshest conclusions of the *First Essay*" (italics and a capital supplied). This member of the trinity is Moral Restraint, very narrowly defined as one of "the preventive checks, the restraint *from* marriage which is not followed by irregular gratifications" (italics supplied). With this one vitally important modification, the old claim to exhaustiveness is repeated: "the checks which repress the superior power of population ... are all resolvable into moral restraint, vice and misery" (Malthus, 1802, vol. I, p. 240).

To complete his theoretical structure Malthus makes the point that the values of the various possible checks do not vary entirely independently: "The sum of all the positive and preventive checks, taken together, forms undoubtedly the immediate cause which represses population ... we can certainly draw no safe conclusion from the contemplation of two or three of these checks taken by themselves because it so frequently happens that the excess of one check is balanced by the defect of some other" (1802, vol. I, p. 256).

Although his general statements about the relations between the various checks considered as variables are usually, like this one, curiously weak, his particular arguments again and again depend on the subsistence of far stronger connections. Thus in the *First Essay* he remarks that the failure of Richard Price, after supposing that all the checks other than famine were removed, to draw "the obvious and necessary inference that an unchecked population would increase beyond comparison, faster than the earth, by the best directed exertions of man, could produce food for its support" was "as astonishing, as if he had resisted the conclusion of one of the plainest propositions of Euclid." Again, in the *Second Essay,* Malthus quotes with approval the remark of a Jesuit missionary: "if famine did not, from time to time, thin the immense number of inhabitants which China contains, it would be impossible for her to live in peace". Most significant of all, the whole force of the argument for Moral Restraint lies in the contention that this check might be substituted for those others which Malthus classed as species of Vice or Misery.

The second stage itself involves two steps: first, to underline the similarities; and then to indicate how Malthus was led astray by his natural scientific model.

In both schemes the master question is in form negative: "The natural tendency to increase is everywhere so great that it will generally be easy to account for the height at which the population is found in any country. The more difficult, as well as the more interesting, part of the inquiry is, to trace the immediate causes which stop its further progress ... What becomes of this mighty power ... what are the kinds of restraint, and the forms of premature death, which keep the population down to the level of the means of subsistence?" Earlier in this same *Second Essay* Malthus had quoted the question which Captain Cook asked of New Holland in his *First Voyage,* "By what means are the inhabitants of this country reduced to such a number as it can subsist?"; remarking that, "applied generally", it may "lead to the elucidation of some of the most obscure, yet important, points in the history of human society. I cannot so clearly and concisely describe the precise aim of the first part of the present work as by saying that it is an endeavour to answer this question so applied" (1802, vol. II, p. 240).

Newton might have spoken in parallel terms. For, as stated in Book I of the *Principia*, the First Law of Motion runs: "Every body continues in its state of rest or of uniform motion in a right line *unless it is compelled to change that state by forces pressed upon it*" (italics supplied). Since in actual fact all bodies are in motion relative to some other bodies, and since this motion never continues for long in a right line, the questions arise: Why do bodies *not* continue in a state of rest or of uniform motion in a right line, what forces operate to prevent this, and how?

Again, in the *1817 Appendix* Malthus defends his talk of a natural tendency, which in fact is always to a greater or lesser extent checked by counteracting forces, by appealing to the practice of "the natural philosopher ... observing the different velocities and ranges of projectiles passing through resisting media of different densities". He complains that he cannot "see why the moral and political philosopher should proceed upon principles so totally opposite" (Malthus, 1817, vol. II, p. 405).

We must have the more sympathy with his complaint when we see how he has been treated by one well regarded modern critic: "The invalidity of Malthus' ratios could never have escaped detection if he had stated the real series of increase and hence deduced all that it implied" (K. Smith, 1951, p. 234). One might as well argue the invalidity of the First Law of Motion on the ground that real bodies do not for long continue in a state of rest or of uniform motion. For Malthus laying down his Principle of Population perfectly parallels Newton laying down his First Law of Motion. Both were propounding ideal limiting cases, and then going on to ask why it is that that ideal is never in fact realized. This exercise generates the heuristically fertile notions: in the one case of checks; and in the other of impressed forces.

The same method has been followed by others; usually, no doubt, without realizing that Newton and Malthus were among their predecessors. Above all Weber made much of the notion of ideal types. These had for him a primary classification purpose: authorities were classified as legal, traditional or charismatic; and economic systems as – among other possibilities – handicraft, city economy, capitalism, or socialism. Ideal types also served to generate questions: in what ways, and why, does this or that particular instance fall short of the ideal? It is important to recognize that the ideals here are purely theoretical, not practically prescriptive: there can be ideal types of social forms which all would agree to be unadmirable.

Nevertheless, this said, everyone needs to be alert to the fact that some famous ideal types or theoretical limiting cases have been for some at the same time ideals which ought to be realized in practice. It is, for instance, many years now since the logician father of the economist Maynard Keynes observed in a treatise on *The Scope and Method of Political Economy* that, perhaps especially in England, there had been a tendency to accept the conceptual ideals of laissez-faire theory as moral norms (Keynes, 1904, pp. 50–1). Today there is, even more certainly, a tendency to see the theoretical limiting case of ideal social equality as, simultaneously, the prescriptive imperative. Courses are advertised and taught on the assumption that any kind of social inequality is self-evidently bad, and hence that the task of social science is to show, both how such inequalities arise, and how they might be abolished (Flew, 1976a, pt I, ch. 4; and compare Flew, 1981, chs. I–IV).

So much for similarities; we have next to notice a crucial dissimilarity. This lies in the difference: between the power of a human population to multiply if "left to exert itself with perfect freedom"; and the kind of natural power described by the First Law of Motion. It is a difference of which Malthus began to take account when he admitted the possibility of Moral Restraint. But this admission demands theoretical adjustments much more drastic and pervasive than he ever recognized to be required. There is also a difference which was pointed out by contemporary critics, and somewhat half-heartedly accepted by Malthus, between two related senses of the word 'tendency'.

As was hinted at the end of chapter 3, above, it is essential to distinguish two senses of the word 'power'. In one sense, the only sense in which the word can be applied to inanimate objects and to most of animate nature, a power simply is a disposition to behave in such and such a way, given that such and such preconditions are satisfied. Thus we might say that the bomb ('the nuclear device') dropped at Nagasaki possessed an explosive power equivalent to that of so many tons of TNT, or that full-weight nylon climbing rope has a breaking strain of (a power to hold up to) 4,500 pounds. Let us, for future ready reference, label this 'power' (physical). In another sense, the sense in which the word is typically applied to people, and perhaps to people only, a power is an ability at will either to do or to abstain from doing whatever it may be. Let this be 'power' (personal). Notice too, and resolve to adopt, the good practice of giving easily remembered names to senses distinguished. The example to follow is that of the colloquial distinction between 'funny' (ha ha) and 'funny' (peculiar) – eschewing the esoteric and obfuscating self-indulgence of those too indolent to offer anything but eminently forgettable numbers and letters.

More, much more, has to be said about what is presupposed and implied by asserting that someone possesses "an ability at will either to do or to abstain". But first we have to distinguish two senses of the word 'tendency'. This distinction was well made in 1832 by Archbishop Whately in the ninth of his *Lectures on Political Economy*. In one sense a tendency to produce something is a cause which, operating unimpeded, would produce it; in the other to speak of a tendency to produce something is to imply that that result is in fact likely to occur.

Malthus, misled perhaps by his favourite physical paradigm, seems to have slipped without distinction: from the first interpretation, which comes easily to the theoretical natural scientist, to the second, which belongs rather to the discussion of practical and human affairs. It is as if one were to argue that, because the First Law of Motion is, in the first sense, a law of tendency, it must therefore follow that it is probable or certain that everything, in the second sense, tends to remain at rest or to move uniformly, in a right line. In a similar way, especially but not only in the *First Essay,* Malthus was inclined to construe the multiplicative power of human populations as a natural force rather than as, what it is, a power (personal).

It is these confusions which mainly determine the gloomy conclusions actually drawn in the *First Essay*. For if the Principle of Population really were a power (physical), then this presumably would imply what we may in mischievous flattery christen Parkinson's Law of Population – the doctrine that always and everywhere human populations must press hard up against whatever resources can be made available for their support. It was this doctrine which Malthus employed to shatter all utopian dreams of universal egalitarian abundance.

It must, surely, have been precisely and only because Malthus was throughout this *First Essay* construing his Principle of Population on a Newtonian model, and in a way which made it imply population Parkinsonism, that he became unable to recognize any possibilities of voluntary control, any possibilities of individual or collective policies for the inhibition of, this mighty and menacing power of multiplication. Certainly it has to be seen as a fact crying out for explanation that so able and so concerned a writer should for so long have failed to recognize the possibility in this area of any form of Moral Restraint. For Malthus was never committed to any general doctrine of hard determinism, requiring him to deny the possibility of choice in this and all other particular cases. On the contrary: even in the *First Essay* itself he has a bit to say about the avoidable wrongness of choosing vicious rather than virtuous alternatives.

Once the fundamental distinctions have been made, and their implications understood, the true practical moral emerges. It is still, more than ever, both hugely important and extensively uncongenial. William Nassau Senior, another of the classical economists, summed up the agreement achieved in his own controversy with Malthus in this way: "... no plan for social improvement can be complete, unless it embraces the means both of increasing production, and of preventing population making a proportionate advance."

2 The inescapable reality of choice

The practical importance of that undeniably sound yet perennially neglected moral, especially for the peoples of the poorest countries, would be hard to exaggerate. But our present concern is with what must be, in the first instance, a more theoretical implication. Whereas in studying natural selection Darwin could, as he saw, afford to discount choice, choice is something of which every social scientist should forever be mindful. For it is involved in every human action; in the sense that all agents must in some sense be able to do other than they do do. So it is not possible for the behaviours of agents to be inexorably necessitated. An introduction to the philosophy of the social sciences cannot, therefore, pretend to be complete unless it tackles head on the question of what agency implies.

Perhaps the best way to bring out, both what is meant by "an ability at will either to do or to abstain", and that we are all of us throughout our waking hours possessed of more or less wide ranges of such abilities, is with the help of Book II, chapter xxi, 'Of Power' in *An Essay concerning Human Understanding*. John Locke (1632–1704) writes in its section 5: "This at least I think evident, that we find in ourselves a *Power* to begin or forbear, continue or end, several actions of our minds, and motions of our Bodies ... This *Power* ... thus to order the consideration of any *Idea*, or the forbearing to consider it; or to prefer the motion of any part of the body to its rest, and *vice versa* in any particular instance, is that which we call the *Will*" (Locke, 1690, p. 236).

   Locke's explanation continues in section 7, marred only by the fact that he sees himself as spelling out what is meant by 'a free agent' rather than, more simply and more fundamentally, by 'an agent'. The three Latin words refer to St Vitus's dance: "... everyone, I think, finds ... a power to begin or forbear, continue or put an end to several actions in himself ... We have instances enough, and often more than enough, in our own bodies. A Man's Heart beats, and the Blood circulates, which 'tis not in his Power ... to stop; and therefore in respect of these motions, where rest depends not on his choice ... he is not a *free Agent*. Convulsive Motions agitate his legs, so that though he wills it never so much, he cannot ... stop their motion (as in that odd disease called *chorea Sancti Viti*), but he is perpetually dancing: he is ... under as much Necessity of moving, as a Stone that falls or a Tennis-ball struck with a Racket" (p. 237).

   Now, let us call all those bodily movements which can be either initiated or quashed at will movings, and those which cannot motions. Obviously there are plenty of marginal cases. But so long as there also are, as there are, plenty – indeed far, far more – which fall unequivocally on one side or the other, we have stubbornly to refuse to be prevented from making a distinction of enormous practical importance by any such diversionary reference to marginal cases.

This particular stubborn refusal is a token of a more general type. For most of those distinctions which are of the greatest human interest refer to differences of degree; in the sense that the two opposed extremes are linked by a spectrum of actual or possible closely resembling cases, such that it is not possible to draw any clearcut and non-arbitrary dividing line at any point in the middle zone of the spectrum. This applies not only to actions as opposed to necessitated behaviours but also to the distinctions between riches and poverty, age and youth, sanity and insanity, a free society and one in which everything which is not forbidden is compulsory, and so on. So it manifestly will not do: either to dismiss all such differences of degree as *mere* differences of degree; or to profess to be unable to discern any decisive differences save where clearcut and non-arbitrary lines can be drawn (Flew, 1975, secs. 7.13–7.24).

If, having thus seized the high ground, we remain inflexibly resolved to hold it, we are positioned to see off any and every necessitarian counter-attack. For, once 'action' has been ostensively defined in terms of movings, there remains no possibility whatsoever of denying: either that all of us often are agents; or that, when we are, we must be able to do other than we do. ('Ostensive definition' is definition by reference to actual examples satisfying the requirements of the definition.)

The most doctrinally infatuated necessitarian theoreticians can scarcely hope to bring themselves to deny that some of everyone's bodily movements are movings rather than motions; and, this given, there is no room for doubt but that with respect to these movings, and in the most fundamental sense, ostensively defined precisely and only by reference to such movings, they can do other than they do do.

Locke is in this chapter indicating a way of defining a long string of closely associated notions: 'choice'; 'action'; 'agent'; 'an ability at will either to do or to abstain'; 'could do otherwise than they do do'; and so on. But he is at the same time also indicating how to define 'physical necessity'. (The implicit contrast with 'logical necessity' will be explained in chapter 5, below.)

By thus showing that (the members of) these opposing (sets of) notions both can and indeed have to be defined ostensively, Locke demonstrates that we do all have experience both of this sort of necessity and of choice. It is, therefore, just not on to maintain that everything in the Universe, including the senses (directions) of all human actions, is subject to ineluctable physical necessitation.

Against this philosophically sophisticated yet totally direct appeal to experience, other philosophers would argue that it is always conceivable that we are mistaken about what is or is not in fact subject to our wills; that some of us in the past have been afflicted by sudden paralyses, and all unwitting we may be now; or that any of us may suddenly have acquired powers of psycho-kinesis. Certainly this is all conceivable: we are none of us either infallible or all-knowing. But the great mistake is to assume that knowledge presupposes infallibility; that, where we may conceivably be mistaken, there it is impossible for us ever to know. The truth is that actually to know we need only to be in a position to know, and to be claiming to know something which is in fact true. If it really were the case that, where it remains conceivable that we might be mistaken, there we could never truly know; then we could, as fallible human beings, never know anything – not even that we could never know anything (Flew, 1971, ch. VIII, secs. 1–4 and ch. IX).

Anyone doubting whether it is correct to claim that these notions can be defined only by ostension must be challenged to provide alternative explications not referring to our experience of necessity and choice. These two ideas, although opposed, are connected and almost complementary. For how could creatures living in a world of total physical necessitation find any intelligible contrast against which to understand that actually, by the hypothesis, all-pervasive feature? And how is it that we in our different world acquire the idea of making things happen, of making this physically necessary and that physically impossible, if it is not by acting in one way while being all the time aware of the possibility of not so acting?

The concept of the contrary-to-fact, of what would have happened had some condition been satisfied which in fact was not, is essentially involved in that of this causing that to happen. Wherever such causal propositions are asserted, some contrary-to-fact propositions are entailed. If I say that the cause of the explosion was my pressing down the plunger, then I imply that, all other things being equal, had I not pressed down the plunger, the explosion would not have occurred. But then again, how could this key notion of contrary-to-fact alternatives be acquired by any creatures which were not, in the sense just now explained, agents? (Compare Flew, 1982a.)

Having said this much about causation it is worth adding, as it were between parentheses, that it is, though often tempting, false to say that historians and other social scientists can have no truck with what might have been. To the extent that they have anything to say about causes, and are not mere annalists, they cannot but say things which carry implications about what might have been but was not. John Grigg's *1943: The Victory that Never Was* was thus unfortunate in its reviewers. A. J. P. Taylor in *The Observer* wrote: "It is hard enough to find out what happened, without dreaming what might have happened." In the *Chicago Sun-Times* David Kahn spoke of such dreaming as, while "one of the most fascinating of intellectual pastimes", nevertheless, "probably the most fruitless undertaking in historiography" (Compare Oakeshott, 1966, p. 206). Weber knew better (Runciman, 1978, pp. 117ff; and compare Nagel, 1961, p. 589 and Hook, 1975, p. 205).

We noticed at the beginning of the previous section that Locke saw himself as explicating the meaning of 'a free agent' rather than of 'an agent'. This was a mistake. It is a perennially persistent mistake, which has led to the traditional misrepresentation of the philosophical problems arising in this area. These are thus wrongly described as problems about freewill or the freedom of the will rather than about agency and choice. Before we can go on to see just what the admission of these realities does imply for social science, we have to correct both this fundamental misconception and various consequent or otherwise connected errors.

The first necessary step is to appreciate that, in ordinary untechnical English usage, action of one's own freewill is contrasted: neither with physically necessitated nor with merely predictable behaviour; but with action subject to coercion or compulsion – these typically consisting in pressure from other human beings. Both persons who act of their own freewill and persons who act under compulsion act. So, in the more fundamental sense, definable in terms of the distinction between movings and motions, they could have done other than they did. Their behaviours, therefore, are not in either sense to be categorized with the spasmodic and involuntary tics, jerks, quivers, tremblings, flutters and twitches which are conventionally but misleadingly labelled 'reflex actions' or 'compulsive actions'. All these are, presumably, what no true action can be, physically necessitated.

So when we say of someone who did in this most ordinary sense act under compulsion that, as things were, they had no choice, or that, considering all the circumstances, they could not have acted otherwise than they did, these common and easily charitable expressions need to be construed with caution. If they really did act, albeit under compulsion, then it cannot be true: either that they literally had no choice at all; or that, in the more fundamental sense, they could not have done otherwise. The point, rather, is: not that they had no alternative at all, but that they had no tolerable alternative; and not that, in that more fundamental sense, they could not have done otherwise, but that, although of course they could, it was in every way unreasonable to expect that they either would or should. The case, for instance, of the recalcitrant businessman, receiving from *The Godfather* "an offer which he cannot refuse", is vitally different from that of the errant mafioso, who is without warning gunned down from behind. The former is an agent, however reluctant. But the latter, in that very moment of sudden death, ceases to be.

This whole batch of idioms really is quite extraordinarily misleading. We have no business to be surprised that so many even of the wise and good have been, and are, misled. For the clear implication of the previous two paragraphs is that, when we say, in the ordinary everyday sense, that someone had no choice at all, or that they could not have done other than they did, we are not saying that, in the most fundamental sense, they did not have any choice, or that they could not have done other than they did. On the contrary: we are presupposing that they did and that they could.

"Here I stand. I can no other. So help me God." So spoke Martin Luther before the Diet of Worms. To misinterpret this as evidence for a necessitarian determinism, as both Freud himself and his official biographer were inclined to do, is to require that we read Luther as at the same time both explaining and excusing what appeared to be, yet was not, an act of defiance; upon the memorably implausible grounds that he had been suddenly afflicted with a paralysis rendering him physically incapable of retreat! (See Flew, 1978, chs. VIII–IX.)

In this case, as in many others where expressions like 'could have done otherwise' are employed in their secondary sense, what is in question is not only the (impartial) explanation of conduct but also its (partial) justification. So it becomes worth distinguishing two senses in what is often a key word, 'expect'. Mr Worldly Wiseman will often not (descriptive) except people to do what he may quite consistently (prescriptive) expect them to do (Flew, 1975, secs. 5, 9 and 6.11). In his signal before Trafalgar Nelson was, surely, playing on this ambiguity? Since he was undoubtedly the darling hero of the whole fleet he must, by issuing that signal, have increased, at least marginally, the chances both that its prediction would be fulfilled and that its prescription would be obeyed. It remains for us only to insist, against the denials of among others many sociologists of education (Young, 1971, ch. 5), that, in so far as we are agents, we are not the completely helpless creatures of our environments. Nelson's signal had its desired effect, in so far as it did, because he was respected and even loved. But I myself reacted to my teacher's uttered prediction of my certain failure in O-level French in such a way that this in fact caused me not to fail but (only just) to succeed. (Maybe he even – descriptively – expected that it would!)

In saying, in the penultimate sentence of the previous paragraph, that "my teacher's uttered prediction . . . caused me not to fail but (only just) to succeed", I am of course asserting that I made that particular speech act my reason for launching an all-out effort. This provides occasion for distinguishing two fundamentally different senses of the word 'cause'. When we are talking about the causes of some purely physical event – an eclipse of the Sun, say – then we employ the word 'cause' in a sense implying both physical necessity and physical impossibility: what happened was physically necessary; and anything else was, in the circumstances, physically impossible.

Yet this is precisely not the case with the other sense of 'cause', the sense in which we speak of the causes of human actions. If, for instance, I give you good cause to celebrate I do not thereby make it inevitable that you will celebrate. To adapt a famous phrase from Gottfried Leibniz (1646–1716), causes of this second, personal sort incline but do not necessitate. So it remains entirely up to you whether or not you choose to make whoopee. Certainly knowledge of such causes, especially when combined with some familiarity with the persons to whom they are presented, may provide both historians and plain laypersons with overwhelmingly strong reason to expect (descriptive) some one particular response.

Given these two fundamentally different senses of the word 'cause' it becomes clear that we now need, if only within the human sphere, to distinguish two correspondingly different senses of 'determinism'. To be committed to the doctrine that absolutely everything that happens, including all human behaviour, is completely determined by the causes of the first or physical kind must be, surely, to be committed to a strong doctrine of the ultimate inevitability of everything.

But determination by causes of the second, personal sort has to be another matter altogether. It was in fact just such a non-necessitating determinism which Freud labelled 'psychic', although he then at once went wrong by assuming that this psychic determinism was nothing but the psychological particular case of a universal determinism of physical causes. No one would suggest that psychic determinism applies to anything except those elements in human behaviour (and possibly some brute behaviour) which are or could be actions; while anyone recognizing and adopting this fundamental distinction between kinds of cause has to conclude that psychic determinism is incompatible with, rather than a particular case of, the universal determinism of physical causes (Flew, 1978, chs. 8–9).

By failing to make these crucial distinctions, first between two senses of 'cause' and then between two corresponding senses of 'determinism', many are misled into the enormous mistake of construing all explanations of conduct in terms of personal causes as providing support for a doctrine of universal, physical, necessitarian determinism. That this is the main move being made, and that it leaves no escape from a doctrine of universal historical inevitability, comes out very sharply in E. H. Carr's Cambridge lectures on *What is History?* But the same unsound move to a disastrous and false conclusion has been and is being made more obscurely and more fuzzily by other historians, as well as by social scientists of other sorts (Carr, 1961; and compare Flew, 1978, ch. III).

3 Natural laws determining human action?

The Dedication of Popper's *The Poverty of Historicism* reads: "In memory of the countless men and women of all creeds or nations or races who fell victims to the fascist and communist belief in Inexorable Laws of Historical Destiny." The one expression of such a belief cited in the text is drawn from the Preface to *Capital*: "When a society has discovered the natural law that determines its own movement, even then it can neither overleap the natural phases of its evolution, nor shuffle them out of the world by a stroke of the pen. But this much it can do: it can shorten and lessen the birth-pangs" (quoted Popper, 1957, p. 51).

These two passages together show that the historicism against which Popper is polemicizing actually consists in a belief in natural laws of historical development. Historicism in this Popperian sense was the basis for Nikita Khrushev's famous boast, or notorious threat: "Communism lies at the end of all the roads in the world; we shall bury you!" Yet Popper's own official definition is totally different: "It will be enough if I say here that I mean by 'historicism' an approach to the social sciences which assumes that *historical prediction* is their principal aim, and which assumes that this aim is attainable by discovering the 'rhythms' or the 'patterns', the 'laws' or the 'trends' that underlie the evolution of history" (1957, p. 3).

The articles from which *The Poverty of Historicism* was developed were originally turned down by *Mind,* and first published some years later in *Economica.* G. E. Moore, the then Editor of *Mind,* presumably refused to accept them until and unless this and other similarly gross faults were remedied. 'Gross', surely, is not too strong a word? For Popper was proposing to introduce a fresh sense for an already somewhat overworked word. It behoved him to supply an accurate and unequivocal account of the meaning which he wanted it to be given.

Instead he first brings in and gives heavy emphasis to the irrelevant idea of *"historical prediction"*. This is irrelevant, because many commentators have succeeded in making, and in deploying tolerably good reasons for making, correct predictions, without pretending to derive these from putative natural laws of historical development. Here, as elsewhere in discussions of choice, it is a mistake to focus on predictability as such. For what, if anything, precludes choice is not the possibility of predicting the senses of choices yet to be made, but the possibilities of prediction on the basis of knowledge that movements in those senses will be physically necessitated. No one, for instance, should think that the possibility of predicting my future voting behaviour on the basis of my known political convictions is a reason for fearing that I shall not be able, in the more fundamental sense, to do other than vote as predicted.

It is, again, irrelevant, or worse, to bring in rhythms, patterns and trends, as if these were on all fours with the vastly stronger notion of laws of nature. Since it is hard to see how there could be any intelligible and illuminating historical writing if we had to abandon all these weaker notions too, Popper's wretched definition gives purchase to charges of obscurantism from such hostile and (according to Popper's actual usage) historicist critics as Carr. Perhaps it is in hopes of forestalling these charges that Popper proceeds to present what he holds to be "a really fundamental similarity between the natural and the social ..." This putative "fundamental similarity" arises, he thinks, thanks to "the existence of sociological laws or hypotheses which are analogous to the laws or hypotheses of the natural sciences" (1957, p. 62).

By thus insisting on the subsistence of natural laws determining human action Popper deprives himself of the most direct and decisive refutation of historicism. For, if there is a conceptual incompatibility between action and necessitating determination, then there can be no such laws; hence it must be even less possible to have an especially grandiose sort determining macroscopic historical development. There are hints of such a more decisive refutation both in earlier and in later works. Thus in *The Open Society* it is claimed that "it is necessary to recognize as one of the principles of any unprejudiced view of politics that everything is possible in human affairs"; while one of the three volumes of what has been nicknamed his *Concluding Scientific Postscript* is entitled, boldly, *The Open Universe: An Argument for Indeterminism* (Popper, 1945, vol. II, p. 197; and compare Popper, 1982).

What is in fact offered in *The Poverty of Historicism* is an argument for the inherent unpredictability of future scientific advances: "The course of human history is strongly influenced by the growth of human knowledge"; but "We cannot predict, by rational or scientific methods, the future growth of our scientific knowledge. (This assertion can be logically proved . . .)" (Popper, 1957, pp. ix–x). This logical proof is best grasped by quoting Humphrey Lyttleton's reply to an interviewer asking him where jazz was going: "If I knew it would be there already." Popper's logical proof may be sufficient, though it is not quite as strong as at first it seems. For what is of historical importance is, in the main, not theoretical advances but technological applications. And we may well be able to predict that something will become technically possible, without first solving all the problems which will have to be solved in order to make it so.

Popper attempts to dispose of the suggestion that there are no sociological laws in a characteristically forthright and straightforward way: "I will now give a number of examples" (1957, p. 62). But he makes his self-imposed task more formidable by stressing, quite rightly, that a proposition expressing a law of nature must carry entailments of physical necessity and physical impossibility. Thus he says, on the previous page: "As I have shown elsewhere, every natural law can be expressed by asserting that *such and such a thing cannot happen*; that is to say, by a sentence in the form of the proverb: 'You can't carry water in a sieve'" (p. 61).

The reason why so many otherwise alert and well-girded writers have failed to see any problem about laws of nature in the social sciences, and have thought that an introduction to the philosophy of the social sciences could be completed without coming to terms with any questions about choice, is that they have accepted Humian analyses both of (physical) causation and of laws of nature. These, as we saw back in chapter 1, reduce such causation and such laws to mere regularities of accompaniment or succession, denying that we have any knowledge of practical necessity or practical impossibility.

If these regularity analyses were correct,then there would perhaps be no problems here. Certainly no one could suggest that there might be a conceptual incompatibility between action, on the one hand, and laws of nature or (physical) causation, on the other. Certainly too, if physical necessity is not necessity but only unconnected and unnecessitated regularity of succession, then the "reconciling project" of Hume's first *Enquiry* goes through at the trot: total 'necessity' and liberty or choice become fully compatible (Hume, 1748, sec. VIII; and compare Flew, 1961, ch. VII). It is, surely, only upon these Humian assumptions that so many philosophers have been able to be, what I myself once was, Compatibilist. (Compatibilists maintain that there is, after all, no incompatibility between universal necessitating determination and the realities of choice; while Incompatibilists, unsurprisingly, contradict that contention.)

The most persuasive of the several supposed specimens deployed by Popper is: "You cannot have full employment without inflation." No doubt it is true that wherever you do have full employment you will also find some measure of wage-push inflation; and that there are no measures, or at any rate no tolerable measures, which government can take which will completely neutralize this inflationary pressure. There is, however, no call to argue about this in the immediate present context. For if Popper had really laid his hands upon a true law of nature determining social actions, then the practical necessities and practical impossibilities entailed by that law would have to constrain all the agents concerned. It is not enough that such necessities should apply only to those in and around governments, and then only to governments inhibited by some scruples against, or some constraints upon, the totalitarian full employment of state power. The necessities of a genuine law of nature would have to apply equally to all, including all those outside government whose several individual determinations to do the best they can for themselves sum up to the pressure for wage-push inflation. And, however strong and well-grounded our confidence that they – that we – will never in fact suppress our unrelenting drive to better the condition of ourselves and our families, we do nevertheless all know equally well that, in the more fundamental sense already explained, we could.

"You cannot have full employment without inflation" is Popper's most promising candidate for the position of a true sociological law of action. It is, as we have just seen, not nearly good enough. Some of the others are so terrible that it is hard to understand how Popper ever brought himself to enter them. Take, for instance, "You cannot introduce agricultural tariffs and at the same time reduce the cost of living" (1957, p. 62). Of course you can; always supposing that you are – perhaps in your capacity as a minister in the cabinet of Saudi Arabia – so fortunate as to possess the means for effecting some more than corresponding reductions in the prices of some other items in the cost of living index. If we are now told that this wretched candidate has to be assessed as if it had contained an all other-things-being-equal clause, then let us come back hard with the reply that this makes the claim true but only at the cost of making it tautological. Certainly it is true – all too true – that any increase in the price of any item in a cost of living index will result, all other prices remaining the same, in an overall increase in that index. But if a candidate is to be accepted as a law of nature it has to be not tautological but substantial.

Or again, take "You cannot introduce a political reform without strengthening the opposing forces, to a degree roughly in ratio to the scope of the reform" (1957, p. 62). This one is simply not true. Nor is there here any parallel possibility of withdrawal beckoning into the sanctuary of tautology. For there are plenty of reforms which, once implemented, win the more or less grudging acceptance of those previously opposed. There are also reforms which create interests or institutions which make reversal politically impossible.

Consider, for instance, either the Reform Bill of 1832 or the measures of economic liberalization through which in 1948 Ludwig Erhard unleashed the really quite unmiraculous German 'economic miracle'. In both cases the implementation of the reforms transformed the whole balance of political forces. That Reform Bill created a mass of new electors who never would vote for their own disfranchisement; while many diehard opponents discovered that, even after its passage, the heavens did not fall. The extent of the Erhard transformation is demonstrated most strikingly by the decisions taken only eleven years later at Bad Godesberg by the former doyen of Marxist parties. For there in 1959 the Social Democratic Party of Germany decided that, if ever they were to be elected to office, they had to repudiate their monopoly socialist aims; and they did. (In that same year the British Labour Party rejected a much weaker move by its then Leader, Hugh Gaitskell; instead reaffirming, with insubstantial amendment, its commitment, by Clause IV of its constitution, to the public ownership of "all the means of production, distribution and exchange".)

All the other examples presented by Popper can be collapsed in the same way. Either, that is, they are just false; or they make insufficiently universal claims about physical necessities; or, in order to be made true, they have to be so amended and so qualified that they become tautological. His own suspicions ought to have been aroused – at latest – when he found that he was having to construct candidates out of his own head, and that there were no ready-named specimens pushing themselves forward. For why is it that textbooks of sociology index no references to Comte's Law or to Spencer's Law; paralleling those to Boyle's Law, to Ohm's Law and all the others which we can find in any textbook of physics? (Such suggested exceptions as Gresham's Law, Parkinson's Law, and Michel's Iron Law of Oligarchy – exceptions rarely if ever mentioned in textbooks – can all be collapsed by the methods just now demonstratively employed.)

The moral for us to draw is that proposed already. The reason why Popper can neither find any established and accepted socio-logical laws in the textbooks, nor excogitate presentable substi-tutes on his own account, simply is that there neither are nor could be any laws of nature necessarily determining social action; and that this fundamental truth, together with the inexpugnable reality of such action, constitute the surest bases for the decisive disposal of (in Popper's sense) historicism. (Nevertheless, see also Hook, 1943.)

4 *What can and cannot be discovered*

There is no call to be depressed by the upshot of the previous section. For that still leaves plenty of room for the discovery of any number of true propositions of all the various kinds so far, in the process of establishing these latest conclusions, distinguished from law of nature nomologicals. Yet a full realization of the truth of these conclusions must lead us on to perhaps surprising and certainly important insights. We shall come to see that many of what are retailed as the fruits of social scientific enlightenment neither are not could be truths; and that some of the proposed objects of inquiry neither are nor could be there to be found. The common cause of all these troubles is the refusal to recognize, and to take appropriate account of, the realities of choice. The reason why these popular propositions neither are not could be true, and these sought-after objects neither are not could be there to be found, is that their truth, or their existence, presupposes, what is manifestly false, that we are not creatures which make, and which cannot but make, choices (Locke, 1690, bk II, ch. xxi, sec. 23, pp. 245–6).

The logical fact that, in so far as people are agents, their actions cannot be completely necessitated, does not by any means rule out all possibility of making true assertions about the physical necessities circumscribing social action. Nor does it foreclose on the possibility of inferring, from such and such statements about their character and circumstances, that, it follows necessarily, so and so did act or will act thus and thus. (Retrodictions and predictions of this form do not assert physical necessities: the necessity qualifying 'it follows' is, as we shall see in chapter 5, of quite another kind.)

One example of the realization of the former possibility is provided by Popper's "You cannot have full employment without inflation"; if suitably supplemented by an account of the far less than universal reference of the 'you'. Another promising vein is that of propositions about the possibly unintended consequences which must be produced by various patterns of social action. Here the necessities, since they are not determining the actions themselves, might be completely universal: they would obtain, that is, wherever and whenever social actions were performed forming these specified patterns; and this universality is not prejudiced by the fact that the same patterns are not found in all times and places. It is curious that sponsors of laws of nature in the social sciences have not been more eager to present candidates of this most promising kind.

Nor is there any shortage of true premises of the second sort, yielding similarly true predictive and retrodictive conclusions. What, however, arguments of this form cannot provide is covering law explanations of conduct of the type standard in the natural sciences. This will distress all, but maybe only, those committed to contending that there must be no fundamental differences between the natural and the social sciences. Covering law explanations explain by showing that and how the truth of the explanandum can be deduced from the truth of the conjunction of one or more law of nature nomologicals and statements of the circumstances. Explanations of conduct cannot be of this type since, as has been insisted ad nauseam and beyond, there cannot be laws of nature determining particular courses of action. (For further discussion, with particular reference to historiography, see Gardiner, 1952 and Dray 1957).

Some historical writers, by reason of their commitments to what they saw as the presuppositions of any genuinely scientific history, have been misled to believe that their own researches have warranted unwarrantably strong nomological conclusions. The distinguished Victorian, H. T. Buckle, for instance, in a much quoted passage from the first chapter of his *History of Civilization in England,* commended the belief "that every event is linked to its antecedent by an inevitable connection, that [every] such antecedent is connected with a preceding fact; and that thus the whole world forms a necessary chain, in which indeed every man may play his part, but can by no means determine what that part shall be" (Buckle, 1903, vol. I, p. 9).

Later, after citing some remarkable year-to-year regularities in vital statistics, he continues: "In a given state of society, a certain number of persons must put an end to their own life. This is the general law; and the special question of who shall commit the crime depends of course upon special laws . . ." Nevertheless, "the power of the larger law is so irresistible, that neither the love of life nor the fear of another world can avail anything towards even checking its operation" (p. 28).

In his Preface to the third German edition of *The Eighteenth Brumaire of Louis Bonaparte* another Victorian – rarely described as such and even more rarely, though with equal truth, described as a retired shareholder/manager of a mini-multinational – commended his friend the author for composing "a concise, epigrammatic exposition that laid bare the whole course of French history since the February days . . . [and] reduced the miracle of December 2 to a natural, necessary result". It is greatly to the credit of that recently deceased friend, and highly significant, that, in his own Preface to the second edition, the only claim made was much more modest: "I . . . demonstrate how the class struggle in France created circumstances and relationships that *made it possible* for a grotesque mediocrity to play a hero's part" (Marx, 1852, pp. 8 and 6: italics removed and supplied).

In chapter 1, section 1, the author of *Thinking about Crime* was quoted as arguing that "if causal theories explain why a criminal acts as he does, they also explain why he *must* act as he does" (J. Q. Wilson, 1977, p. 58). This argument is valid iff the word 'cause' is being employed not in its personal but in its physical sense. But that is not a distinction made either by Wilson or by the many other writers whose work he is reviewing. So, while they are apt, on finding personal causes of criminal behaviour, invalidly to infer that they have thereby shown that and why these criminals *must* act as they do, Wilson, for all his stubborn common sense and conservative concern for the victims, fails to put his finger on the fallacy.

There is a similar failure in dealing with the sort of criminologist for whom "the individual who is confronted with a choice among kinds of opportunities does not *choose,* he 'learns deviant values' from the 'social structure of the slum'" (p. 63). This refusal to recognize that people make choices, that we are none of us the totally helpless creatures of our environments, that different people, or even the same people at different times, may respond differently to the same environments, is seen as a perverse individual eccentricity. Perverse it most certainly is, since the facts which criminologists of this sort are refusing to recognize are within the common everyday experience of us all. Yet it is not a mere minority aberration.

No doubt the historians and the economists are for the most part immune: in any case they tend neither to think of themselves nor to be thought of as social scientists. But among the sociologists, the social policy researchers and their like, as well as among those boasting of having acquired some social science background in the course of their professional training, such refusals are not found solely as the oddities of licensed eccentrics. Instead they are largely unnoticed features of a whole climate of opinion. Skinner, as we saw in section 3 of chapter 2, puts forward a bold and explicit formulation of these refusals, insisting that they must be the presuppositions of any human science. But for what sometimes seems to be the great majority, both of practising social scientists and of those who have merely suffered some instruction in the social sciences, they are, rather, rarely if ever formulated, continually misguiding, deep background assumptions.

Consider, for instance, the following report of a conversation between two modern mothers: "One mentioned how, on a visit to her child's school, a particular seven-year-old appeared to be in the process of dismantling the classroom while the teacher stood passively by. 'Can't you stop him?' asked the mother. 'He comes from a broken home', the teacher fatalistically replied. 'Well,' said the mother, 'he can bloody-well learn, can't he?" (Morgan, 1978, p. 57).

No doubt that fatalistic teacher had been told, either during some Sociology of Education course at college and/or by some social worker who had also got it from some similar source that there is, as indeed there is, a high positive correlation between broken homes and bad school behaviour and low achievement. But even if this were allowed to be enough to warrant the conclusion that a particular misbehaving seven-year-old from a broken home is misbehaving because he comes from such a wretched home, it does not even begin to show that he could not, given firm discipline and good teaching, become one of those who, all handicaps notwithstanding, perform up to the top level of their native abilities. Such sociological correlations only seem to warrant fatalistic conclusions when people fail to make and to insist upon crucial distinctions: between physical and personal causes;

between the more and the less fundamental senses of 'can no other'; between the prescriptive and the descriptive meanings of 'expect'; and so on.

The most that such correlations show is that it is very likely that people from homes of such and such a sort – rich or poor, close-knit or broken, bookish or bookless, working-class or whatever else – will in fact act in this or that way. They cannot show that they will not be acting at all, but behaving instead under an absolute necessitation. In fact the correlations, even when they are both significant and positive, are always a lot less than perfect; that is to say, one to one.

So when someone claims, on the basis of the actual or alleged subsistence of such a correlation, that such and such a condition is the, or a, cause of this or that sort of behaviour, they should always be challenged to tell us why the minority behaves differently. This question is especially to the point, and perhaps most often unasked, when the behaviour of the majority is in some way deplorable, and the practical reason for seeking its causes lies in the hope of discovering cures. Why do not ALL the members of such and such a set become delinquents? And how might the non-delinquent minority – or majority – be increased?

The refusal to recognize that people make and cannot but make choices, and that people who are in most ways similar may choose in different sense, infects all the work on equality mentioned in section 2 of chapter 1. For to deduce inequalities of opportunity directly from inequalities of outcome, as all these otherwise sober and uninfatuated workers do, is to assume that inclinations and abilities – to say nothing of qualities like determination, and persistence with ventures once undertaken – are found in substantially the same distributions in all the various sets which are being compared. It is this same false assumption which misguides all those – and today their name is legion – who insist that there cannot but be racist or sexist discrimination wherever the sexes and the races are not in every subset distributed in the same way as in the whole set of the population.

There is in fact an enormous amount of usually neglected evidence, drawn from many countries and many cultures, showing how big these differences of inclination and of actual choice can be. For instance: thanks to various forms of what, in the slimy

euphemism currently fashionable, is called 'positive discrimination' many Chinese Malaysians have to study abroad. Nevertheless, "although there are approximately equal numbers of Chinese
and Malays in Malaysian colleges and universities, the Chinese
out-number the Malays by more than eight-to-one in the sciences
and fifteen-to-one in engineering" (Sowell, 1983, p. 139). Again:
"Back before World War I, a study in New York City showed that
German and Jewish school children graduated from high school at
a rate more than a hundred times that for Irish or Italian children"
(Sowell, 1981c, p. 9). Now that really was for the Irish and Italians
an achievement in under-achievement! Nor, in view of the later
rises of both the Irish-Americans and the Italian-Americans, is it
plausible to try to diminish this negative achievement by postu-
lating any genetically determined inferiorities.

An even more striking example of this besetting occupational
reluctance to admit the importance of choice, and of the differences between the senses of choices made, is provided by the
monumental study reported in *Inequality: A Reassessment of the
Effect of Family and Schooling in America*. This is most remarkable among sociological works for its willingness to admit, at least
as between individuals, large genetically determined differences in
abilities. Yet, in examining factors favouring financial success, the
researchers collapse into one residual miscellany, called "varieties
of luck and on-the-job competence", all those various human
differences which they either cannot measure or have not tried to
measure (Jencks and others, 1973, p. 8). Into this discounted
category of unmeasured unequalizables are flung all disregarded
differences in respect of inclination and choice; to say nothing of
those regarding the supposedly officerlike qualities of drive, initia-
tive, energy, resource, enterprise, creative imagination, and – you
name it.

Economists, by contrast, are professionally concerned with
choices between alternative employments of scarce means; and
perhaps also inclined to believe that, at least typically, people
make their choices in the senses which – on the basis of the
information available to them – appear most likely best to serve
their several individual ends. Given these commonsense convictions, economists are further inclined to believe that the Royal
Road to reducing the amount of any kind of disfavoured behav-

iour must be to decrease its perceived rewards and/or to increase its perceived costs.

It would be hard to find any assumptions more alien to most sociologically oriented criminologists. They often believe that social scientists have discovered that no potential criminal is ever deterred (Rockwell, 1974, p. 51). Apart from the general occupational disbelief in the reality of choice, this particular 'discovery' seems to depend on two quite inadequately supportive particular facts: that the death penalty does not seem to deter murders within the family; and that present prisoners, who are the persons most accessible to criminological investigation, were not deterred from committing the offences which landed them in prison. (Curiously, our 'discoverers' never reflect how they can themselves be deterred from parking illegally by a credible threat to tow away and impound all illegally parked cars!)

It is, therefore, not surprising that, when the American Enterprise Institute organized an incursion of economists into criminological preserves, the results were intellectually exhilarating; sufficient to restore anyone's faith in the possibilities of wholly realistic and doctrinally unblinkered social science. (See Rottenberg, 1973: not only for several further references to silly statements about the ineffectiveness of all deterrents; but also for calculations showing that, given the present condition of the American criminal justice system, a criminal career is for many the course of supreme economic rationality.)

5   Matters of Fact, and Relations of Ideas

All the objects of human reason or enquiry may naturally be divided into two kinds, to wit, *Relations of Ideas,* and *Matters of Fact.* Of the first kind are the sciences of Geometry, Algebra and Arithmetic; and, in short, every affirmation which is either intuitively or demonstratively certain. *That the square of the hypothenuse is equal to the square of the two sides,* is a proposition which expresses the relation between these two figures. *That three times five is equal to the half of thirty,* expresses a relation between these numbers. Propositions of this kind are discoverable by the mere operation of thought, without dependence on what is anywhere existent in the universe . . .

Matters of fact, which are the second objects of human reason, are not ascertained in the same manner; nor is our evidence of their truth, however, great, of like nature with the foregoing. The contrary of every matter of fact is still possible; because it can never imply a contradiction, and is conceived by the mind with the same facility and distinctness, as if ever so comfortable to reality. *That the sun will not rise tomorrow* is no less intelligible a proposition, and implies no more contradiction than the affirmation, *that it will rise.*

David Hume, *An Enquiry concerning Human Understanding,*
see IV, pt i, pp. 25–6.

The challenge presented in the motto passage above is known as Hume's Fork. It is a merit of this nickname that it suggests, correctly, that Hume is engaged in forceful inquiry. He is not just claiming to have noticed, what is manifestly not the case, that every assertive utterance which is to any extent intelligible falls unequivocally into one or other of these two mutually exclusive and together exhaustive categories. He is, rather, insisting that it is always possible and often necessary to force ourselves and others to decide which of these two utterly different sorts of assertion we are really wanting to make. This insistence was fundamental to the Logical Positivism of the Vienna Circle, formed shortly after the end of World War I, and dispersed when National Socialist Germany enforced its Anschluss with Austria. Logical Positivism, as thus defined, is not to be confused with the unqualified Positivism of Comte and his nineteenth-century followers.

1 Logical necessity, logical possibility, and logical impossibility

Several further possible occasions of confusion call for brief attention before we can begin to put Hume's Fork to use. First, in speaking of the relations of ideas Hume is concerned with the logical relations between concepts rather than with likenesses and unlikenesses between mental images. It is not a matter of psychological fact but of what follows or does not follow, what is or is not incompatible with what.

Second, both the two fundamental catch-all categories include both true and false propositions. Since it is intolerably paradoxical to say that something is both a matter of fact and yet not the case, it is best to think, on the one hand, of propositions stating *or purporting to state* the relations of ideas, and, on the other hand, of propositions stating *or purporting to state* matters of fact.

Third, in the present context, the word 'possible', along with such associated terms as 'necessary' and 'impossible', are all employed in senses less familiar than those explained in chapter 4, above, and there characterized as practical or physical. To say that some suggestion is logically possible is to say that it is coherent, that it makes sense, that making it involves the maker in no self-contradiction, that what is suggested is conceivable. Even if it cannot be pictured, it can at least be intelligibly described.

Propositions stating the true relations of ideas are said to be necessarily true or to express necessary truths. If this proposition can be validly deduced from that, when this proposition is said to follow necessarily from that. And a valid deductive argument is, by definition, an argument such that to assert the premises while denying the conclusion is to contradict yourself. For anyone who is serious about attempting to think soundly about anything, it is essential both to master these several notions and to appreciate their interconnections. What a proposition means must be the sum of all that can be immediately deduced from it, while both 'valid deduction' and 'logical necessity' are defined in terms of meaning and of self-contradiction.

The key notion here is self-contradiction. Where contradiction occurs it is – pace G. W. F. Hegel and all his direct and indirect disciples – a feature not of the non-linguistic world but of language. It is statements and propositions which may be in contradiction one to another. Material things are (sometimes) under tension, while people are (often) in conflict. (It was typical of the output of Penguin Education in the seventies that one writer in *Counter Course* should have complained that "our philosophers" ignored social conflict; not by concentrating on, but by "avoiding the idea of contradiction"! See Pateman, 1972, p. 120.)

Self-contradiction has to be an intolerable scandal to all, but only, those who – like Bertrand Russell's pedant – prefer their statements to be true. Such persons cannot endure to hear *p* simultaneously both asserted and denied. For, above all, we want to know, now and always, what truly is the case.

Deduction being what deduction is, definable in terms of self-contradiction, it follows that valid deductive argument can never reveal anything which was not already implicit in its premises. One mildly interesting corollary is that the explanation of a series of facts can never be deduced from any set of statements simply recording the facts to be explained. Any such 'explanans' would have to be dismissed on the grounds that it told us no more than we knew already, that it was at best only a partial or perhaps complete restatement of the explanandum. In this sense, if only in this sense, the explaining of facts cannot but be an essentially creative activity.

Because to contradict any true proposition stating only the relations of ideas is to contradict yourself, to assert such a proposition is not to assert anything substantial about the Universe around us. It would therefore seem that all the necessarily true propositions of formal logic and of pure mathematics must be, at bottom, tautologies. The reason why they do not all look as empty and as obvious as textbook examples of tautologies is that even the best of us humans are endowed with rather poor powers of reasoning and logical intuition.

It is as easy to confound the two senses of 'necessary' and of its associates as it is important that they should not be confounded. Hume employed his Fork first in order to establish that anything may be the cause of anything; in the sense that it is not logically necessary for any thing or sort of thing to be the cause of any other thing or sort of thing. Unfortunately he was so keen to defend this insight – an insight which, as we have seen, is essential to the progress of the social sciences – that he refused to allow that we all have experience of a second sort of necessity, the practical or physical or contingent.

It is also tempting and common to make the mistake of thinking that, when one proposition follows necessarily, as a matter of logic, from another proposition, then either the former or the latter or both must themselves be making some assertion about necessities, in either the second or the first sense of 'necessity'. This is what was going on, and going wrong, in all those arguments which purported to deduce the massively substantial conclusion of a universal, physically necessitating determinism from tautological premises stating only the logically necessary relations of ideas. It is the same vicious yet seductive move which is made whenever anyone infers what will in fact be done from premises making no claims about physical necessity; and then, falsely, takes it that they have shown that the persons concerned will not be able to behave in any but the predicted ways. (It is in fact as wrong to think that some sort of necessity must characterize any conclusion following necessarily from a premise as it is to think that the premises from which conclusions follow necessarily must be themselves either logically necessary propositions or else nomologicals asserting practical necessities.)

Arguments of the first of the two sorts just distinguished are at least as old as Book IX of Aristotle's *On Interpretation*. Let us, however, work here with a specimen familiar to an earlier generation of filmgoers. It comes in a theme song sung by Miss Doris Day beginning: "Che sarà, sarà. Whatever will be will be"; and concluding that there is nothing which anyone can do to stop anything. Spell this out in a clarifactory notation and it becomes obvious that the tautological premise is that, for all values of X, from X *will be* it follows necessarily that X *will be*. Indeed it does. But it does not follow necessarily that X *will necessarily be*. It simply does not follow: neither if the second 'necessarily' is construed, as in its new context is natural, in the physical sense; nor if it is construed, much less naturally, in the same logical sense as the first.

It is much more difficult to spot that and how things are going wrong when the premise or premises are not tautological but substantial; and when other words of the sort which Immanuel Kant (1724–1804) loved to call apodeictic are employed, as well as 'necessarily'. That was the pedagogic reason why, in the previous paragraph, we began with a cartoon-simple textbook example, dissecting the invalid argument in order to display its nerve in a clarificatory notation. (By the way: 'apodeictic' is an adjective referring to logically compulsive demonstration: such expressions as 'must be' and 'cannot but be' therefore score as apodeictic.)

It should always have, but has not, been obvious to everyone that no substantial conclusions about matters of fact ever could be validly deduced from purely tautological premises. But, when we start from factual premises, it is easier not to notice when these are making no assertions about practical necessities. Thus we are tempted to argue that, since these people are members of a social set which always behaves in such and such a way, therefore it follows: not just that they will so behave; but that they cannot but, that they necessarily must, that it is inevitable (even by them), and so on.

We have just considered one type of fallacious move, by which usually false conclusions about inexorable practical necessities may be invalidly derived from insufficient premises. There is another similar mistake, equally persistent and with an equally ancient ancestry. This consists in failing to distinguish causal from criterial senses of the word 'make'; and then, mistakenly, assuming that having the criteria is the cause of all the phenomena which satisfy those criteria. People notice that it is the law which makes crimes and, hence, criminals; in the sense that certain sorts of behaviour, and hence certain kinds of behaver, are correctly describable as crimes, and criminals, only and precisely because they are by the criminal law so defined. In this criterial sense of 'make', the law does indeed make both crimes and criminals.

But, thus understood, this is a pretty pedestrian truism. How much more dashing it is to suggest, or even outright to say, that the same sentence still expresses a truth when the 'makes' is construed in the causal sense. In this interpretation the claim is being made that it is the criminal justice system itself, or perhaps only the criminal justice system of "capitalist society", which is the ultimate cause of all the behaviour which it defines as criminal; that, if only we could get rid of the whole system, then there would – the Revolution accomplished – be no rapes, no muggings, no assault and battery, no robbery, no murder; nothing, nothing but idyllic sweetness and light.

Once again, once the nerve of the fallacious argument is thus clearly displayed, it becomes difficult to believe that anyone could, sincerely and with a straight face, either argue so outrageously or assert such nonsense. But, of course, the distinction between these two senses of 'make' has to be made. Even Plato himself, without making it, spoke of the Form or Idea or Essence of Justice as if it might be – must be – both the criterion and the cause of whatever is in fact just. Nowadays those who are still committing the same fallacy wrap it up both with empirical material and with other confusions. They argue, for instance, and just as wrongly, that whatever is legally defined as criminal must be so defined quite arbitrarily, or in the interests solely of the class enemy (Quinney, 1970, pp. 1–14, 204–50 and 316; and compare S. Cohen, 1972 passim).

The same ruinous failure to distinguish causal from criterial senses of the word 'make' is also found in widely circulating and strongly recommended works in the sociology of education. As in the criminological case the conclusion of the fallacious argument is supported, and its fallaciousness to some extent concealed, by further falsehoods and confusions. Nell Keddie, for instance, appears to believe that, since (of course) pupils do not differ in their actual abilities, the differences (not produced but) revealed by IQ tests and other kinds of categorization are merely apparent (Young, 1971, ch. 5).

But Bernard Coard, in a book recommended by the Inner London Education Authority (ILEA) in documents circulated during 1983 to all its employees, undertook to explain *How the West Indian child is made educationally sub-normal in the British School System*. Here the differences allegedly made are real not apparent, while the conclusion that they are so caused is also supported both by the general assumption of environmental omnipotence and by a more particular belief that pupils are creatures of the expectations of their teachers. (If only this were true we should all of us be able to become 100 per cent successful teachers by an easy adjustment of our expectations!)

2   Putting Hume's Fork to use

In Act I Scene 5 of *Hamlet* the hero responds to a question about the ghost by saying:

> There's ne'er a villain dwelling in all Denmark
> But he's an arrant knave.

To this uninformative information Horatio very reasonably responds with a complaint:

> There needs no ghost, my lord, come from the grave,
> To tell us this.

There needs no ghost, because Hamlet's utterance is of the first Humian kind: it is a proposition stating only the relations of ideas. In another terminology it is analytic, its truth-value knowable apriori. To say this is to say that we can tell whether it is true or false – in this case that it is necessarily true – simply by analyzing the meanings and hence the implications of the various symbols employed in its expression, and without any appeal to extra-linguistic experience.

It is, perhaps, just worth emphasizing what sort of appeal to experience is *not* required. For the author of *Anti-Dühring* was certainly not the last to believe that he could dispose of the contention that pure mathematics and abstract economic analysis consists in universal apriori truths by pointing out, perfectly correctly, that the concepts employed could not themselves be acquired without experience (Engels, 1878, pp. 46ff.; and compare pp. 103 and 134ff.).

What Horatio wanted was a proposition of the second Humian sort; synthetic, with its truth-value knowable only aposteriori. Had Hamlet claimed, unpoetically and anachronistically, that all Danish villains are the products of maternal deprivation, then his proposition would have been both synthetic and aposteriori. It could be known to be true or – much more likely – false only by reference to some actual empirical study of the home background of Danish villains.

The distinction embodied in Hume's Fork has already been employed in our examination, in chapter 4, section 3, of Popper's candidates for the diploma title 'Law of Nature in the social sciences'. But it has a much wider application. In the first place, as was hinted during that examination, people who have offered some generalization about supposed matters of social fact will often, under the pressure of falsifying counter-examples, so amend their too bold generalizations that these come to express nothing but made-to-measure tautologies. That all concerned shall appreciate exactly what is going on, and going wrong, the resolute and persistent application of Hume's Fork is most strongly indicated. In the second place, we frequently find one and the same form of words interpreted ambiguously: on some occasions as expressing a necessary truth; and on others as purporting to state a matter of fact. To the extent that Hume's Fork is not applied to these manoeuvres, resolutely and repeatedly, it will appear that the second proposition is both as necessary and as true as the first.

Sometimes what are in fact tautologies are offered either as explanations of facts or as fresh factual findings from empirical research. Harassed by Opposition MPs during Prime Minister's question time, James Callaghan once opined that the reason why increased employment in British industry had resulted in no increase in output might be low productivity. Werner Sombart – another person capable of better things – even ventured the suggestion that the rise of capitalism might be attributed to the growth of the Spirit of Capitalism – something which cannot be identified except as epitomizing the phenomena to be explained.

Such standing-start presentations of tautology are relatively rare, and can be recognized and discredited with little difficulty. For, though tautologies do not contain substance, they are analytic and do at least have a sense. Much more troublesome is the production of whole paragraphs leaving the reader at a loss to divine what, if any, determinate meaning the author wishes to convey. Andreski's *Social Sciences as Sorcery* is a very rich secondary source of such material.

Here the most important warning is against misplaced humble-mindedness. Confronted by a piece of specialist writing in any of the natural sciences, intelligent and literate laypersons will, typically, have little or no understanding of what is being said. That is because we do not know the first thing about the subjects under discussion, and are not masters of the required technical vocabularies. With studies of human conduct and human affairs, however, our situation is entirely different. All of us have a great deal of knowledge and experience, although there are also enormous differences between the amounts of that knowledge and the width of that experience. That is why we should expect to understand not only history books written for a general public but also most historical papers published only in the specialist journals. The serious difficulties to be expected are with accounts of the application of sophisticated research techniques and, in particular, of statistical analyses. The same, surely, should hold for most of the other social sciences; certainly for anthropology and sociology, as well as for policy studies and political science.

This point made we should recall two others mentioned earlier. First, by far the most effective tactic for bringing out what, if anything of substance, actually is being asserted is to discover what would have to have happened or to be happening or to be going to happen to require the asserter to concede that the original assertion was false. Since not not p ($\sim \sim p$) is equivalent to p, a proposition which denies nothing about the Universe around us asserts nothing either (Flew, 1955). In the gnomic words of the *Tractatus Logico-Philosophicus*: "The propositions of logic are tautologies. The propositions of logic therefore say nothing. (They are the analytical propositions)" (Wittgenstein, 1922, secs. 6 and 6.11).

Second, remember that Maxim of the Marquis de Vauven argues: "For the philosopher clarity is a matter of good faith." So it is for the social scientist, and for everyone else as well. All those who prefer their statements to be true, and in particular everyone who is investigating in good faith, wants it to be clear to all what is being asserted. How else can those assertions be criticized and, if false, shown to be false? For all such persons, as above all for the Socrates of Plato's *Apology*: "The unexamined life is for a human being not worth living" (38 A 5).

The continually neglected truism embodied in this Maxim gives us the key to understanding our failure to understand a crucial paragraph in Nicos Poulantzas. He was, in 'The Problem of the Capitalist State', labouring to maintain a central Marxist doctrine; which, as a believing and practising Leninist, if for no other reason, he must himself at some level have realized to be untrue. He was, that is to say, trying, no doubt unconsciously, to ensure that neither he nor his readers should be forced to attend to the falsity of the contention that wielders of political and military and bureaucratic power are always and everywhere completely the creatures of class interests outside the state machine.

We have, therefore, to suffer this painful piece of near meaningless mystification: ". . . although the members of the state apparatus belong, by their class origin, to different classes, they function according to a specific internal unity. Their class origin – *class situation* – recedes into the background in relation to that which unifies them – their *class position* – that is to say, the fact that they belong precisely to the State apparatus and that they have as their *objective function* the actualization of the role of the State. This in turn means that the bureaucracy, as a specific and relatively 'united' social category, is the 'servant' of the ruling class, not by reason of its class origins, which are divergent, or by reason of its personal relations with the ruling class, but by reason of the fact that its internal unity derives from its actualization of the objective role of the State. The totality of this role itself coincides with the interests of the ruling class" (Blackburn, 1972, pp. 246–7).

Although tautologies and other utterances empty of determinate (would be) factual content are often launched from, as it were, a standing start, it is more common to discover that what certainly began as a hefty empirical generalization has, under the pressure of falsifying counter-examples, been so qualified as to become now emptily tautological. Perhaps someone starts by contending, in the context of a discussion of religious education, that those who have been raised to be Christians will be better citizens than the rest. Then an objector points out that those claiming to have been raised as and to be Roman Catholics have long been heavily over-represented in British prisons and Borstal institutions. One possible but deplorably evasive response is to make The No-*true*-Scotsman Move (Flew, 1975, secs. 3.1–3.7, 3.13–3.15 and 4.1): 'No *true* Roman Catholic becomes a criminal.'

Again, we are continually bombarded with assurances that under full socialism all manner of things will be well. To the objection that in the existing fully socialist countries all manner of things are far from well, and in many cases much further from well than the corresponding things in countries not yet fully socialist, the pat reply is all too often that precisely this is what makes those failed paradises not *truly* socialist.

The key point to seize is that if any general proposition – All such and suches are so and so – is to be satisfactorily substantial, then such and suches have to be identifiable entirely independently of so and sos, and the other way about. For instance, the *Communist Manifesto* asserts: "The ruling ideas of each age have ever been the ideas of its ruling class" (Marx and Engels, 1848, p. 102). In so far as this is put forward as a contribution to social science, we cannot begin to determine its truth-value until and unless we have been provided or have provided ourselves with criteria for identifying the ruling ideas, and for doing so without either implicitly or explicitly assuming that these just are the ideas of whoever we are proposing to pick out as members of the ruling class. Once thus clearly stated, the present point, like almost all the others made in this chapter 5, will appear too obvious to merit our labouring. Yet all are being overlooked all the time, not only in popular but even in professional social thinking.

Another kind of occasion for the employment of Hume's Fork s where we find one and the same form of words ambiguously interpreted: sometimes expressing a necessary truth; at other times purporting to state a matter of fact. All too often the truth of the necessary truth is then mistaken to prove the truth of the more substantial proposition. One favourite token of this type of fallacy

is the popular putative demonstration of the demoralizing conclusion that there can be no such thing as a genuinely unselfish
action. In a made-to-measure sense of 'want', every action is
defined as done solely because the agent wanted to do it. But that
is not, of course, the everyday sense in which you can properly be
credited with unselfishness for giving up your Saturday afternoon
to sick-visiting; although that was in truth just about the last thing
you wanted to do.

A currently important sub-class of this type of fallacy takes off
from the logically necessary connections between correlative
terms. It is, for instance, only in so far as something can be (said to
be, relatively,) large that anything can be (said to be, relatively,)
small; only in so far as there is (actual or possible) development
that there can be (said to be) underdevelopment; and so on. The
temptation is, through failing to distinguish either the criterial
from the causal sense of 'make', or tautological from substantial
interpretations of key utterances, fallaciously to conclude that the
richer must everywhere be responsible for the absolute levels
achieved by the poorer, the more developed for the absolute levels
achieved by the less developed, and so on. But, if ever or wherever
any of this is in fact the case, it has to be shown to be so: not by
apriori and fallacious argument; but by citing hard and particular
empirical evidence. To attempt anything else is like assuming that
mice can be smaller than elephants only because the elephants
have eaten all the food which would otherwise have fattened the
mice.

A major reason why so many people, while deploying little if
any relevant evidence, are so apt to be persuaded that poverty and
underdevelopment are always and everywhere the results of
exploitation by the less poor and the more developed is that they
insist that what has to be explained is why so many people, and so
many countries, have so little, and are so backward. They thus
presuppose, as a socio-economic analogue of the First Law of
Motion, that the natural condition of humanity, all deviations
from which demand explanation in terms of anti-social forces,
must be one of sustained economic growth, in which everyone
enjoys a high and rapidly rising standard of living. Yet this, as the
slightest acquaintance with world history should teach us, is the
opposite of the truth.

The whole approach is, in the most literal construction, preposterous. It was looking-glass logic to argue "that in the self-same relations in which wealth is produced, poverty is produced also; that in the self-same relations in which there is a development of the productive forces, there is also a driving force of repression" (Marx, 1847, p. 104).

For our second collection of occasions for the strenuous employment of Hume's Fork we turn to Robert Michels' *Political Parties*. This is the source of the supposed Iron Law of Oligarchy. The first edition was published in 1911, an English translation from the 1915 edition appeared in the same year, while the most recent republication seems to have been in 1959 and by a New York firm specializing in reprints of classics of science and mathematics. It is called "a classic of sociology". It would be as well described, or as ill, as a classic of political science.

The most disappointing feature of an over-long and rather wretched book is that we are offered no straightforward statement of the thesis proposed; no straightforward statement of what it is which, according to the supposed law, is supposed to be practically necessary, and what practically impossible. So there simply is no official formulation, provided by its eponymous discoverer, of Michels' Iron Law of Oligarchy. In so far as the claim is that, in any centralized and hierarchical organization, those occupying positions of power and influence must always be a minority, then all we have is a logically necessary truth; on all fours with the modest and unadventurous assertion that the winners of races involving more than two competitors must always remain, among all the runners, a minority. If the claim is that the same people tend to stay in positions of power and influence, and that, once they are in, it is often very hard to get them out, then this is perfectly true. But it is not a truth with the semantic force and the implications of a law of nature. If the claim is that no one is ever got out of any such position by pressures from below, or that, even if they are, successors always maintain all the policies and practices of predecessors; then these claims are simply false.

"As long as any organization is loosely constructed", we are told, "no professional leadership can arise. The anarchists . . . have no regular leaders" (Michels, 1959, p. 36). But if the Michels thesis is to be applied only to hierarchical and centralized organizations, then it is tautological. He proceeds to proclaim "the *logical impossibility* of the 'representative' system" (p. 36: italics supplied).

Having offered Rousseauian reasons for saying this, Michels goes on to suggest that it is a matter of fact that representatives always take their own lines, ignore the actual wishes of their electors, and cannot be by those electors effectively replaced. But thee would-be factual assertions are then tacitly admitted to be less than universal truths. Britain, for instance, is accused of being an untrustworthy ally because of changes in party control (p. 103). So some representatives can, after all, be replaced by others, pursuing different policies? Sometimes too representatives do, it seems, change course, in deference to the wishes of their constituents. This concession also is dismissed as of no account. For, Michels argues, they do this *only because* they do not want to be replaced by rivals (pp. 164–5). By the way: it is remarkable how many people will, like Michels here, attempt to show that something is not the case by offering their own account of why it is! Maybe it would prove useful to christen this move (Flew, 1975). I therefore name it now, The It-is-not-*only-because*-it-is-Riposte.

Eventually we get around to considering socialism and, in particular, syndicalism: "All that the syndicalists have written upon political parties in general . . . applies to themselves as well, because it applies to all organizations as such, without exception" (Michels, 1959, p. 347). This universal truth is, of course, the original tautology. But that is, almost immediately, granted superfluous support from a proposition which might plausibly be put forward as a sociological nomological. For this proposition makes a claim about the supposedly inevitable consequences of actions, which cannot be themselves necessary. However, both it and the reasonings from which it is derived are, with acknowledgement, borrowed from the neglected writings of Gaetano Mosca (1958–41): ". . . social wealth cannot be satisfactorily administered in any other manner than by the creation of an extensive bureaucracy. In this way we are led by an inevitable logic to the flat denial of the possibility of a state without classes. The administration of an immeasurably large capital, above all when this capital is collective property, confers upon the administrator influence at least equal to that possessed by the private owner of capital . . . always and necessarily there springs from the masses a new organized minority which raises itself to the rank of a governing class" (Michels, 1959, pp. 390–1; and compare, for instance, Andreski, 1975 and Djilas, 1958).

Michels finally concludes by repeating what he still does not see to be a mere tautology: "Who says organizations says oligarchy" (p. 401). It was, surely, too harsh a judgement upon either of those disciplines to describe such an uninformative and misinformative shambles as a classic of either sociology or political science.

Our third and last case study is drawn from yet another area. Nowadays innumerable courses are taught and taken under rubrics such as 'Sociology of Literature', 'Social History as seen through the Contemporary Novel', 'Drama and Society in the Age of So and So', and the like. Unfortunately these courses almost never draw on the latest and best work of the relevant specialists in economic and social history; while those specialists themselves either complacently believe that their findings are getting through or, irresponsibly, do not care whether they are or not (Jefferson, 1975).

The consequence of these mutual withdrawals is that the pictures of past periods usually presented to pupils have been shaped not by actual historical evidence but by prejudices, and, inevitably, by prejudices applied to a relatively small selection of all the productions of those periods (Jefferson, 1974; and compare West, 1975, and Hayek, 1954). All such selections must be arbitrary too in so far as they are made on the basis of literary merit, or of anything else but an assessment of the evidential value of works cited. And, here as properly everywhere, prejudices are convictions formed in advance of any scrutiny of the evidence, not strong but presumably misguided beliefs peculiar to other people.

Many of those teaching these courses are, to a greater or lesser extent and in one interpretation or another, Marxist. (See, for instance, Laurenson, 1978, as well as Routh and Wolff, 1978.) They are therefore, and perhaps reasonably, committed to maintaining some sort of physical or metaphysical priority of stuff over consciousness, of the material over the ideological. (See pp. 31–2, above.) But then, much more questionably, they construe this as sustaining the contention that ongoings in the ideological superstructure must, always and *ultimately*, be determined by prior or simultaneous ongoings in the material foundations; and, hence apparently, any representations in the former must, albeit often in much distorted forms, *reflect* the latter.

That last crucial corollary has been defended in a recent and respectfully received book by Joan Rockwell, *Fact in Fiction*: "To say that writers necessarily reflect their own time, which I must repeat is the justification for using their fictions to study the facts of their society, is to say that they are bound to do so, and cannot choose to do otherwise" (Rockwell, 1974, p. 119). Rockwell's own immediate appeal is to scriptural authority: what are offered as the proof-texts are all drawn from George Lukács, *The Historical Novel*. Nevertheless her hypothesis itself is one which should excite all those who are *For Science in the Social Sciences*, and who interpret this as requiring the discovery of laws of nature determining human action. For it does hypothesize physical as opposed to logical necessities, and it obviously is susceptible of experimental disconfirmation.

Certainly as a hypothesis this has to be construed as implying that all writers of historical fiction, of science fiction, or of fantasy are bound to give themselves away: the well-girded sociologist will always be able to discern marks of the lurking bourgeois beast in all the works of any writers whom she is putting down as such; while writers of historical fiction are bound to reveal, presumably through the admission of anachronisms, the actual periods of their compositions. A moment's thought reveals, both that there is a very simple and straightforward way to test this claim, and that it is in the last degree unlikely that it would not, if subjected to such simple and straightforward testing, be shown to be false. It is, therefore, distressing, indeed alarming, that neither Joan Rockwell herself nor any of her sociologist or 'cultural studies' reviewers seems to have had a moment to spare for such thought.

The simple and straightforward way is this: first, to work out the principles on which we are supposed to be able to infer contemporary social facts from fiction of every kind; and, second, to apply these detective principles to a variety of works the actual social background of which is known, but not to the appliers. Suppose that the principles were found to work. Then they could be employed to achieve definitive solutions to several famous problems: when, for instance, and perhaps where the Homeric poems were composed; and so on. The reason why the Rockwell hypothesis is implausible is that any detective principles discovered or discoverable by sociologists could presumably be either communicated to or discovered by the authors themselves, and then employed by them to cover their sociological tracks. We have here one more example of the importance in the social sciences of what has been named most aptly the Oedipus Effect: "the influence of an item of information upon the situation to which the information refers" (Popper, 1957, p. 13; and compare Hume, 1748, p. 94).

Rockwell's own nearest approach to direct empirical investigation is not very near. Thus she asserts: "The assumption in fiction that a given institution exists may be supported by other evidence . . . but the deductions may justifiably be made even in the absence of this support . . ." (Rockwell, 1974, p. 122). She then proposes to show what might, she thinks, be thus reliably deduced from "the following group of fictional and personal accounts: *The Life and Times of Frederick Douglass*; *Uncle Tom's Cabin*; *Huckleberry Finn*; various works of William Faulkner; *Gone with the Wind*; and the recent *Confessions of Nat Turner*".

The first of these, however, does not belong to a study of *Fact in Fiction* at all. It is the autobiography of an escaped slave who became active in the Abolition Movement, and it has long been recognized as an invaluable primary source. About the rest the important point is "that they were written over a period of a hundred years by writers . . . living up and down the Eastern seaboard from Maine to Missisipi". So, if Rockwell's detective principles were correct, the times which those of these writers who belong to our century "necessarily reflect" must be our times, and not those of "the USA in the first half of the nineteenth century" (1974, p. 122). Slavery, therefore, must have survived into the early nineteen-thirties, to be 'reflected' in the writing of *Gone with the Wind*!

How then does Rockwell manage to be so sure that her hypothesis – which is not so much bold as reckless – cannot but be right? Clearly this confidence is not based on empirical evidence. Part of the answer lies in the fact that she sees it as founded on the Marxist revelation. But in part it seems to be another case of a single form of words being interpreted without distinction in two different ways: expressing on one occasion a necessary truth; and, on another, a would-be factual falsehood – a falsehood believed to be true primarily on account of the confounding of these two interpretations. Since Rockwell's intellectual equipment does not include Hume's Fork, she moves easily, and without observing any difference of substance: from saying, in one sentence, that a society's literature "is an integral part of it and should be recognized as being as much so as any institution, the Family for instance, or the State"; to saying, in the next, and as if this were an equivalence or a logical consequence, that "Narrative fiction is an indicator, by its form and content, of the morphology and nature of a society, just as the structure and function of the family in a society will be an indicator of how that society differs from others" (1974, pp. vii–viii).

3   Deductive conceptual schemes: pure and applied

The motto quotations at the head of the present chapter 5 are drawn from Hume's first *Enquiry*. Later in the same part of the same section IV Hume discusses how the calculi of pure mathematics, and, in particular, that of (Euclidean) geometry, can be and are applied in the natural sciences. All the propositions of pure mathematics belong, of course, to the first of Hume's two fundamental categories; whereas some of those in what we would call applied but what he described as "mixed mathematics" must fall into the second. "Every part of mixed mathematics proceeds", Hume says, "upon the supposition that certain laws are established by nature in her operations; and abstract reasonings are employed ... to determine their influence in particular instances, where it depends upon any precise degree of distance and quantity. Thus, it is a law of motion, discovered by experience, that the moment or force of any body in motion is the compound ratio or proportion of its solid contents and its velocity ... Geometry assists us in the application of this law, by giving us the just dimensions of all the parts and figures which can enter into any species of machine; but still the discovery of the law itself is owing merely to experience, and all the abstract reasonings in the world would never lead us one step towards the knowledge of it" (Hume, 1748, p. 31).

Although he does seem to have the heart of the matter in him, Hume's formulation here is – putting it gently – unsteady and a shade crude. It is, nevertheless, sufficient to point what has to be, for us, the main moral. The validity of deductive arguments passing through calculi of pure mathematics constitutes no guarantee of the truth either of any supposedly factual premises from which those arguments begin, or, therefore, of any supposedly factual conclusions derived therefrom. Nowadays both the most important and the most frequent occasions for keeping this moral in mind are when we are told 'what the computer says'; that the final results in the elections in which the count has just begun will be such and such; that, on the NIESR or the Treasury of whoever else's model, GNP will next year increase by something point something percent; and so on.

It is most unlikely, although not altogether impossible, that there will have been any sort of computer failure: what the computer has in fact 'deduced' from its programmed input will, almost certainly, have been 'deduced' validly. What is much more likely is that there was something wrong with that input: that the model employed by the NIESR or the Treasury does not, after all, faithfully and adequately represent the economy which it is supposed to represent; that false assumptions were built into the original programme, or that false information was supplied later. The computer-wise whizz-kids have a slogan: "Garbage produces garbage." There is also the acronym GIGO – which, being explicated, becomes "Garbage In, Garbage Out".

Towards the end of his *Logic* J. S. Mill disclaims any attempt "to decide what other hypothetical or abstract sciences, similar to Political Economy, may admit of being carved out of the general body of the social science" (Mill, 1843, bk VI, ch. ix, sec. 4: vol. II, pp. 497–8). The insight revealed in this disclaimer is the more remarkable in that the previous discussion had not brought out at all clearly that economic analysis is a kind of pure mathematics, a deductive conceptual scheme which may or may not find application. This is, of course, true only of economic analysis, and not of many other activities pursued in Departments of Economics and of Economic History.

Nor is it any the less true for the fact that the basic notions have been abstracted and refined from some of those employed in the very concrete and down-to-earth business of producing and exchanging goods and services. For it is notorious that much the same holds of arithmetic and geometry. Most of us learn to collect and to count physical things, as well as to sum such collections together or subtract one from another, before we manage to compass any abstract numerical calculations; while it appears to be certain that Egyptian surveyors had discovered that in a rectangular field with sides as 3 to 4 the diagonal would be 5 well before Pythagoras – if it was Pythagoras – proved the Theorem of Pythagoras. Wheras the logical progression, both in mathematics and in economics, is from pure to applied, in the history of the race, and in the biography of individuals, this order is reversed.

In that previous discussion Mill lays it down that "Political Economy considers mankind as occupied solely in acquiring and consuming wealth . . ." (1843, bk VI, ch. ix, sec. 3: vol. II, p. 492). In the following year, in his *Outlines of a Critique of Political Economy,* Engels gives another and less sober account: "Political Economy – the science of how to make money – was born of the mutual envy and greed of the merchants. It bears on its brow the mark of the most loathsome selfishness" (Engels, 1844, p. 148).

This furious misdescription suggests that the classical economists were all trying to write the sort of book which might have been marketed as *How to Make your First Million* or *Getting Rich: a Guide for Everyman – and Every Woman*! But the full title of Smith's economic masterpiece was significantly different, *An Inquiry into the Nature and Causes of the Wealth of Nations.* Not for nothing was what we now call economics known traditionally as political economy. For Smith was investigating: not how he and his readers might become millionaires; but the political arrangements needed if "the natural effort of every individual to better his own condition" is to lead to self-sustaining economic growth, the increase of wages, and general prosperity. The findings of this kind of inquiry, making no strident demands for state-to-state charitable handouts but speaking only of unhindered self-help and self-reliance, should interest and appeal: not to would-be plutocrats, though it is surely no sin either to be or to want to be rich; but rather to all those, both in the Third World and out of it, who really do long to see poor countries climbing out of their poverty (Bauer, 1976 and 1981).

Where Mill and Engels were both wrong, however, was in limiting economic analysis to the acquisition and consumption of wealth. It is this limitation which provides purchase for, though it can scarcely justify, John Ruskin's dismissal of Adam Smith as "the half-bred and half-witted Scotchman" who taught "the deliberate blasphemy . . .: 'Thou shalt hate the Lord thy God, damn his laws, and covet his neighbour's goods'" (Ruskin, 1876, pp. 516 and 714). Earlier Thomas Carlyle too had had a lot to say on the same lines, and in a similar tone of voice: one or two of his choices phrases were even adapted and adopted by the authors of the *Communist Manifesto*.

The truth, as Lionel Robbins made clear in his masterly *Essay on the Nature and Significance of Economic Science,* is that the key notion is not wealth but scarcity. Both are essentially relative: nothing can be either scarce or "valuable in itself . . . any more than a thing can be distant in itself without reference to another thing" (Robbins, 1949, p. 56). It is, however, human wants and human needs in relation to which things are scarce or valuable. In chapter 2, section 4, John Watkins was quoted as saying: "Whereas physical things can exist unperceived, social 'things' like laws, prices, prime ministers and ration-books, are created by personal attitudes. (Remove the attitudes of food officials, shopkeepers, housewives, etc., towards ration-books and they shrivel into bits of cardboard.)" The same is true of such social 'qualities' as scarcity. "Value", as Robbins puts it, "is a relation, not a measurement" (p. 56). So much, therefore, for the labour theory of value; which maintains that the value of any good is the (measured) quantity of labour needed for its production.

Economic analysis is relevant wherever four conditions are satisfied. First, several different ends must be desired. Second, these ends must not all be equally important to those who cherish them. Third and fourth, the time and the other means required for attaining these ends must be both limited and capable of alternative applications. "But when time and the means for achieving ends are limited *and* capable of alternative application, *and* the ends are capable of being distinguished in order of importance, then behaviour necessarily assumes the form of choice. Every act which involves time and scarce means for the achievement of one end involves the relinquishment of their use for the achievement of another. It has an economic aspect" (Robbins, 1949, p. 14).

Once this is appreciated it becomes obvious that economic analysis may find application in areas remote from those which would be considered to be economic either by the contemporary layperson or by the classical economists and their critics. This was observed well before World War I by the logician father of the more famous Lord Keynes (Keynes, 1904, p. 300). Yet it seems to have been only in World War II that people trained as economists began to play a part in Operational Research teams attached to the staffs of various very senior commanders. Again, what is called in Britain *The Economics of Politics* and in the USA the study of Public Choice did not really begin to flourish before the late fifties (Seldon, 1978). James Buchanan and Gordon Tullock, however, and other leading figures of that flourishing, are scrupulous to give due credit: both to anticipations in Adam Smith, and in other British classical economists; and to Machiavelli, as well as to several Italian successors in the tough-minded study of the workings of state machinery.

Mill was, as we have seen, reluctant to commit himself on the question whether "other hypothetical or abstract sciences . . . may admit of being carved out of the general body of the social science". The most promising candidate to emerge in the years between is the mathematical theory of games, although some might want to disqualify this as constituting no more than a fresh branch of political economy. By far and away the most exciting application of any part of this theory is the work of Robert Axelrod on *The Evolution of Cooperation*. For this shows how cooperation can evolve without requiring, either self-sacrificing altruism, or machinery for making and enforcing contracts. Hume, and the other Founding Fathers considered in chapter 3, would have loved this book.

The particular game which Axelrod examines is Prisoners' Dilemma. The two players are supposed to have been charged with a crime which they have in fact committed. Both are urged to confess, and neither is allowed to communicate with the other. If neither either confesses or implicates the other, then neither will be convicted and punished: this is winning through cooperation, and each scores three. If each confesses and implicates the other, each gets a 'punishment' score of one. If one confesses, implicating the other, whereas the other – the 'sucker' – does neither, then the latter scores zero whereas the former scores five – the 'temptation' payoff. The aim is to develop a strategy which enables the player to score high in a run of games, when the score in every game is revealed to both players at the end of every game, but when neither is ever able to communicate with the other.

What Axelrod did actually involved almost no mathematical theory: perhaps the further development of this will, as in other cases mentioned earlier, have to follow practice. For he asked assorted theoreticians how they would over a long series play Prisoner's Dilemma. He then set a University of Michigan computer to calculate which of these more than seventy-five suggested strategies would be most successful. TIT FOR TAT, submitted by Canadian psychologist Anatol Rapoport, won out against all comers.

This strategy begins on the first round by cooperating; that is, by neither confessing nor implicating the other. After that, it always does what the other player did in the previous round. If the other player cooperated on the previous round, TIT FOR TAT cooperates. If the other player defected, TIT FOR TAT 'punishes' the other player by defecting on the next round – but *only* the next round. And so on.

TIT FOR TAT thus has four fundamental characteristics. First, it is, as Axelrod puts it, "nice"; or, perhaps it would be better to say, optimistic. That is, it never betrays first, preferring to assume good intentions until proved wrong. Second, it is retaliatory: it does not ignore betrayals, but retaliates at once. Third, although retaliatory, it is not vengeful. It extracts only an equal amount of vengeance for each betrayal. (The principle of "an eye for an eye, a tooth for a tooth" was originally established to limit vengeance: it is only much later that some have come to think it too severe!) Fourth, it is easy to understand: many of the others failed because they conveyed no intelligible message to the other player.

This optimistic and generous yet never foolishly self-sacrificing strategy, neither spiteful nor exploitative, is, surely, that of Hume's

"Two men who pull the oars of a boat", and "do it by an agreement or convention, tho' they have never given promises to each other". It is, it seems, in this way that "recognitions of common interest will lead to the regulation of conduct in ways which are not, and often could not be, derived from prior contracts." What Axelrod calls "niceness" the altogether English George Orwell would have commended as common sense and simple decency.

Analysing his computer printout, Axelrod made further discoveries. For example, when played against each other in lengthy computer tournaments, the strategies quickly separated themselves into two categories. The first was that of those alled "nice" – the ones that assumed goodwill on the part of the other player and did not betray first. The second was the "not nice" strategies, which were generally built around a plan for *not* cooperating, but shrewdly trying to betray the other player.

The former always did better. With only one exception (which turned out to be a kind of anomaly), the "nice" strategies were all bunched at the top, while the "not nice" strategies formed a separate sub-class at the bottom. Moreover, when played over an evolutionary time sequence, the "not nice" strategies eventually faded into extinction, while the "nice" strategies all survived.

Actual games with and among his students revealed something else. Both Axelrod and his students found that they were strongly tempted to behave as if Prisoner's Dilemma were a zero-sum competitive game, which it was in fact deliberately designed not to be. They were strongly tempted, that is to say, to assume that, in order to do better for yourself, you had to do better than the other fellow; and, hence, that any gain on his side had to be at the expense of a loss on yours. But, of course, if they succumbed to this temptation, then their 'betrayals' provoked 'counter-betrayals'; and so both players, until and unless this spoiling strategy was reversed, proceeded to do progressively worse. Axelrod draws the moral that in Prisoner's Dilemma the first rule is to eschew envy: "Envy is self-destructive."

The important moral for Political Economy depends on the logical truths that, while commercial competition has to be, precisely as competition, a zero-sum game, the uncoerced exchange of goods or services is not. It is as wrong as it is common to say or to assume that "Whenever material gain follows exchange, for every plus there is a precisely equal minus" (Ruskin, 1899, p. 131). No one makes such an uncoerced exchange save in so far as they believe that they will be, in their own eyes, and by their own standards, better off if it is made than they would be if it were not. Each party, therefore, must, in consequence of the exchange, be taken to be better off than they would have been otherwise. If this is to be called exploitation, then both parties are equally guilty. For both have made themselves better off through the willingness of the other to cooperate in the exchange. In this sort of social cooperation for one party to envy the gains of the other is indeed paradigmatically self-destructive.

6 Facts and Values

In every system ... which I have hitherto met with, I have always remark'd, that the author proceeds for some time in the ordinary way of reasoning ... when of a sudden I am surpriz'd to find, that instead of the usual copulations of propositions, *is* and *is not,* I meet with no proposition that is not connected with an *ought,* or an *ought not.* This change is imperceptible, but it is, however, of the last consequence. For as this *ought,* or *ought not,* expresses some relation or affirmation, 'tis necessary that it should be observ'd and explain'd; and at the same time that a reason should be given, for what seems altogether inconceivable, how this new relation can be a deduction from others, which are entirely different from it.

David Hume, *A Treatise of Human Nature,*
bk III, pt. i, sec. 1, p. 469

Euclid has fully explained all the qualities of the circle, but has not in any proposition said a word of its beauty. The reason is evident. The beauty is not a quality of the circle ... It is only the effect which that figure produces upon the mind, whose peculiar structure renders it susceptible of such sentiments.

David Hume, *An Enquiry concerning the Principles of Morals,*
App. I, pp. 291–2

The interdict indicated in the first of the two motto passages above has come to be called Hume's Law. What is by this law ruled out as illegitimate is any attempt strictly to deduce conclusions about what ideally *ought* to be so from any premise or premises stating only what, it is supposed, actually and already *is* the case. Any neutral and non-partisan assertion about what in fact has been, is or will be can, therefore, without self-contradiction be conjoined with any contention, whether positive or negative, dealing only with the supposedly ideal.

Some interpreters betray themselves by missing Hume's irony. As in dealing with Hume's Fork, considered in chapter 5, so here, they mistakenly think that he was maintaining – what is quite obviously not true – that this fundamental distinction is always made, and that it was left to him only to notice the practice and to point the moral. This does scant justice to Hume. The truth is that he was insisting that, although it very often is not, the distinction always can and often should be drawn, and is "of the last consequence" (Hudson, 1969, pp. 135–43).

Once this is understood, it becomes obvious that claims that some favourite guru has 'resolved Hume's supposed dichotomy' or has 'transcended this positivist distinction' must be preposterous. For these supercilious pretensions are now revealed as euphemistic and evasive alternatives to a forthright and impious admission that your guru either wholly failed to make, or else collapsed, a distinction which it is scarcely possible to deny to be both fundamental and indispensable (Popper, 1945, vol. II, pp. 394–5).

Invalidly to deduce an *ought* conclusion from *is* premises is to commit what G. E. Moore christened the Naturalistic Fallacy. This is a good name, notwithstanding that his own account of the matter is curiously constipated. Most remarkably, it neither quotes the now hackneyed passage from which our first motto is drawn nor makes any reference to Hume. By contrast Hume himself had at once gone on to show that equivocations upon the word 'nature' constitute the nerve of many tokens of that particular fallacy type. For instance, though this is not one of his instances, we need to distinguish – as many of the wise and good have not – prescriptive from descriptive understandings of such expressions as 'natural law' or 'law of nature'. It must be absurd to hold that anything determined by a descriptive law of nature could sensibly be either prescribed or proscribed by a law of the moral or legal kind. Such prescriptions are bound to be redundant, and such proscriptions futile. They cannot but be, because everything determined by a descriptive law of nature occurs by physical necessity.

Another thing for which Moore's *Principia Ethica* became at first famous and later notorious was his contention that goodness is a simple, non-natural quality like, and yet at the same time very unlike, yellowness. In default of any explanation of what it might be for a quality to be non-natural, other than the one which Moore himself later dismissed as "utterly silly and preposterous", the adjective 'non-natural' has to be construed as *alienans*: non-natural qualities are no more qualities than non-tauroid bulls would be bulls. A more sophisticated philosophical objection is that, whereas of two otherwise identical objects one may be red and the other yellow, one cannot be good and the other not. This is because things are (said to be) good solely in virtue of their (other) good-making characteristics.

Thus in the case of beauty, which may perhaps be regarded as the aesthetic kind of goodness, and in those of virtue and vice, the moral forms of good and evil, Hume sees the actual characteristics of what is (called) beautiful or virtuous or vicious as causing our reactions. But the beauty or the virtue or the vice itself somehow consists in those same reactions. Thus, he argued, "morality consists not ... in any *matter of fact,* which can be discover'd by the understanding ... Take any action allow'd to be vicious: Wilful murder, for instance. Examine it in all lights and see if you can find that matter of fact, or real existence, which you call *vice* ... The vice entirely escapes you, as long as you consider the object. You can never find it, will you turn your reflexion into your own breast, and find a sentiment of disapprobation, which arises in you towards this action" (Hume, 1739–40, bk III, pt. i, sec. 1, pp. 468–9).

Both here, in his explanation of the nature of value characteristics, and elsewhere, in his parallel account of what he took to be the misconception of causal necessity, Hume's model was the treatment in the great natural scientific works of the previous hundred years of such supposedly secondary qualities as colour. Thus in the *Opticks* Newton had written: "The ... light and rays which appear red, or, rather, make objects appear so I call rubrific or red-making ... And, if at any time I speak of light and rays as coloured or endued with colours, I would be understood to speak not philosophically and properly, but grossly, and according to such conceptions as vulgar people in seeing all these experiments would be apt to frame. For the rays, to speak properly, are not coloured. In them there is nothing else than a certain power and disposition to stir up a sensation of this or that colour" (Newton, 1704, bk I, ch. ii, Definition to the second theorem under the second Proposition, pp. 124–5). These sensations, as our private experiences, really are in our minds only; or, as Newton himself preferred to say, our sensoria. But we, vulgarly, project such private sensations out onto a public world which is in itself altogether colourless.

1 What is meant by 'value-freedom'?

It is in the Humian perspective, sketched in the immediately preceding paragraphs, that we can best consider the issues so clearly and so forcefully raised in Weber's classic paper 'The Meaning of "Value-Freedom" in Sociology and Economics' (Weber, 1917, pp. 1–47). In deference to him the German 'Wert-freiheit' is in such discussions frequently employed rather than the English 'value-freedom'. He maintained two theses here.

The first was substantially that of Hume. There is, that is to say, an unbridgeable logical gulf between partisan prescription and non-partisan description, between assertions that something actually *is* the case and insistences that it ideally *ought* to be. Since the values which we put on things are not in truth qualities of those things, sciences concerned to describe what actually happens, and to explain why, cannot truly report that things have such intrinsic qualities, which they do not and cannot have. Of course sciences can and must take note of what individuals and groups do in fact value. But they cannot, in the nature of things, truly record that this or that *is* intrinsically valuable, and therefore categorically *ought* to be valued.

Confessing himself "quite unable to understand how it can be conceived to be possible to call this part of Max Weber's method-ology into question", one leading economist enforced the crucial point with a homely yet historically contentious example: "We can", he urged, "ask people whether they are prepared to buy pork and how much they are prepared to buy at different prices. Or we can watch how they behave when . . . exposed to the stimuli of the pig-meat markets. But the proposition that it is *wrong* that pork should be valued ... is a proposition which we cannot conceive being verified at all in this manner." He concludes, in words which might have been adapted from Hume, yet probably were not: "Propositions involving the verb 'ought' are different in kind from propositions involving the verb 'is' (Robbins, 1949, pp. 148–9).

Weber's second thesis was frankly prescriptive. He never claimed that values were either dispensable or unimportant. Nor did he assert that everyone, or even that all social scientists, should always and everywhere eschew value-judgements. On the contrary. What he insisted was that the difference between fact-stating and evaluation should be neither concealed nor blurred. When anyone expresses a value-judgement, they must not pretend that it is scientifically warranted; because it cannot be. If scientists, and in particular social scientists, make recommendations for action – and they are as much entitled and indeed obliged to do this as any other citizen – then they should be scrupulous to make plain, what in what they are saying is put forward as a scientific finding, and what has the very different status of a policy proposal. This is an imperative of intellectual honesty and respect for truth.

2   Repudiations of value-freedom

No wonder, surely, that the future Lord Robbins was at a loss to understand how people wishing to be accounted social scientists could bring themselves to challenge either of these two proposals. Those who have in our day dismissed all talk of value-freedom with confident contempt appear either not to have studied Weber, or not to have understood him, or perhaps to have chosen to misunderstand. He himself had to complain of "the constantly recurring and almost incredibly wrong-headed misunderstanding of those who think it is being maintained that empirical science cannot treat men's 'subjective' value-judgements as objects (whereas the whole of sociology and, in economics, the whole theory of marginal utility are based on the opposite assumption)" (Runciman, 1978, p. 78).

Even more incredibly wrong-headed are some of the statements which appeared in widely circulating Penguin Education Specials in the seventies; and which have been, it seems, accepted as the new gospel in many Departments both of Sociology and of Education. Thus, in a volume offered as a 'Handbook for Course Criticism', in a contribution trendily entitled 'Class Struggle among the Molecules', the author informs us that "The employees of a chemical company ... include research chemists. Nobody pretends that the chemistry they do is value-free" (Pateman, 1972, p. 212). His sole, preposterously irrelevant reason for saying this is that their employers hope that some of their discoveries can be made "useful (i.e. profitable)".

A more complicated example, but potentially more instructive, can be found in another Penguin Education Special, *Academic Freedom*. the author begins with a slightly grudging concession to "objectivity, in the sense of respect for facts, and a certain standard of honesty in the treatment of evidence". This, he is ungraciously prepared to allow, "is an obviously desirable quality for education to cultivate". But then, with enthusiasm now, he goes on to list what he sees as unacceptable consequences of what is denounced as "the quite mistaken belief that value-judgements could be eliminated" from the social sciences. He says: "... neutrality, or impartiality, in the sense of a demand that teacher, and students do not take sides and do not allow interpretation or opinion (or bias, or prejudice – call it what you will) to con-taminate the pure stream of facts is an absurdity. The role of theory, or hypothesis, and interpretation is now generally accepted to be an irreducible element in even the most dispassionate and factual sciences" (Arblaster, 1974, p. 17).

There is no room here to re-establish all the distinctions which this outburst collapses, and all the subtleties which it blunts. The essential is to recognize that "theory, or hypothesis, and interpre-tation" too, all belong to the world of facts rather than to that of values. So to show that these are "an irreducible element in even the most dispassionate and factual sciences" is not to show that those cannot be value-free.

That this is so becomes manifest the moment that we get down to concrete cases. The theories or hypotheses of historians, for instance, are theories and hypotheses about what in fact hap-pened, and how, and why. Certainly matters of opinion are sometimes contrasted with matters of fact. But in these contrasts the former involve opinions about what was or is or will be the case. The opposition is between belief and knowledge rather than between value and fact: there are (disputatious) matters of opinion; which are contrasted with (established, known) matters of fact. So to show that the social sciences must accommodate some of the former as well as some of the latter would not be to show that, in any understanding obnoxious to Weber, they either are or ought to be value-laden.

Before moving on to a third example of the ignorant and hasty dismissing of Weber it is worth protesting briefly against refusals to recognize any distinctions between prejudices, biases and points of view. Earlier we took issue with the slovenly practice of abusing all disfavoured beliefs as prejudices, instead of reserving the word for convictions formed prior to any examination of the evidence. A prejudice in this strict sense is not at all the same as a bias. With both this latter term and the expression 'a point of view' we should do well to bear in mind the literal meanings.

Thus a bias in a bowl is built-in and permanent; although it can, of course, be recognized and regularly offset by a skilful player. A bias in thinking should be regarded in the same way: it is a disposition to underestimate or to overestimate in one particular direction. As such, a bias can be recognized and systematically compensated for; just as prejudices can be and will be identified and open-mindedly examined by all those who prefer their beliefs to be, even if uncomfortable, well-evidenced and, hopefully, true.

Literally construed the expression 'a point of view' refers to a position and a direction of observation. What is or is not visible from a particular point of view, while looking in a particular direction, is not subject to the control of the persons in that position, while looking in that direction. There is, therefore, nothing irredeemably subjective about differences between observations made by observers observing from different points of view. Again, while everyone is at every moment bound to have some point of view, and while it is no doubt practically impossible to dispose of absolutely every prejudice, we are not, surely, all subject to strong biases which we cannot possibly recognize and for which we are genuinely unable to compensate.

In both the 'Handbook for Course Criticism' mentioned above, and in another volume of Radical essays from a different publisher, professional historians refer to what is supposed to have been established in E. H. Carr's *What is History?* (Compare Flew, 1978, ch. III). In the former one of these tells us: "It is now generally realized that the claim to record facts and reconstruct the past 'as it happened' is not tenable. Carr . . . argues that 'facts' are defined as worth recording at all, in terms of some model in the historian's mind" (Pateman, 1972, p. 284).

The Editor of the latter promises that Gareth Stedman Jones, a future Fellow of Kings, will show that "the assumption that there exists a realm of facts independent of theories which establish their meaning is fundamentally unscientific." Jones himself writes: "Carr attacked the notion that 'facts' and 'interpretation' are rigidly separable. Pointing out that all writing of history involves a selection from the sum of facts available, he demonstrated that any selection of facts obeys an implicit evaluative criterion. 'Facts' are thus inseparable from 'interpretations', which in turn are determined by 'values'" (Blackburn, k1972, pp. 10 and 113).

On page 27, above, we quoted a preposterous passage from a professing socialogist. In his new version of philosophical idealism the Honoured Society of the sociologists usurps the role of Berkeley's God: " . . . it is not an objectively discernible, purely existing external world which accounts for sociology; it is the methods and procedures of sociology which create and sustain that world" (Young, 1971, p. 131). To this anyone who is *For Science in the Social Sciences* has to respond that, on the contrary, there is "an objectively discernible, purely existing external world which accounts for sociology". It cannot be, and it is not, "the methods and procedures of sociology which create and sustain that world".

A similar response is required when professional historians dare thus slightingly to dismiss the great Leopold von Ranke. For it was he who claimed, famously and truly, that his and their professional business was to discover and to tell, "wie es eigentlich gewesen" [how it really was]. Anyone who truly believes that it is, necessarily and in all cases, impossible "to reconstruct the past 'as it happened'", and who nevertheless accepts employment as a historian should ask himself, and tell us, what reason he has left us for believing anything which he chooses to say about the past.

Nor is it compatible with any sort of science, whether social or other, much less less required by it, to deny "that there exists a

realm of facts independent of theories". For if it was not possible –
as of course it is – to describe experimental and other data in ways
logically independent of rival theories offered to explain such data,
then no one could ever show that any theories are inconsistent
with the facts, and, therefore, false. There is, surely, some giveaway significance in the fact that Jones covers his embarrassment
over the finding that real wages rose between 1790 and 1850 with
bluster, sneering, and abuse (Blackburn, 1972, pp. 107–9). For to
demonstate the falsity of one of its main logical consequences, the
'Immiseration Thesis', is, necessarily, to falsify the cherished
theory of *Capital*.

The more immediately relevant objection to what is alleged to
have been established in *What is History?* is that nothing of this
sort follows from the proposition "that all writing of history
involves a selection from the sum of facts available". Certainly
such selection is always involved: not only in "all writing of
history"; but also in all other descriptive discourse, both written
and oral. For there is no limit on the number of true propositions
which could be formulated and asserted about anything. This is,
perhaps, what Lenin and others have had in mind when maintaining that the properties of matter are infinite.

It does not, however, follow: either that every statement of the
facts in the case must be more or less viciously selective and
misleading; or that every such statement and every interpretation
put upon it has to be either equally value-loaded or – what is
often, though wrongly, thought to be a further implication –
equally arbitrary. When, for instance, you are as a witness sworn
to tell "the truth, the whole truth, and nothing but the truth" you
have not undertaken the impossible task of uttering an infinite
collection of truths. What the court wants, and what in this and in
other cases is meant by 'telling the whole truth', is that you should
reveal everything which you know, *which is relevant to the
business in hand*.

Notice well that here, as everywhere, both relevance and
importance are essentially relative. But we must not succumb to
the temptation to hold that what is relative is, necessarily, also
subjective; and hence, it is thought, arbitrarily determinable.

Many people find this temptation too strong to resist. It is, for
instance, common to take it that, if what is right or wrong is

relative to time and place, then it will follow that there is nothing right or wrong but each particular individual's (entirely arbitrary) thinking makes it so. Whether this common conclusion is true or false it certainly does not follow. For motion too is essentially relative. Yet from this we cannot infer that the question whether this is now in motion relative to that is a question not of objective physical fact but of the psychology of possible observers. Even some of the classical philosophers, however, have made fallacious inferences of this form: "... *great* and *small, swift* and *slow,* are allowed to exist nowhere without the mind; being entirely relative ..." (Berkeley, 1710, bk I, sec. 11, p. 263).

A big mouse – a mouse, that is, which is bigger than the usual run of mice – will be very small when compared with even a small hippopotamus – a hippopotamus, that is, which is small relative to the usual run of hippopotami. In the same way what is relevant and important relative to one set of interests may be unimportant or altogether irrelevant relative to another, different set of interests. Nevertheless, given any one particular set, what is relevant and important is just as much a question of objective fact as any of those otherwise very different questions about the bigness or smallness of mice or hippopotami.

Certainly, what interests we are to have, and when, is a matter for our individual choice; which may or may not be arbitrary. So too the selection of points of view from which to take their photographs is something for the photographers to decide. But then, as in a better moment Berkeley went on to say, "When in broad daylight I open my eyes, it is not in my power to choose whether I shall see or no, or to determine what particular objects shall present themselves to my view: and so likewise to the hearing and other senses; the ideas imprinted on them are not creatures of *my* will (1710, bk I, sec. 29, p. 273).

In the light of what has just been said both the objectivity and the relativity of both relevance and importance, it becomes easy to appreciate that, although every account of anything can constitute only an infinitesimal selection from the infinity of true statements which conceivably could have been formulated and uttered, still there is never either need or excuse for that kind of selectivity which truly is scandalous.

There is, to take a rather old-world illustration, no excuse for certain professing and pretending historians who have written and published scandalously selective biographies of Jesuit missionaries martyred during the reign of Queen Elizabeth I. They have managed not to mention that these had all sworn obedience to the Pope: who had both declared that anyone assassinating her, "with the pious intention of doing God service . . . not only does not sin but gains merit"; and who was all the time giving full support to Spain in its ongoing war with her kingdom (Trevor-Roper, 1957, pp. 108–18).

Certainly historians have to choose what periods they are going to study, into what aspects of those periods they want to inquire, and what questions they are trying to answer. So we might say that, by choosing in whatever sense they do choose, they are also choosing what is going to be relevant to and important in their inquiries. But, if we do choose to say this, then we must be more than ever resolved to insist that what actually is relevant or important relative to some given set of interests is so relevant or important *altogether independent of the will of persons who have chosen to pursue those interests*. We also need to be aware that, since historians even of the same periods may be and often are pursuing very different sets of interests, two very different history books may both contain equally sound and objective history. The fact that historians have to choose what they will investigate "is no reason whatever . . . why historians at different times, but possessing the same information, should answer the same question differently" (Hayek, 1949, p. 75).

Nor is this fact, which is just as much the fact about both other social scientists and all other investigators, any reason for holding that their investigations cannot be value-free, or have always to be corrupted by a sort of subjectivity both peculiar to history and the other social sciences, and vicious. Sir Lewis Namier, therefore, misleads when he argues that "The function of the historian is . . . not to reproduce indiscriminately all that meets the eye . . . History is therefore necessarily subjective and individual, conditioned by the interest and the vision of the historian" (Namier, 1952, p. 7).

Weber himself, who demanded Wertfreiheit both in sociological investigation and in the presentation of findings, was, quite consistently, just as strongly committed to Wertbeziehung – value-relevance – in the choice of subjects for inquiry. Another of his classic articles deals with '"Objectivity" in Social Science and Social Policy'. It is entirely right and proper that sociologists should by their well-known enthusiasm for educational insti-tutions and by their notorious hostility to criminal behaviour be led to study these topics. What concepts they find applicable in so doing will then be determined by those interests; although those concepts should not by them – at least not in their working hours – be defined in even partially prescriptive or evaluative terms. "In the mode of their use," Weber concludes, "the investigator is obviously bound by the norms of our thought just as much here as elsewhere. For scientific truth precisely is what is *valid* for all who *seek* the truth" (Weber, 1904, p. 84).

It is just because the subject-matter of social science and social policy is so value-relevant that value-freedom becomes so vital. Because we are all human, we are all apt to become ego-involved in any position upon which we have once taken a stand, and disinclined to admit that we have been proved wrong. But, again because we are human, whereas most of us have few strong desires to believe this or that about positrons or iguanas or any other elements in the subject-matter of the natural sciences, all of us would very much like to believe, and/or would very much like others to believe, all manner of different things about social affairs and social policies. In these areas, therefore, the desire to discover and to tell the truth, letting the chips fall where they may, needs to be much stronger. Very often it is not. Indeed very often it is so weak as to be indiscernible.

3 Are all cultures equal?

It would seem that it is nowadays widely believed either that the social sciences must presuppose, or even that they have discovered, that all cultures are equally good or equally valid. Thus in a collection of essays under the title *Race, Culture and Intelligence* the sociologically trained Professor of Education in the Open University concluded: "And finally we cannot accept quality distinctions between cultures" (Richardson and Spears, 1972, p. 156).

Again, presumably after receiving some such academic misguidance, the Education Committee of the London Borough of Brent, in a document entitled *Book I: Education for a Multicultural Democracy,* issued a ukase to all its teachers: "The recognition that all peoples and cultures are inherently equal must be a constant from which all educational practice will be developed" (p. 7). It is obvious that acceptance is thought to be essential to a total rejection of racism; which is, presumably, why the Committee at once goes on to insist that this "is not a negotiable principle" (p. 7).

Since that Brent document is typical of the productions of what the mischievous Peter Simple would have us call the race relations industry, it is worth making one or two remarks especially relevant to that context, before proceeding to more general issues.

First, the associations of race with culture, and of all peoples with all cultures, suggest some failure to appreciate that there is an enormous difference between racial and cultural identification. Certainly there are many social sets all of whose members share what sociologists and anthropologists would, in their extremely broad and comprehensive sense, count as a culture, and all or almost all of whose members happen to have skins of roughly the same colour. But if and where any culture is racially exclusive, and cannot be shared by members of any but the most favoured race, there we have a culture which truly is, and is surely to be condemned as, paradigmatically racist. For, as the activists of the race relations industry so often need to be reminded, racism just is, and is to be unreservedly abominated precisely and only in so far as it consists in, the advantaging or disadvantaging of individuals for no other or better reason than that they happen to belong to some favoured or disfavoured racial set.

The distinction between race and culture is here crucial. For many people would like to explain all inter-set differences in economic or educational success or failure by referring to hostile discrimination against members of the sets which in the event prove unsuccessful. Certainly there has been, and is, plenty of hostile discrimination against members of disfavoured racial sets; and of that any at all is too much. But there is now a vast accumulation of evidence of often quite huge inter-set differences in success and failure; differences which simply cannot be accounted for in terms of racial discrimination, whether friendly or hostile. (See, for instance, Sowell, 1981a.) It is, surely, in order both to conceal the decisive importance of cultural differences and to exaggerate the extent and effects of racial discrimination by whites for whites that activists in the race relations industry are urging a redefinition of the word 'black'. This is in the future to include: not only both blacks and all other non-whites; but perhaps also some sets of whites qualifying as "minorities" (Flew, 1983b).

The second point to be made here, about what for Brent Education Committee "is not a negotiable principle", is that it is flat inconsistent with their own crusading commitments. For there certainly are cultures – in the relevant, most comprehensive sense – which are both racist and sexist: indeed the Brent Committee-persons would themselves bring both charges against that of, or against some of those of, contemporary Britain. So how can they, how can anyone, say that male chauvinist macho cultures and racist cultures are equally good or "equally valid" (p. 10), when compared with cultures sexually egalitarian and wholly colour-blind?

These attempts to marry a pretence that everything is equally good with insistence that some things are very definitely better than others may be instructively, but ruefully, compared with the combination in so much of the criminal justice world of a pretence to be working for the reform and rehabilitation of offenders with a horrified rejection of any desire "to impose our values on them" (Morgan, 1978, ch. 9).

If the word 'impose' is felt to be too harsh and too authoritarian, then it can without much loss be jettisoned. But if the Probation Officers and others involved in this business are not even trying somehow to bring it about that offenders come to prefer a non-criminal to a criminal way of life – come, that is, to value the one and to disvalue the other – then why do we as taxpayers have to go on employing these 'public servants'; and why do they have no scruples against accepting their salaries, and regularly asking for more? The fact is that Brent Education Committee actually is, and the Probation Officers ought to be, trying to get those under its, or their, charge to accept certain values: anti-racist and anti-sexist in the one case; and anti-criminal in the other.

It is rare for those who proclaim that all cultures are of equal value to state the source from which they derive this revelation. In the two cases cited so far it was presumably derived, by way of some confusing of culture with race, from a doctrine of racial equality; and that probably a doctrine construed as in the first instance descriptive rather than prescriptive (Flew, 1976a, pt I, ch. 5). But where no question of race is involved the source or sources must be different. Perhaps one is the jurisdictional claim that the scope of the social sciences embraces all societies, everywhere and at all times. Adapting an advertising slogan from Britain's most popular Sunday newspaper: "All social life is here!" A more elevated formulation was provided by Ranke, referring only to the writing of history. Every age, he ruled, "is equal in the sight of God".

Once this picturesque utterance is duly demythologized there is little temptation to read it as either constituting or entailing any claims about the equal goodness or validity of all cultures. A somewhat more persuasive suggestion is that we have here another case of something quite often found in the history of ideas; namely, the transformation of a methodological rule into a metaphysical assertion – an assertion, that is, about ultimate reality.

Way back at pp. 73–4, above, we quoted Malinowski's explanation of "The functional view". It was that "in every type of civilization, every custom, material object, idea and belief fulfils some vital function, has some task to accomplish, represents an indispensable part within a working whole. "Now it is one thing to urge, as a methodological maxim, that the anthropologist – like the biologist – should always search for such vital functions. It is quite another to maintain, as a piece of metaphysics, that these are, ultimately and in the last analysis, always there to be found. The temptations are: both to offer the metaphysics as unsupported support for the maxim; and to replace the maxim by the metaphysics. So the suggestion is that at least in some cases the doctrine of the equal goodness of all cultures may be an illegitimate derivation from functionalist methodology. If every feature of every culture "has some task to accomplish, represents an indispensable part within a working whole", then every culture, as an efficiently working whole, must be equally 'valid'. Of course this does not follow. Yet someone might well think that it did.

The most influential current particular application of this general doctrine seems to be in Linguistics. Thus, in an Open University setbook on *Accent, Dialect and the School,* we read: "During the past several decades, people working in linguistics have studied a good proportion of the world's languages ... From this study it has emerged that there are no linguistic reasons for saying that any language is superior to any other. All languages, that is, are equally 'good'" (Trudgill, 1975, p. 24).

Notice first that the word 'good' in the passage quoted is wrapped in what have to be read as sneer or disclaimer quotes. Presumably these were introduced to indicate the distaste of the value-free, professionally neutral scientist for all such normative notions. But this distaste should have led him to say: not that all languages are equally good, or equally (sneer) 'good'; but that no such normative terms are to be found in the vocabulary of the (properly value-free) science of Linguistics. Instead he appears to have fallen – like so many others – into the error of holding that, while to say that this is superior to that is, to say that this and that are of equal worth is not, a value-judgement.

Notice, second, and perhaps more surprising, that, although Trudgill speaks at the beginning of extensive empirical studies, and although he says there that his conclusion "emerged ... from" these studies, and although he later tells us that we have already seen that there is no way in which one variety of language can be considered superior to any other" (p. 27); still he never either gives his own account or otherwise specifically refers to any of those particular pieces of more or less esoteric work by which this conclusion is supposed to be sustained. The truth is, surely, that it has no such foundation. Instead, in so far as it has any basis at all, this is in invalid derivations from methodological maxims, an uncomprehending commitment to value-freedom, and some manifesto of the comprehensive scope of linguistics.

Another relevant error is to hold that a value-free social science has to disown all consideration: not only of absolute but also of instrumental good; not only of categorical but also of hypothetical imperatives. Failing to make and to appreciate the importance of such distinctions Trudgill, like too many of his colleagues, feels he has to avoid admitting as relevant what are undeniable facts of comparative linguistics. It is not to the point, he has to insist: that a speaker of Eskimo (Inuit) is far better equipped to make nice distinctions between different kinds of snow than a speaker of Arabic; that such highly inflected languages as Lithuanian require complex machinery to do jobs which are more economically done in English and Chinese; and so on (Bodmer, 1943).

Again like too many of his colleagues, he also becomes by his failure to employ these distinctions committed to denying the vital instrumental importance for anyone proposing to make their life in Great Britain of a mastery of Standard English (Honey, 1983). Certainly other dialects and other languages might have served us equally well. But Standard English is what we actually have, and not Urdu or Creole or Japanese or anything else at all. So, although these others might or might not have been or be equally good or equally valid, this is what anyone wanting to become British now has to learn.

An absolute good is something which is (thought to be) good in itself, and independent of consequences. An instrumental good is one which is an effective means of securing something else (thought to be) good in itself. The distinction between categorical and hypothetical imperatives was first drawn by Immanuel Kant. A categorical imperative rules that something categorically must be done, quite regardless of the possibly different or even contrary desires of the agent. A hypothetical imperative asserts that, iff the agent wants this, then, in order to get it, he must do that. It is, therefore, obvious that both propositions asserting that this is instrumentally good, that this is an efficient means to get that, and propositions asserting hypothetical imperatives, that if you want this then in order to get it you must do that, must be, in Humian terms, propositions belonging in the *is* category rather than the *ought*; that they describe or purport to describe our actual world, rather than recommend actions which (it is thought) would make it more ideal.

7 Subjective or Objective, Relative or Absolute?

There is nothing good and nothing bad absolutely speaking;
everything is relative, this is the only absolute statement.

Auguste Comte, *L'Industrie*, bk III, ch. 2;
quoted in Hayek, 1979, pp. 238 and 389

Scholars who have traditionally sought to discover 'objective'
knowledge have had to contend with the fact that the search for
and discovery of such knowledge is socially organized ... The
implication is this: if objective knowledge is taken to mean knowledge of a reality independent of language, or presuppositionless
knowledge, or knowledge of the world which is independent of the
observer's procedures for finding and producing the knowledge,
then there is no such thing as objective knowledge.

Alan Blum, 'The Corpus of Knowledge
as a Normative Order'; in Young, 1971, p. 128

Often nowadays it is said or suggested that in the areas of social
science and social policy – indeed perhaps in other areas too –
there can be no such thing as objective knowledge; knowledge,
that is, of "how it actually was", or is. It is also urged, in support
of this conclusion, that everything is always and necessarily in
some way relative; and that this results in an inescapable subjectivity. Although these are sometimes presented as philosophical
implications of work in the social sciences – in particular the
sociology of knowledge, anthropology and the history of science –
practitioners tend to respond with petulant impatience when
confronted with the obvious and devastating objection. This is

that this is to make the whole enterprise self-refuting. For it is to say, on the basis of supposed findings of social scientific investigations, that no such findings are to be relied on as real knowledge. For example, the two intervening sentences in the motto quotation from Alan Blum read: "Philosophically, this has often constituted a dilemma. Sociologically, it is not so much a dilemma as an inescapable fact of enquiry."

Since any sincerely truth-seeking inquirers, fully persuaded of the impossibility of attaining knowledge in their chosen field, would presumably construe this conviction as a decisive reason for frankly abandoning the quest, we are forced to infer that those who do not react in this forthright and realistic way either have a commitment to truth-seeking which is something less than total and overriding, and/or cannot entirely persuade themselves that these alleged implications are true. Yet even a half-belief in the hopelessness of the whole enterprise is demoralizing. If objectivity is anyway impossible, and the truth forever undiscoverable, then why bother to be strenuously and painfully self-critical? Anything goes; or, rather, nearer to the bone, anything sitting comfortably with our own values and interests is quite acceptable.

To appreciate just how demoralizing such a half-belief in such conclusions can be, consider again the response which Margaret Mead made when she was confronted with the evidence proving that all her main claims about Samoa in the period of her visit were false. *Coming of Age in Samoa,* she insisted, "must remain, as all anthropological works must remain, exactly as it was written, true to what I saw in Samoa and what I was able to convey of what I saw, true to the state of our knowledge of human behaviour as it was in the mid 1920s; true to our hopes and fears for the future of the world" (For more on this great anthropological scandal, and on some of the still more scandalous attempts either to cover it up or to pretend that there are no lessons to be learnt, see Freeman, 1983b and 1984, Caton, 1984 and Wendt, 1983.)

Many of the weapons needed for dealing with those challenges to the possibility of social scientific knowledge which are being considered in the present chapter have been deployed already on various occasions in its predecessors. The first and almost always neglected essential is to insist that anyone proposing to employ any of the various key terms must begin by making clear what usage they propose, and must then stick to that usage. This is essential because, although they sound like established technical terms, the words 'subjectivist', 'objectivist' and 'relativist' possess in fact only whatever meanings may be supplied for them ad hoc in some particular context. We have therefore to demand to be told what precisely it is which is being said to be subjective or objective, and exactly what it is which makes it count as such. Again, what is it which is supposed to be relative to what, and in what way?

Once that first fundamental is seized, we are positioned to grasp a second. Notwithstanding widespread assumptions to the contrary, to say that this is necessarily relative to that is by no means to imply that the relation between this and that is only in the minds of observers, or is determinable by their arbitrary fiat. To maintain, for instance, that what anyone ought to do must depend upon time, place and circumstance is not at all the same thing as maintaining that there is no right or wrong about it, and that it is entirely a matter of individual or even collective taste. The general maxim, 'Do in Rome as the Romans do' is not a licence to please yourself alone; unless, of course, the particular place and period in question is that of *La Dolce Vita,* in which precisely that is what the Romans do do! Again, motion is everyone's paradigm case of the essentially relative. Yet, once both the object and the reference point have been specified, nothing, surely, could be more a matter of mind-independent objective fact than whether and in what direction, and how fast, that body is in motion.

A third fundamental concerns the concepts employed in articulating our beliefs, and us as the subjects of those beliefs. It is, certainly, true: that we understand and have to understand whatever we do understand in terms of whatever concepts we have; that it is, and cannot but be, we who believe or who know whatever we do believe or know, and who possess whatever concepts we do possess; and, consequently, that facts of both these two unexciting sorts are facts about ourselves as subjects. But from all this, when presented in an unfevered fashion, it does not even seem to follow that propositions involving our concepts cannot constitute, and be by us known to constitute, statements of objective, mind-independent truth.

1 *Subjective idealism and the sociology of knowledge*

Blum's article on 'The Corpus of Knowledge as a Normative Order' comes in *Knowledge and Control*, a collection aspiring to set "New Directions for the Sociology of Education". In it, according to the Editor, "sociology of education is no longer conceived as an area of enquiry distinct from the sociology of knowledge" (Young, 1971, subtitle and p. 3). So, apparently, we must "explore the implications of treating knowledge, or 'what counts as knowledge', as socially constituted or constructed", insisting that "the subversion of absolutism by sociology is of crucial importance for the sociology of education" (pp. 5 and 6).

Knowledge and Control is not a book to be lightly dismissed. For, as was emphasized earlier (pp. 26–8), for fifteen or more years the obscurantist and educationally subversive doctrines commended by its Editor have been preached as revealed truth both from the electronic pulpits of the Open University and in the more conventional lecture halls of the University of London Institute of Education. So by now a substantial proportion of all Britain's present or potential schoolteachers must have been exposed to these doctrines. The key contention, the misguiding thread, is never formulated in a properly terse, explicit, or completely categorical form. It is, nevertheless, perfectly clear what it is: namely, that the mere possibility of developing some sociological account of the desires and interests supporting the making of some kind of discrimination constitutes a sufficient demonstration that there is no objective basis for anything of the kind; that there are, that is to say, no corresponding differences 'without the mind'.

Thus the Editor faults the authors of "an otherwise excellent paper" for "drawing on a *metaphysical* 'out there' in terms of which, they claim, we must check our theories against our practice" (Young, 1971, p. 43n). Again, Nell Keddie, one of his favourite contributors, after noting that "teachers differentiate . . . between pupils perceived as of high and low ability", forthwith dismisses the very idea that corresponding differences might actually subsist between those teachers' pupils: "The origins of these categories are likely to lie outside the school and within the structure of the society itself in its wider distribution of power"

(p. 156). Finally, in Blum's own commended contribution, we have, as we have seen twice already, a reckless manifesto of total subjective idealism: ". . . it is not an objectively discernible, purely existing external world which accounts for sociology; it is the methods and procedures of sociology which create and sustain that world" (p. 131).

The justification for describing these doctrines as educationally subversive is, therefore, quite simply, that they are. For *Knowledge and Control* forecloses on the possibility that any distinctions made by examiners may correspond to actual differences in the quality either of the work examined or of the candidates. So we now find teachers of intending teachers in Chelsea College concluding a *New Society* article: "The point is fundamental. There are no universal standards; there are only people's perceptions of standards" (24 February 1977, p. 384).

So what, please, are our intending teachers supposed to be going to be trying to bring about, if not real improvements in the capacities and performances of their pupils? Our immediate concern here, however, is not with the educational or anti-educational implications. (But see Flew, 1976a, chs. 2 and 3; and compare Dawson, 1981). It is, rather, with the reasons which have been offered or suggested for reaching these obscurantist and preposterous conclusions.

Take Blum first. The main source of trouble in the motto quotation lies in his failure to appreciate how vast a difference in meaning can in an English sentence be produced by a small change in word order. Like so many others he would benefit from exercising with Marghanita Laski's exemplary utterance, "The peacocks are seen on the western hills." (Eight clearly distinct meanings can be generated by inserting the word 'only' in eight different positions.) After training himself in this way Blum might have become able to recognize the enormous difference: between, on the one hand, "knowledge of a reality independent of language"; and, on the other hand, knowledge, independent of language, of a reality.

For it is just plumb grotesque to maintain that – say – the stars in their courses are in any way dependent on what we say or do not say; and it is not for any sociologist to deny the claims of the natural scientists to know that this earth existed long before it bore any language-using creatures. If, on the other hand, Blum really intends to deny only propositional knowledge independent of language, then this is unexceptionable. Or, rather, it is unexceptionable so long as it is not mistaken to imply that the truths which we have to express in a particular form of words would not be true at all until and unless someone had formulated those truths in these or equivalent words. The crucial distinctions are: first, between knowing, and the truths which are known; and, second, between knowledge of a reality which is independent of language, and knowledge which is itself independent of language.

It is one thing, and scarcely disputatious or exciting, to say that the extent of our knowledge must be limited by, among other things, the quality and quantity of the conceptual equipment which happens to be available to us. It is quite another and, as we have been reminding ourselves, utterly paradoxical and preposterous to hold that every reality of which we can have knowledge must be dependent upon our presence, and our activities, and our "observer's procedures", and our having the concepts required to possess and to express that knowledge. Embarrassing though the observation is, it does appear to be true that the shamefully simple confusions removed in this and the previous paragraph have been and remain perennial chief sources of the demoralizing dogma that any knowledge which we do possess must be, in some depreciatory and emasculating sense, essentially and only relative and subjective opinion; the dogma – to put it in a brief, brutal and straightforward way – that there really neither is nor can be any such thing as, without prefix or suffix, knowledge.

Certainly there are several other sources, and some of these are more particularly concerned with the fields of social science and social policy, and with the alleged impossibility in these of "objective knowledge"; knowledge, that is, and not merely perceived knowledge, of mind-independent realities.

The first of these other sources is the identification of investigator-produced pseudo-phenomena; the identification, that is, of what has been mnemonically nicknamed The Buggery in Bootle Effect. Young begins: "It is a statistical truism that ... half a population of kidney beans will be of shorter than average length

... despite efforts of breeders to produce longer beans ..." (1971, pp. 9–10). It is an unauspicious beginning. For if the word 'average' is to be interpreted in its ordinary sense, in which it is equivalent to the 'arithmetic mean' of mathematicians, then it is not necessarily true, but plain false, that half of any population must be below average. Where one is a mere five foot and everyone else is a six-footer, there all but the first must be above the arithmetic mean height. It is the median, not the arithmetic mean, which (nearly) half of any population has to be at or below.

Young proceeds: "the methodical character of marriages, divorces and suicides is seen and made possible by the organized practices of sociologists: likewise the inevitable normal distribution of kidney beans ... and the regular 50–60 per cent of passes in General Certificate are seen and made possible by the organized activities of breeders and examiners" (p. 10).

The initial ill omens are thus fulfilled. For these three cases are all different. First, the phenomena of marriage, divorce and suicide were all going strong long before there were any sociologists to see and make them possible. Second, any social scientists recording any of the necessary truths or necessary falsehoods of logic or mathematics as if they were propositions stating or purporting to state matters of fact and real existence make fools of themselves. (See chapter 5, section 2, above.) It is only the third case which does seem to be one of an investigator-produced pseudo-phenomenon; which is what Young is contending that they all are.

For the examiners for the General Certificate of Education have apparently been obeying an instruction from the whilom Secondary Schools Examinations Council to ensure that in every year in each subject roughly the same proportions of all candidates are awarded the various different grades. This ukase has had the effect, as it was presumably intended to have, of invalidating direct year on year comparisons as a means of determining whether levels of learning achievement are rising or falling: such comparisons can, therefore, not be used to throw light on the question whether the so-called 'comprehensive experiment' has been, from an educational point of view, a success or a failure (Shaw, 1983).

A little later Young refers approvingly to a "discussion of how 'official statistics' on crime are produced" (p. 25). He suggests, though he does not outright say, that crime is another investigator-produced pseudo-phenomenon. Certainly everyone with a sophisticated interest in the subject knows that some, though not of course all, increases or declines in the recorded numbers of offences may refer rather to features of the system of reporting than to actual variations in the popularity of these offences. Thus, in the bad old pre-Wolfenden days, a sudden jump in the number of successful prosecutions for homosexual offences in – say – Bootle might have indicated, not a real explosion of unnatural vice, but the appointment of a Chief Constable with 'a thing about queers'. Young and his associates, with the over-enthusiasm of the freshly initiated, are inclined to see everywhere nothing else whatever but this Buggery in Bootle Effect. (It should, by the way, be carefully distinguished from the England Expects Effect identified on p. 95, above, which is itself a special case of the more general Oedipus Effect. For, surely, Nelson by issuing his most famous signal actually made some difference to morale in the British fleet?)

It is, as has been emphasized before, a fundamental fact about the peculiar subject-matter of the social sciences that as near as makes no matter all distinctively human activities are concept-guided, in the sense that they can be performed only by persons possessing the relevant concepts. This carries two important consequences. First, all social scientific explanation must accept as fundamental the reasons which agents themselves had for acting. Hence, second, whatever further concepts and explanations social scientists find it necessary or possible to introduce, they must always begin by mastering the action-guiding concepts employed by the subjects of their studies (chapter 2, section 1).

In part no doubt it was a badly focused appreciation of these truths which, with the help of the three kinds of intellectual malpractice reviewed in the preliminary paragraphs of the present chapter, led Blum to maintain that "the methodical character of marriage, war and suicide is only seen, recognized and made possible through the organized practices of sociology" (Young, 1971, p. 131). But, surely, another part of the story is that many notions originally devised by social scientists, slipping out of their sometimes strikingly uncloistered cloisters, have been adopted as action-guiding by what Blum would call "societal members". This is the less surprising since so many of the leaders have, like Smith and Malthus, combined and sometimes confused quests for theoretical undersanding with commitments to practical policies.

Thus, for instance, a Weberian ideal type, originally offered primarily or purely as an instrument of neutral and non-participatory understanding of some society, may become the normative ideal of some members of that society and may in this way guide both their social activities and their understanding of these activities: this surely happened with Smith's ideal picture of a dynamic, private, pluralist and competitive economy. Again, consider a characteristic statement by Lenin: "The history of all countries shows that the working class, exclusively by its own effort, is able to develop only trade-union consciousness ... The teachings of socialism, however, grew out of the philosophic, historical and economic theories elaborated ... by intellectuals" (Lenin, 1902, p. 80; and compare Hayek, 1952 on the concurrent development of sociological science and socialist ideals).

Nevertheless, whatever the present and future influence of notions devised by social scientists, we cannot accept any Revised Version of Genesis 1:27: "And sociologists created societal members in their own image ... male and female societal members created they them." What we can do is take further and fuller note of the Oedipus Effect: "the influence of an item of information upon the situation to which the information refers" (Popper, 1957, p. 13; and compare p. 126, above). For there have been, and certainly will be more, important cases in which the publication of social scientific findings to the people to whom those findings refer has drastically affected the future behaviour of many of those people. The most familiar and most discussed examples are of the influence of the publication of opinion poll findings upon the electoral behaviour of the populations (sample) polled. Thus in the 1948 US Presidential election it was thought that polls suggesting that Dewey would win in a landslide led a lot of lazy Republican voters to stay at home, letting Truman scrape back. But then there was also reason to believe that the samples had been unrepresentative. The clearer cases are from British bye-elections – notably at Orpington in 1962 – where published polls showing how many electors really preferred a third-party candidate have encouraged them to plump for that first preference, instead of settling for their second best 'for fear of wasting their vote'.

Everyone always insists that sociology of knowledge – which, according to *Knowledge and Control,* "is no longer conceived as an area of enquiry distinct" from sociology of education – is not directed specifically and exclusively at knowledge. It is not, there is to say, concerned always and only with rationally justified true belief. Indeed the author of one unusually powerful essay, although himself privately persuaded that all positive religious beliefs are at best false and at worst incoherent, nevertheless commends as a model "Durkheim's classic study 'The Elementary Forms of the Religious Life'": this, it is asserted, "shows how a sociologist can penetrate to the very depths of *a form of knowledge*" (Bloor, 1976, p. 2: italics supplied).

Although the treatises and the textbooks usually begin by disclaiming concern with knowledge as such, sociologists of knowledge are stubborn in their resistance to proposals to rename their discipline, correctly, sociology of belief. The maximum concession which most of them will allow is: either actually to put such key words as 'reality' and 'knowledge' between quotation marks; or else, and more often, to admit that perhaps this is what they ideally ought to do, but not to do it (Berger and Luckmann, 1971, Introduction). The significance of the inverted commas here would be to indicate that the sociologists are dealing only with perceived reality and believed knowledge. They are dealing, that is to say, with whatever their subjects think is the case and whatever they believe that they know; altogether without prejudice to the questions whether what they believe is true and whether they really do know.

This said, it should at once be interjected that social scientists who insist on obeying this perverse self-denying ordinance thereby prevent themselves from raising exciting questions and discovering what are likely to be revealing answers. How do so many otherwise sensible people continue to harbour so many beliefs which it should be obvious to them are, and could by them be known to be, untrue? (Compare pp. 23–4, above.) But the more immediately relevant and widely important need is to attack the irresponsible insouciance of employing the word 'knowledge' when what you are supposed to be meaning is, without prejudice, belief. This objection – like a similar objection on pp. 48–50, above – may be met with complaints about merely verbal purism and sneers at Linguistic Philosophy. Yet it is in truth one the force of which social scientists ought to be peculiarly well fitted to appreciate.

For they of all people should be most aware of the enormous strength of long and firmly established habits. But the habits of association formed in mastering the established usage of a term, and hence its established meaning, habits strengthened by then following that established usage, and understanding the term in that sense, such verbal and semantic habits are no less habits than all other habits. It is, therefore, wildly unrealistic to expect to be able to change your own and other people's actual usage of a word, and hence your own and other people's understanding of it, even if only in one limited context, by simply saying that this is what you propose to do, and want the others too to follow you in doing.

Consider, for example, a similar project from another area of sociology. Thorstein Veblen (1857–1929) insisted upon introducing into *The Theory of the Leisure Class* what is, given his and our established habits of association, the heavily offensive expression 'conspicuous waste'. He then immediately and perhaps somewhat disingenuously protested that, since what and all he was doing was value-free social science, this phrase from now on was to be read as a detached and evaluatively non-committal description. No one should be surprised, however, to find that his own actual usage is not consistent with this stated intention; while his readers have always in fact construed that key phrase as an expression of emphatic, and often well-warranted, disapproval (Veblen, 1899, pp. 97ff.).

It should not be surprising, therefore, that much confusion and many misconceptions have been, are, and will be generated by such irresponsible abusages. In the present particular case confusion is the worse confounded in two other ways. In the first place, most people only begin to seek possible social or psychological causes for (what are always other people's) beliefs after they have already somehow satisfied themselves that these beliefs are either false or at least held with a degree of conviction disproportionate to the evidencing reasons available to the believer. The temptation is to infer that any belief for which some sociological explanation is offered or sought is thereby revealed to be: not what Milton once called "real and delightful knowledge"; but, rather, rationally unjustified false belief. This temptation is further strengthened by the fact that it has been only in comparatively recent years that sociologists of belief have in fact addressed themselves to the hard sciences and to mathematics. (See, for instance, Bloor, 1976 and Barnes, 1974; and compare Flew, 1982b.)

The second reinforcing temptation is provided by the inverted commas around such words as 'reality' and 'knowledge'; when, that is, rather rarely, anyone remembers that these are supposed to be there. It is all too easy to misread them as indicating that what is being talked about is: not, without prejudice, perceived reality and believed knowledge; but beliefs which are already unequivocally discredited.

These, surely, are the main reasons why contributors to *Knowledge and Control* reach the remarkable and altogether devastating conclusions which they do reach. Thus they assume that what they still insist on calling the sociology of knowledge is an essentially subversive activity, necessarily discrediting every belief to which it can be applied: "the subversion of absolutism by sociology is of crucial importance" (Young, 1971, p. 6). Still more remarkable, and still more devastating, is the conclusion that it is by this same discipline revealed that we do not and cannot have any objective knowledge; any knowledge, that is, of mind-independent realities. On no account is there to be any "drawing on a *metaphysical* 'out there' in terms of which . . . we must check out our theories . . ."

The false assumption is supported by another common misconception, that to be critical is to reject. The assumption is false, since we can consistently say: both that Jones has an interest, maybe even a social class interest, in making that distinction or asserting this proposition; and that he knows both that the proposition asserted is true and that there are actual differences being thus distinguished. The short though in the longer run insufficient way with the common misconception is to ask whether, in order to qualify as a Shakespearian critic, you have to condemn his collected works.

"Much research in education", we are told, "starts from an

absolutist view of cognitive categories such as 'rational' and 'abstract'. This view in effect prevents these categories from being treated as themselves socially constructed and therefore open to sociological enquiry" (Young, 1971, p. 11). Certainly, if the word 'absolute' is to be construed thus, as precluding sociological inquiry, then the absolutist is indeed exposed as an obscurantist. Whatever the merits or demerits of these or any other concepts, it should be obvious that there is room for questions about how we in fact come to have and to use those which we do have and use.

So far, which is not very far, so good. But then a little later on, we meet a general objection to the work of philosophers of education – Paul Hirst in particular. "The problem with this kind of critique" is, apparently, that since it neither begins nor ends by rejecting, it is not truly critical; and, hence, that it is, but now in a quite new sense, absolutist. Hirst himself has "an absolutist conception of a set of distinct forms of knowledge which correspond closely to the traditional areas of the academic curriculum and thus justify . . . what are no more than the socio-historical constructs of a particular time" (Young, 1971, p. 23).

The word 'absolutist' is thus no longer employed in the original sense. For Hirst is being faulted: not for obstructing sociological investigation of how we come to make the distinctions; but for concluding that the distinctions made do in fact refer to actual differences. Not having noticed this crucial shift in meaning, Young has omitted to offer any reason for his own confident insistence: that the various concepts under discussion "are no more than the socio-historical constructs of a particular time"; and hence, presumably, that they do not correspond to any actual, objective differences.

The fallacious move made here is extremely common in all areas, although no doubt it is here eased by some of the more particular muddles and misconceptions examined previously. The heart of the matter is that, while it is one thing to say that certain notions are "the socio-historical constructs of a particular time", it is quite another to add that they are *no more than* "the socio-historical constructs of a particular time". It cannot be right to proceed from a premise stating only that this is that, direct to the richer conclusion that this is *merely* that, that this is *nothing but* that, that this is that *and nothing else*. Let us, therefore, introduce the appropriately shaming nickname 'The Debunker's Fallacy'.

That is the fallacy committed when anyone moves direct from 'That is your opinion' to 'That is *merely* your opinion'; with the implication that the proposition asserted has no other and better evidential support than your own bold, bald asserting. It was committed, for example, in a polemic entitled 'Popper's Mystification of Objective Knowledge'. This maintained that: "To appraise an argument for validity is to apply the standards of a social group. It cannot be other, *or more,* than this because we have no access to other standards" (Bloor, 1974, p. 75: italics supplied). This is preposterous. For it is to infer: from the fact that, although by applying the only available standards, we have determined that the argument is valid; the conclusion that in truth it cannot actually be so!

Elsewhere in *Knowledge and Control* Pierre Bourdieu, who does not share the peculiar convictions common to the Editor and his most approved contributors, quotes a relevant passage from the psychologist Kurt Lewin: "Experiments dealing with memory and group pressure on the individual show that what exists as 'reality' for the individual is, to a high degree, determined by what is socially accepted as reality ... 'Reality' therefore, is not an absolute. It differs with the group to which the individual belongs" (Young, 1971, p. 195). This is both true and important. But it is true only when read correctly. What Lewin is saying is: not what reality is not an absolute, because it differs with the group to which the individual belongs; but that 'reality' – that is to say what someone believes about reality – is not an absolute, because it differs with the group to which that individual belongs.

The distinction between reality and 'reality' or, if you prefer, between reality as it objectively is and perceived or believed reality, is, though often perversely collapsed, manifestly fundamental. While it is, therefore, all very well to speak of our concepts and categories "as themselves socially constructed"; it is very far from very well to slide from this to saying that the realities to which those concepts refer and which those categories categorize are created and sustained similarly. So Berger and Luckmann were both asking for and making trouble when they gave their best-selling textbook the title *The Social Construction of Reality,* and then proceeded to compound that initial fault by defining the words 'reality' and 'knowledge' in terms of our (subjective) recognitions and our (subjective) feelings of certainty (Berger and Luckmann, 1971, p. 13).

2   Anthropology, the relative and the rational

Sometime in the fifth century BC Darius, Great King of what would now be described as the Iranian Empire, staged a dramatic confrontation to show the extreme diversity of the norms to which different social sets are committed, often equally strongly. He summoned "those Greeks who were with him and asked them what sum of money would induce them to make a meal of their dead fathers. And they said that nothing would induce them to do this. Darius then summoned the . . . Callatian Indians, who do eat their parents and, in the presence of the Greeks . . . asked them how much money they would take to burn their dead fathers in a fire. And they raised a great uproar, telling him not to speak of such a thing" (Herodotus III 38, p. 229).

From Plato's generation onwards facts of this sort, or in our own day – as in the case of Mead's bestselling books about Samoa – often only supposed facts of this sort, have led many to adopt positions about values of the kind indicated in our motto quotation from Comte. Although there have always been some who have wanted to extend such relativism to embrace not only values but facts and truths also, this desire seems to have become much more widespread in recent years, and to have captured many of those working in the social sciences, and even the natural. Upstanding and forthright formulations are, nevertheless, hard to find. This is perhaps because the most straightforward relativistic claims can be so quickly and so easily discredited.

To say, for instance, that one and the same proposition – let it be christened, conservatively, *p* – is true for me (and my associates) but not for you (and yours) is to contradict yourself. For it is to say that one and the same proposition is both true and false. This catastrophic claim presumably arises from a confusion: between what is true of Smith but not Jones; and what is thought to be true *for* Smith but not *for* Jones. But, of course, nothing is true *for* anyone; or, if you prefer, everything which is true at all is true for everyone, and hence for no one in particular. It may be in some election be true of Smith that he voted Conservative and true of Jones that he voted Labour. Since, however, Smith and Jones are different people the proposition 'Smith voted Conservative' does not contradict the proposition 'Jones voted Labour (and not Conservative)'. (Compare Hollis and Lukes, 1982, pp. 106–22.)

Slightly more complicated versions rely on confusing some of the fundamental distinctions laboured in Section 1, above. What can by me be known to be true is in part a function both of my spatio-temporal position and of my intellectual equipment; while all knowledge presupposes a knowing subject. But none of this even begins to show that any truths which may or may not be known in any way depend on or are somehow relative to anyone's spatio-temporal position or anyone's intellectual equipment; or that what actually is or is not true is always determined by some subject.

Again, perceived knowledge and hence perceived truth are totally different from, without prefix or suffix, knowledge and truth; while there is, similarly, a great gulf between truths about 'reality' and truths about reality. So to show that and how the former are socially constructed or essentially relative is not at all to show – what most surely cannot be shown – that the same is true of the latter.

Various writings by Peter Winch have, since the publication in 1958 of *The Idea of A Social Science,* attracted an extraordinary amount of attention. As becomes a professional philosopher, he propounds a somewhat more sophisticated reading of relativism. This starts by emphasizing the fundamental importance here of what we discussed in chapter 2 'Our Reasons for Acting'. In consequence rationality becomes a key concept in all the social sciences. So far, so excellent.

But then, in a paper disquietingly entitled 'The Reality of Magic', Winch proceeds to raise "certain difficulties about Professor E. E. Evans-Pritchard's ... classic *Witchcraft, Oracles and Magic among the Azande*" (B. Wilson, 1970, p. 78). These involve Winch faulting Evans-Pritchard for wanting to say "that the criteria applied in scientific experimentation constitute a true link between our ideas and an independent reality, whereas those characteristic of other systems of thought – in particular, magical methods of thought – do not" (pp. 82–3). Poor culture-bound Evans-Pritchard was, apparently, in error when he maintained that in their beliefs about withcraft the Azande "attribute to phenomena supra-sensible qualities ... *which they do not possess*" (quoted p. 85: Winch's italics).

In a second part, on 'Our Standards and Theirs', Winch tries to justify this conclusion: "Something can appear rational to someone only in terms of *his* understanding of what is and is not rational. If *our* concept of rationality is a different one from his, then it makes no sense to say that anything either does or does not appear rational to *him* in *our* sense ... MacIntyre seems to be saying that certain standards are taken as criteria of rationality because they *are* criteria of rationality. But whose?" (pp. 97–8).

Enough has been said already about the wrong-headedness of the move: from the necessarily true premise that whatever I sincerely assert must be my opinion; to the conclusion that those assertions must therefore be, if not false, at any rate not known to be true. Yet it is perhaps worth underlining one disturbing consequence of the collectivist version of this invalid reference. If "to appraise an argument for validity" and to assess a proposition for truth or falsity really is "to apply the standards of a social group", and if it really "cannot be other, or more, than this"; then, no doubt, "the objectivity of knowledge resides in its being the set of accepted beliefs of a social group" (Bloor, 1974, pp. 75–6).

To say this, however, is to imply that there neither is nor could be any standing ground for dissident individuals. Given such absolute collectivism it becomes doubtful whether Orwell's Winston Smith could without self-contradiction even muse privately over his doubts about the truth of the historical revisions authorized by Minitrue. For whatever was by due process of collective decision – applying the standards of a social group – tossed down the memory holes must, necessarily, have been false. That, after all, is what under Ingsoc (or English socialism) 'true' and 'false' are supposed to mean. (By the way: let no one be distracted and deceived by any superciliously diversionary suggestion that in *1984,* any more than in *Animal Farm,* Orwell's prime target was anything else but totalitarianism, Soviet style.)

Second, two people, or two cultures, can have two different concept(ion)s of this or that only in so far as there is considerable coincidence between one and the other. For the mere fact that the same vocable – 'rationality' say – is found to be used in two radically distinct ways indicates the subsistence, not of two concept(ion)s of rationality, but of two senses of the word 'rationality'. So if there really are different concept(ion)s of rationality, then the differences between these cannot be either as total or as unbridgeable as Winch assumes.

We are here, it has to be interjected, observing a useful distinction between the concept of such and such and a conception of it. The concept of – say – justice is given when we have been equipped with some traditional definition of 'to do justice'; such as "to live honourably, to wrong no one, and to allow to each their own"; which is to say their several, and presumably often differ-ent, deserts and entitlements (Flew, 1981, chs. III–IV). But people who share that concept, and accept a definition on those lines, may, and sometimes do, have very different conceptions of justice – very different ideas, that is, both about what different people's deserts and entitlements are, and about the proper grounds of desert and entitlement.

Third, Winch continues: "MacIntyre seems to be saying that certain standards are taken as criteria of rationality because they *are* criteria of rationality." Why, please, is this thought to be heinous? Suppose we discover that the Kachin word previously rendered as 'rationality' in fact refers to a wholly different concept, then this merely shows that we have been mistranslating. Suppose that the two terms are perfectly equivalent, then we have no alternatives to choose between. It is only if, though they are not perfectly equivalent, they do have a great deal in common that we are warranted to speak of two concept(ion)s of rationality. But to object now to the insistence that what they have in common – what makes them both concept(ion)s of rationality – is rationality is to align yourself with old Marshal Saxe. (It was he who, according to legend, wanted reassurance that the planet which we all call Uranus really is Uranus.)

Fourth, we must be cautious about following Winch and others in accepting extensive and intractable disagreements as evidence that those who differ thus must have different concepts, or even different conceptions falling under the single concept of rationality. We should remember that people may be awkward or careless in their handling of a concept which they do in fact share with others more careful or more competent. The fact, for instance, that I get nearly all the logical exercises wrong is not good evidence that I am master of an alternative concept of deduction. If in the end we have nevertheless to conclude that the Kachins or the Azande or whoever else have a different conception of rationality, then we certainly do not, whether for that or for any other reason, have to accept that 'our standards and theirs' are equally good or equally bad; and hence that 'their' witchcraft, oracles and magic are cognitively on all fours with 'our' science.

Consider, for example, some of the doctrinally infatuated sayings of one of those currently applying 'A Strong Programme for the Sociology of Belief' to the natural sciences. At the beginning of chapter 2 of *Scientific Knowledge and Sociological Theory* the author writes: "If due weight is given to the preceding arguments, no particular set of natural beliefs [= beliefs about Nature] can be identified as reasonable, or as uniquely 'the truth'" (Barnes, 1974, p. 22; and compare Flew, 1982b). If the passage from which that sentence is drawn stood alone then it might perhaps be construed in some alternative, more charitable, way. But before the chapter ends Barnes brings ridicule upon himself by ridiculing a rival sociologist's claims to know what in my young day our elders used to pick out as 'the facts of life'. Poor Steven Lukes, who might for generational and other reasons have hoped for more gentle treatment, is put down for his "rampant inductivism". More outrageous still, "Lukes refers to the ignorance of physiological paternity among some people and their 'magical' notions of conception; he regards these notions as in violation of objective rationality criteria without making any attempt to show why" (Barnes, 1974, p. 36).

I imagine that Lukes, like most contemporary adults, knows them to be not so much "in violation of objective rationality criteria" as plain false. That is why he does not propose to insult his readers by suggesting that they are, unlike him, still infantile innocents; that they need someone else to spell out for them that, and how, these 'facts of life' are indeed, objectively and absolutely, known to be true.

3   The primacy of the untheoretical language of public description

Winch seems never to have asked himself how the first anthropologists to take the field acquired their knowledge of the languages peculiar to the peoples they wished to study. Of course most of the earliest anthropologists, like most of their successors today, began by employing bilingual or multilingual helpers. But then the question to press is how these helpers first acquired their knowledge of a second language. Certainly the *English–Zande* or *English–Nuer Dictionary* did not descend immaculate from heaven, miraculously endowed with inexpugnable authority. Someone had somehow to master these to them foreign languages before anyone could be in a position to compile such dictionaries of equivalents. And presumably that someone would have started, and indeed would have had to start, by establishing an elementary vocabulary of terms for ostensible objects and ostensible operations; a sort of Basic Zande or Basic Nuer.

All this is fundamental, and carries equally fundamental implications. Let us assume that the would-be language learner is an anthropologist, or would-be anthropologist; and, since he or she will be the foreigner, let us call the persons whose language is to be learnt the natives. Now to understand native utterances the anthropologist has to relate them not only to one another but also to the non-linguistic world. For by simply discovering logical relations between utterances he is not discovering what any of these thus related utterances itself actually means. Suppose that he learns that *p* implies *q,* that *q* is incompatible with *r,* and so on. Then he has learnt to operate what is for him still only an uninterpreted calculus. To establish the bridgehead indispensable for further advance the anthropologist has to discover the meanings of some native sentences. He has, that is to say, to discover what it is that these sentences are used to assert, or to ask, or to command, as the case may be.

   To achieve this the anthropologist does not necessarily have to find any equivalent in his own language, much less any straightforward and not too unwieldy equivalent. After all, when he originally learnt his own mother tongue he had no other language into which to translate anything. What is essential is that the first sentences to be mastered must in some way refer to something which is observable by all concerned, the natives and the anthropologists both. And if we had really been from the beginning born into a world other than that of our parents and teachers, if we had been altogether unable to perceive anything of what is around us and to know truths about that shared environment, then we could never have even begun to learn what is for us our mother tongue.

Maybe there are no widgets where the anthropologist comes from, and maybe his own language previously lacked a single word for these devices. But, unless both he and the natives are able to identify widgets if and when these do make their appearance, then the native equivalent of 'He is carrying a load of widgets round the kraal' cannot serve as one of their bridgehead sentences. Once a bridgehead has been established, however, a whole new world of communicational possibility opens up. Any number of additional notions can be explained either in terms of those already mutually understood and/or by reference to other common or potentially common experience – experience, of course, always and only in what was on pp. 38–9, above, distinguished as the everyday or public sense.

We can even come to understand statements about our own or someone else's experience – in that more artificial and private sense in which a person's dreams are elements in their experience. Yet, here as everywhere else, we can only know that we mean by the words we use what others mean by these same words in so far as there is a permanent possibility of a cross-check. When they report that they are having yellow after-images do they mean the same as I mean by 'yellow'? Yes, surely; but iff they apply that word to describe substantially the same collections of publicly observable objects as I do (Flew, 1961, ch. II).

The implications of all this are of the last importance, both for philosophy in general and for the philosophy of social science in particular. In general, and for a very big start, they must render any non-solipsistic form of philosophical idealism untenable. We just cannot, consistent with these implications, communicate, and know that we are communicating, any disbelief in or sceptical doubt about the mind-independent existence of what philosophers since Descartes have dubbed 'the External World' – what M. F. D. Young and his associates dismiss as "a *metaphysical* 'out there'". For, as we have argued, it is only and precisely in so far as we are able genuinely to perceive (and not merely seem to perceive) and truly to know (and not simply claim to know) truths about objects and ongoings in 'the External World' that we can master any language in which to communicate with one another; or perhaps any language at all (Flew, 1971, chs. IX–X).

It is also notably prejudicial and perverse to describe the situation as represented by such philosophical scepticism about 'the External World' as *our* cognitive predicament. For, for each of us, everyone else must be an inhabitant of that "*metaphysical* 'out there'"; hence, putatively, forever inaccessible. But, once we know that other people share our predicament, then already we must know, both that there really is, and quite a lot else about, that not merely perceived but also actual reality (Lenin, 1908; and compare Flew, 1978, ch. X and 1976a, ch. I, secs. 2–3).

Furthermore, and much more immediately relevant, all the basic notions of logic are and cannot but be involved from the beginning in any learning of a language. Even before we have words for all these ideas we have to be ready to make some distinctions between the true and the false, between the equivalent and the non-equivalent, between what follows necessarily and what is incompatible. So to insist upon logical propriety, rejecting contradiction and requiring validity in proposed deductions, is not arbitrarily to impose some external authority. For to tolerate contradiction in utterance is: not only to speak incoherently, by taking away what you have said out of one side of your mouth by what you are now saying out of the other; but also to reveal your indifference to truth, since you do not scruple to assert both the true and the false indifferently. 'Deduction' is itself defined in terms of contradiction; in as much as a valid deductive argument is one in which it is impossible, without self-contradiction, simultaneously to assert the premises and to deny the conclusions.

It was, therefore, an outrageous violation of the presuppositions of honest communication and truth-seeking inquiry when Herbert Marcuse borrowed a motto from Adorno and Horkheimer – "The general concept which discursive logic has developed has its foundations in the reality of domination" – and went on to contend that we have to be emancipated, apparently willy-nilly, from the allegedly artificial and oppressive doctrine that "contradictions are a fault of incorrect thinking" (Marcuse, 1964, chapter 5; and compare MacIntyre, 1970, pp. 75–9). No wonder that that Modern Master's sympathies were more with *Soviet Marxism* than with the "repressive tolerance" contradictorily attributed to liberal societies!

All the fundamental notions of elementary logic are necessary to the learning of any language because the anthropologist, or any other language-learner, does not know what he can say except in so far as he also knows what he cannot say. That is why his progress is so much faster when he has the help of a native speaker than it would be if he had to try to pick everything up by simply observing the linguistic behaviour of native speakers; just as ours was when we learnt our mother tongues with the assistance of our mothers and other elders. The crux is that the learner can put questions to the helper; and the helper can, when that answer is, as it so often is, correct, give the answer 'No'. 'Have I got it right', the learner can ask, 'and, if not, what should I have said?'

So our conclusion must be that, if our anthropologists really are confronted with different conceptions of rationality, then the common element which makes them all conceptions of rationality must be or include whatever is essential for learning any language, and hence for determining what anyone is saying about anything.

The relativism presented by Winch in *The Idea of a Social Science* and later writings refers in the first instance only to those sciences, and to anthropology in particular. Thomas Kuhn in his enormously influential book *The Structure of Scientific Revolutions* and in later papers, has presented a similar doctrine in the context of the natural sciences. But Kuhn's contentions have been welcomed by many people working in the natural sciences, and applied there too. It will, therefore, be both relevant and rather piquant to end this chapter 7 by bringing out that and why Kuhn himself, as an historian of ideas – and thus under our wide definition a social scientist – cannot consistently maintain the characteristic contentions put forward as fruits of that study.

Giving his 'Reflections on my Critics' Kuhn writes: "Granting that neither theory of a historical pair is true, they nonetheless seek a sense in which the later is a better approximation to the truth. I believe that nothing of that sort can be found." Like Young and his associates, and like other sociologists of belief, he believes that it is (nearer to) the objective truth to deny that there is any such truth; and so, like them, he derides those who "wish ... to compare theories as representations of nature, as statements about 'what is really out there'" (Lakatos and Musgrave, 1970, p. 265).

But, of course, while Kuhn is actually doing historical work he has to recognize that some scientists offer more or less good reasons for or against even what he calls paradigms, and that some paradigms are either more fruitful or themselves nearer the truth than others. Thus, in discussing paradigm changes – shifts of allegiance, that is, from one to another of two supposedly incommensurable theoretical structures not susceptible of any independent critical appraisal – Kuhn tells us: "Because scientists are reasonable men, one or another argument will ultimately persuade many of them. But there is no single argument that can or should persuade them all" (1970, p. 157).

Here a first caveat has to be interjected. Kuhn is, like so many others, collapsing the distinction between proof and persuasion. Certainly all reasonable people should, and to the extent that they are both reasonable and equipped to deal with the particular field will, be persuaded that a valid proof does indeed constitute a valid proof. But the fact that someone, and that someone an otherwise reasonable and relevantly well-equipped person, refuses to be persuaded by some material is not a sufficient reason for concluding that that material does not constitute a valid proof. It is, therefore, always wrong to argue direct from the fact that people are not persuaded to the conclusions that no valid proof has been presented to them; and doubly wrong to speak neither of proving something nor of persuading someone but of proving or failing to prove something *to* someone; when what you mean is that you have failed, perhaps through no fault either of yours or of your presented proof, to persuade them.

The second necessary caveat is that, even where "there is no single argument that can or should persuade them all" there may well be, especially in human affairs, accumulations so overwhelming that the reasonable man has no alternative but to concede that the case is proved to the hilt. Abundant illustrative examples are ready to hand both in the Law Reports and in the writings of historians.

Again, in the same 'Reflections' Kuhn writes: "Something must make at least a few scientists feel that the new proposal is on the right track . . ." (1970, p. 157). How odd it is that he never asks himself: 'On the right track for where? What are the scientists trying to do?' Kuhn is here like those who tell us – oh so knowingly – that science is not concerned to discover truth, because scientists commend certain theories as fruitful rather than as true. Yet what is this good fruit if it is neither truth nor some better approximation to it?

Yet again, Kuhn writes: "The . . . comparison of two successive theories demands a language into which at least the empirical consequences of both can be translated without loss or change . . . that theories can be compared by recourse to a basic vocabulary consisting entirely of words which are attached to nature in ways that are unproblematic and, to the extent necessary, independent of theory." Indeed it does. For, if there really was no available vocabulary uninfected by either of the rival theories, then neither could be tested by reference to theory-independent facts, and maybe falsified. Kuhn, however, denies that any "such vocabulary is available . . . Successive theories are thus incommensurable" (1970, pp. 206–7).

But now, in what vocabulary does Kuhn or any other historian of science begin to describe one of these paradigm changes? Obviously he begins by employing only the ordinary untechnical and untheoretical vocabulary of whatever language he himself is working in. Nor does he find it impossibly difficult to describe the crucial observations and experiments in neutral terms, even though the protagonists perhaps relied on their own loaded technicalities.

They may, in writing up their own experiments, have mentioned gains or losses of phlogiston, or the chemical combinations of oxygen and carbon, whereas the historian can and will describe the scenes in their laboratories in the sorts of ways in which these might have been described by acute but innocent persons totally ignorant of any chemical theory at all. When he wants to introduce any of the theoretical notions of either of the rival paradigms he will do this, as the original sponsors of these paradigms must at some stage themselves have done, by explaining these novelties in the untheoretical and untechnical terms of the vernacular – supplementing his explanations in words with various sorts of showing as and when necessary.

Suppose someone now suggests that even an ordinary, untechnical vocabulary must be itself theoretically loaded. Then the reply has to be that it can be, and is, at least "to the extent necessary, independent of theory". The favourite example here used to be talk about the sunrise, the suggestion being that all such talk is necessarily loaded with pre-Copernican astronomical theory. This example was especially popular in debates about the so-called Ordinary Language philosophy, spokespersons for which frequently employed it to bring out that they were not, in insisting that it is sound, idiomatic, untechnical English to describe a sunrise as a sunrise, committing either themselves or anybody else to any theory for explaining the observed phenomena. Such talk is purely observational rather than explanatory. Its terms can be, and are, defined ostensively.

Even opponents who had been exposed to Ordinary Language philosophy in its Oxford homeland were wont to brandish this same sunrise example in triumph, just as if their exultant objection had never been pre-empted (Gellner, 1959). But nowadays it is usual, in urging the thesis that the vocabulary of even the most concrete and down-to-earth vernacular cannot but be theory-loaded, to offer somewhat more sophisticated grounds. The key idea is that observers, by applying any of these terms in reporting their observations, cannot help making claims which go far beyond the provision of a narrowly non-committal record of their own private experience. To say, for instance, that you can see a glass of milk on the table is to say something which carries a load of implications: both about the origins of the substance in the glass; and about what would or will happen if various things were or are done to or with it. So, it is argued, even this most innocent and detached of observer's reports really involves the application of an elaborate theory; theory necessary in order to classify and thus to some extent to explain that observer's private experience, his sense-data.

The key idea here is certainly correct, even though some might feel uneasy, and hesitate before applying any descriptions hinting speculative precariousness. Nor was it 'theories' at this most fundamental level which Kuhn and others have been discussing. So even the more sophisticated objection constitutes no sufficient reason to withdraw the crucial contention: "that theories can be compared by recourse to a basic vocabulary consisting entirely of words which are attached to nature in ways that are unproblematic and, *to the extent necessary,* independent of theory" (Italics supplied).

Finally, let it be in summary emphasized once again that Kuhn and others, both in presenting their findings and in finding them, make assumptions which they themselves claim that they have found to be false. Some will be reminded of how Sir Karl Popper – a far, far greater man, who was later to publish a book entitled *Objective Knowledge* – apparently became in *The Logic of Scientific Discovery* committed to the intolerably paradoxical, grossly false conclusion that there is no such thing: ". . . we must not look upon science as a 'body of knowledge', but rather as . . . a system of guesses . . . of which we are never justified in saying that we know that they are 'true' or 'more or less certain' or even 'probable'" (Popper, 1934, p. 317; and compare pp. 280–1).

At the start of chapter 4 of *Scientific Knowledge and Sociological Theory* we are assured that we have just been shown "how the culture of natural science may be made intelligible without recourse to externally based 'objective' assessments of the 'truth' of its beliefs or the rationality of its activities" (Barnes, 1974, p. 69). But if, truly, "the sociologist cannot single out beliefs for special consideration because they are *the* truth" (p. 22), then what does Barnes himself think he is doing in thus presenting to a wider public this particular collection concerning *Scientific Knowledge and Sociological Theory*? Are these thus recommended beliefs, too, no more than "the informal understandings negotiated among members of an organized intellectual community" (Young, 1971, p. 117) – one particular Edinburgh sept of the sociological clan?

The truth is, as we have seen, that the anthropologist has to start by establishing some vocabulary shared with his tribe. It is only upon this basis that he can begin to ask his distinctively anthropological questions. In the same way the historians of science investigating paradigm changes has to have some vocabulary shared with both his two tribes if he is to begin to understand what the conflict was about, and perhaps to hope to appreciate its development better than its participants did. If the rival systems really were irredeemably opaque to one another they would both, presumably, be equally or more opaque to the latter-day historian. But no, he and "we are suitors for agreement from everyone else, because we are fortified with a ground common to all" (Kant, 1790, bk I, mom. 4, sec. 19, p. 82).

4 Deploying 'a new machine of war'

In 1569, Gentian Hervet, secretary to the Cardinal of Lorraine, published a Latin translation of the works of Sextus Empiricus. The latter was a physician, living in the second century AD, and his two surviving books constitute a compendium of the arguments of the Classical Greek sceptical philosophers, above all of Pyrrho of Elis. Hervet's aim has been summed up as being "to employ Pyrrhonism to undermine the Calvinist theory, and then advocate Catholicism on a fideistic basis". He and others thus "constructed 'a new machine of war' to reduce their opponents to a 'forlorn scepticism' in which they could be sure of nothing" (Popkin, 1960, pp. 68 and 69).

These tactics were for a time enormously successful. Of course Protestant spokesmen saw, and said, that "The 'new machine of war' appeared to have a peculiar recoil mechanism which had the odd effect of engulfing the target *and* the gunner in a common catastrophe" (p. 79). For, in so far as the demoralizing sceptical conclusions were correct, there could be no sufficient ground for thinking one coherent system of religious belief more likely than any other to be true. (The most that could be offered by way of rational apologetic was something like Pascal's Wager – an argument which, after conceding that "Reason can decide nothing here", concludes that it would nevertheless be insanely imprudent not to endeavour to persuade ourselves into the Catholic faith (Flew, 1971, ch. VI, sec. 7).)

Although theoretically powerful, this Protestant response was in practice ineffective. All were agreed that any indefinite suspension of religious belief was not to be endured: our eternal destiny – Hell or Heaven – depended on believing, and believing right. And the place and period was one in which almost anyone was bound to plump for the Old Firm if he saw himself as having, with no balance of grounds either this way or that, to make a bet.

'This is perhaps all very well', readers may be saying to themselves, 'but why has the author started to go on about the Reformation and the Counter-Reformation and fideistic Catholicism?' The reason is that in recent years some people, very different from Gentian Hervet and his friends, have, from some of the materials tested earlier in the present chapter 7, constructed another 'new machine of war'. For a description of that successor in action, at the Polytechnic of North London, we go to three senior members in – a very apt title! – *The Rape of Reason*.

In chapter 3, 'Attack on Knowledge', they write: "An amalgam of relativism and Marxism is the main weapon. The extreme relativist reduces criteria of knowledge either to personal taste and opinion or to the tenets of the culture ... The concept of academic knowledge ... is a part of bourgeois ideology. This is the corroding of the ... foundations." Again: "There is emphasis on the social construction of reality, and a systematic ignoring of the external objective existence of the natural world." Armed with these weapons it is now Marxist-Leninist Revolutionaries, not Roman Catholic Counter-Reformers, who approach the prospective recruit: "They systematically sneer, argue and threaten him out of any steady beliefs and values ... The emotional pressure is intense, however crude, superficial and ignorant the attacks." Finally: "The security of a tight-knit group and an all-embracing world view are offered, and many are glad to accept" (Jacka, and others, 1975, pp. 41, 43, 41 and 42).

8 Who truly Wants to Know?

Some years before the First World War, a Parisian periodical asked some of the most prominent French figures in the various branches of what we would now call the social sciences, and which were known at that time in France as *les sciences morales,* about what they regarded as the most essential method in their field. While other respondents sent back learned methodological disquisitions, Georges Sorel replied in one word: 'honesty'.

Stanislav Andreski, *Social Sciences as Sorcery,* p. 232

What a man would like to be true, that he more readily believes.

Francis Bacon, *Novum Organum,* bk I, sec. 49, p. 226

Suppose that someone gives vent to utterances which others, whether rightly or wrongly, consider to be perverse, contrary to manifest fact, scandalous, immoral or in some other way beyond the pale. Then, in these permissive and latitudinarian days, someone else is almost bound to come forward with the eirenic suggestion that, whatever else might be said to their discredit, both the beliefs expressed in those utterances, and the believer, must be allowed to have been totally sincere. To this complacently charitable response it would be as appropriate as uncommon to respond in turn that such a concession constitutes a paradigm case of praising with faint damns. For, to anyone seized of the enormous possibilities of wishful thinking, of self-persuasion and of self-deception, to allow that the speaker was at least guiltless of plain, conscious, calculated mendacity can scarcely appear generous. Neither can the fulfilment of so universal and absolute an obligation serve as the basis for awarding any kind of diploma. To warrant that we need something more: perhaps that the speaker's pronouncements were, however mistaken, an outcome of a sincere and open-minded search for the truth; or that he is already obeying his proposed practical imperatives, however unacceptable to us, at some cost of self-sacrifice for himself.

Certainly Georges Sorel was calling for honesty in more than the narrow and minimal understanding. Yet it still needs to be noted, before going after more, that even the minimum is not always supplied – not even in the physical and medical sciences. For instance: under the headline 'The professor is a fraud' *The Economist* recently reported, along with many other cases in what was itself an incomplete collection, how "a highly respected worker in the field of cancer research was exposed as having painted black areas on experimental mice to simulate the results he desired", and that the "federal food and drug administration had to move against one of the country's leading cardiologists, a professor of medicine at the University of California at Irvine, for reporting false results with patients" (21 January 1984).

The most notorious recent British case of what is alleged to have been the direct falsification of test results – in the everyday rather than the philosophical sense of 'falsification' – is that of the late Sir Cyril Burt. But IQ testing belongs to an area adjacent rather than central to the social sciences. What is shamefully common there, or here, is suppression and misrepresentation of a different, less positive and calculated kind. Two specimens from a bulging file will have to, and should, suffice.

First, in a volume of essays professing to examine the record of the 1974–9 Labour administrations in achieving "far greater economic equality – in income, wealth and living standards", none of the professional social scientist contributors so much as mentions the top rates of taxation introduced by Dennis Healey in the first of his thirteen budgets – in partial fulfilment of his wildly applauded party conference promise "to make the rich howl in agony". These top rates were, starting from what were by OECD standards low thresholds, 83 per cent on earned and 98 per cent on investment income. One economist contributor, without making or referring to any attempt to show either that these rates were not high or that they were not in fact paid, simply dismissed, what on his own sheer authority, he called "the myth that the top 20 per cent of household incomes ... are highly taxed" (Bosanquet and Townsend, 1980, pp. 5 and 41).

Three years later, in *Encounter* for April 1983, a social sciences spokesperson – two of his other interventions were scrutinized in chapter 1, section 2, above – accused the 1974–9 administrations of being "unwilling or unable to impose any effective discipline on the rich ..."; but again without mentioning the imposition of those top tax rates; and again without noticing that he and the others had elsewhere tacitly conceded their effectiveness by execrating "the present regime" for its lowering of those rates, in a first budget, to, respectively, 60 and 75 per cent.

Second, in a *New Society* article entitled 'Is Britain turning into a police state?' (2 August 1984), published during an exceptionally violent and protracted strike, a university Lecturer in the Sociology of Law concluded: "The police are bearing the brunt of the miners' resentment, deflecting attention from the sources of the conflict"; which, in his view, apparently, lay in "a law and order government ... unconcerned about destroying the social preconditions of consensus policing" (p. 56). Anyone unfamiliar with either the present state of British sociology or the present editorial policies of *New Society* will, surely, find it hard to believe that nowhere in this article was there any mention of the fact that heavy police casualties have been incurred in defending the something between a quarter and a third of the miners resolved to continue working – defending them and their families against the assaults of striking miners resolved to deny any 'right to work' to this dissenting minority.

To gross misstatements and suppressions committed by able and tolerably well-informed persons the most constructive response is to grasp every opportunity of pointing out that none of them, surely, would resort to illicit or questionable means of persuasion if only they were in a position to put forward a comprehensive and compelling case, straightforwardly establishing whatever it is that they wish to establish. In the same way we ought, both when confronted with sneering misrepresentations of positions dear to us, and when ourselves inclined similarly to misrepresent the positions of opponents, to try hard to remember that all such deliberate distortion is to be construed as tantamount to a confession that the positions actually held by the person or persons thus misrepresented are more difficult, if not impossible, truly to refute. Important though all this is, however, there is much more to be made of Sorel's reply.

1   Sincerity, rationality and monitoring

The essential is to seize and never to let go one very simple point about the necessary relations of ideas. Yet this is one of those simple, fundamental points which have wide and often devastating application. In these respects indeed it resembles the distinction embodied in Hume's Fork (chapter 5, above). For that too was itself a point about the necessary relations of ideas; but one which, put to aggressive use by Hume, enabled him to conclude his *Enquiry concerning Human Understanding* with a famous purple peroration. (This was later to add the sole touch of colour to many an otherwise black-and-white essay in Logical Positivism. It begins by asking, rhetorically: "When we run over libraries, persuaded of these principles, what havoc must we make?" It ends with an instruction which Hume would certainly not have wanted anyone to take literally: "Commit it then to the flames, for it can contain nothing but sophistry and illusion"!)

The essential point to be hammered home here refers to the necessary relations between the ideas of sincerity, rationality and monitoring. Sincerity in any purpose whatsoever absolutely pre-supposes a strong concern to discover whether and how far that cherished purpose has been or is being achieved. Furthermore, if and in so far as the agent becomes aware that it has not been or is not being achieved, we cannot, unless there is a readiness to attempt alternative tactics, truly say that that purpose continues to be sincerely harboured.

Rationality comes into the picture since not Descartes only, but all the rest of us also, preferred, or prefer, to estimate the actual intentions and the sincere beliefs of other people, and even of ourselves, by looking to what is done, or not done, rather than to what – with whatever appearances of impeccable integrity – is merely said. Ultimately there is no alternative. For, as we began to appreciate in discussing the presuppositions of language-learning, we cannot identify a particular belief as such unless we attribute some minimal rationality to the behaviour of the believer (chapter 7, section 3, above).

Suppose, for example, that a member of the tribe under investigation utters words which we are initially inclined to render into English as 'I am a macaw'. And suppose too that, not greatly to anyone's surprise, they do not act as we should expect a rational person to act if they genuinely believed that they had been transformed into something non-human. (Anyone requiring here some imaginative stimulus is recommended to reread Kafka's nightmare novelette *Metamorphosis*.) The moral which the anthropologist should draw is: not that this tribe is, by the making of such strange utterances, shown to harbour a different conception of rationality; much less that, since its members are not rational animals, they are by Aristotelian standards not human at all. Instead, and more modestly, he should recognize that he has misunderstood the utterance rendered as 'I am a macaw'. Presumably it ought to have been construed as an idiomatic way of identifying with the macaw totem. (Compare, perhaps, the restaurant idiom in which diners are said or claim to be their chosen dishes. If I say, in such a context, 'I am a turkey and mushroom pie', then I am neither reporting an unprecedented metamorphosis nor – for that matter – claiming membership of a totem.)

Returning now to the necessary connection between sincerity of purpose and the monitoring of progress towards the end proposed, suppose that someone proclaims a Quest for the Holy Grail. And suppose then that, almost before the fanfares have died, they settle for the first antique-seeming mug offered by the first fluent rogue in the local bazaar. We surely have to say that this neglect of any systematic inquiry, this total lack of interest in either the true history of the purchase put in the place of honour on the mantelpiece or the evidence that perhaps the real thing does survive somewhere, all conspire together to show that, whatever else they may have been after, it certainly was not to unearth and acquire the vessel actually employed in the original Last Supper.

Again, since many find it hard to accept that such a down-to-earth point can be enforced by an illustration so far-fetched, consider two more pedestrian alternatives. Suppose someone professes to be in business in order, no doubt among other things, to turn a profit; or suppose that the captain of a cricket team says that he is playing, no doubt again among other things, in order to win. Then what credence could we give to these professions if there is no care to keep, in the one case, accounts and, in the other, the score?

The next step is to relate the logical linkages displayed above to the main methodological recommendations of Sir Karl Popper. He makes proposals, which are of course close kin the one to the other, for the spheres of both theoretical science and practical policy. In each case Popperian methodology can be seen as the direct and necessary outcome of sincerity in the appropriate purposes. It is the more worthwhile to represent these recommendations in this way in as much as he himself seems never to have done so. His apparent reluctance, and the consequent failure to deploy what is perhaps the most powerful supporting argument, are probably to be explained by reference to a generous yet unrealistic reluctance to recognize discreditable distractions or even sheer bad faith in any of his academic opponents.

The aim of theoretical science is truth. Given this aim the critical approach must follow. The person whso truly wants the truth, like the knight who with pure heart and single mind seeks the Holy Grail, cannot and will not embrace unexamined candidates. He must and will be ever ready to test, and test and test again. But testing for truth is in this context precisely what criticism is.

Although anything subjected to tests always may and sometimes or often will fail to pass those tests, rejection – as has been emphasized more than once before – is neither a necessary nor a sufficient condition of criticism. What is essential is for the critic to be raising and pressing relevant questions. Does what is proposed cohere or are there internal inconsistencies? Is it compatible with whatever else we know or believe that we know? What is the evidence, and is it sufficient to establish what is being asserted? If the claims made are true, then what else follows? And so on; and on and on.

Among those assuming that to be critical it is sufficient to reject, and boasting therefore of their own comprehensively critical approach, it is easy to find performances which tend to support Bertrand Russell's wry aphorism: "Most people would sooner die than think. In fact they do." Thus the second sentence of the first paragraph of the Introduction to a collection said by one reviewer to be rich in "hard, cold, realistic scholarship" reads: "Throughout history the middle and upper classes ... have given to the working classes as little and as poor an education as possible" (Rubinstein and Stoneman, 1972, p. 7). As its sole support for that first claim the paragraph concludes with a statement of the flat contrary. This is from "Lord George Hamilton, a former education minister, who declared that 'what was wanted was to give to the children of the working man a sound, a compact and a thorough education in those subjects which children during the limited time they were at school could master' (*The Times*, 25 November 1891)."

For marginally more exacting meta-critical exercise examine the inference drawn in the second of two sentences to be quoted from an essay on 'Education or Examination'. The author was said by his Editors to have torn up his examination scripts "at Hull ... then led a student occupation of the university buildings". He wrote, in the present essay: "But when some universities have 30 per cent failure rates and others 3 per cent rates, the failure from one institution would have been a success at another. The huge fluctuations between various failure rates indicate one thing clearly: that the existing system of examinations is a *random process of selection*" (Cockburn and Blackburn, 1969, p. 99). The invalidity of this inference, an inference proudly underlined by its drawer, provides a welcome target of opportunity for the reproach of a poet–scholar, who had himself in his younger days suffered at the hands of Finals examiners: "Three minutes thought would suffice to find this out; but thought is irksome, and three minutes is a long time" (Housman, 1931, p. xi).

Whereas the single aim of theoretical science is truth, the purposes of practical policies, and of the institutions established for the implementation of those policies, and the fulfilment of those purposes, are as multifarious as human desires. Yet parallel considerations apply here too. If, therefore, you want to claim that it was in order to secure some particular reliefs of man's estate that the policy was originally introduced, and that it is with those objectives that it is sustained still; then you have to show that both those who first introduced, and those who now support and sustain, that policy, and those institutions, were, and are, eager to monitor their success or failure by that stated standard. Indeed the originators would have been well advised to make sure that the policy itself embraced provisions both for monitoring and for adjustment in response to its discoveries; while those manning the institution, in so far as they are individually devoted to its official collective aims, will, usually anyway, find themselves doing a deal of detailed and informal monitoring every day of their working lives.

From this we can learn something about Popper's advocacy of piecemeal, reformist social engineering; as opposed to its wholesale, revolutionary opposite. It should be recognized as the consequence and expression of his sincere and rational commitment to the welfare of the socially engineered. For his crucial objection to the wholesale Utopian variety precisely is that this must make the monitoring of success, and thus the cybernetic correction of failure, impossible. So we have an obvious Popperian answer to the question, 'Just how wide-ranging and upsetting does a programme have to be before its implementation ceases to count as piecemeal, and begins to rate as wholesale, social engineering?' It is: 'Just so soon as it becomes impossible effectively to monitor success or failure, and to make cybernetic corrections of perceived mistakes.'

Popper himself says: "... the reconstruction of society is a big undertaking which must cause considerable inconvenience to many and for a considerable span of time. Accordingly, the Utopian engineer will have to be deaf to many complaints: in fact it will be part of his business to suppress unreasonable objections. (He will say, like Lenin, 'You can't make an omelette without breaking eggs.') But with it, he must invariably suppress reasonable criticism also" (Popper, 1945, vol. I, p. 160). In this perspective it is easy to see how inept it would be to describe the enormous exercises of social engineering made possible by the Bolshevik October Coup as features of 'that great social experiment in Russia' – notwithstanding that these were in the twenties and the thirties frequently so described. In the compulsory collectivization of agriculture, for instance, there was not and is not any willingness to change course if and when it could or can be shown that non-socialist agriculture is more productive, and/or that people anyway much prefer to work their individual plots.

Especially perhaps in a period when one of the two British parties of government regularly threatens to enforce, just so soon as it can, "irreversible changes", and when more of our academics than ever before claim the Marxist name, there can be no more appropriate ending to the present discussion than a manifesto of Popperian politics; with its cooling card for the trumpeted pretensions of 'Scientific Socialism'. The adoption of his recommendations, Popper suggests, "might lead to the happy situation where politicians begin to look out for their own mistakes instead of trying ... to prove that they have always been right. This – and not Utopian planning or historical prophecy – would mean the introduction of scientific method into politics, since the whole secret of scientific method is a readiness to learn from mistakes" (1945, vol. I, p. 163).

The early part of section 1 above explicated the logically necessary connections between sincerity of purpose, rationality, and the monitoring of success or failure in fulfilling such sincerely adopted purposes. We then saw how a recognition of these connections can be exploited to produce compelling justifications for Popper's main methodological recommendations. We will now begin to show – there is space for no more than a couple of extensive hints – how explosive are the implications for the criticism both of the functioning of the Welfare State machine and of the motivations of many of those who man that machine.

The first hint comes from Britain, and from the world of social work. A recent review is full of material revealing the almost universal unwillingness in that world to monitor results. Thus, referring to a major official report, the joint authors note how "The Committee mention without comment that an irritant to many doctors is the lack of interest of many workers in the social services, and even among the academics, in evaluating the results of their work" (Brewer and Lait, 1980, p. 24). Although they make a point of adding that they themselves share the irritation of these doctors, neither these authors nor the Committee bring out the shocking significance of this indifference. It is, surely, as we are now in a position to see all too clearly, that many such professional benefactors (literally, do-gooders) are not in fact much interested in what and how much good they are actually doing.

This nasty suggestion is, alas, abundantly confirmed by later observations. Referring to one extremely unrepresentative social worker – a potential blackleg is ever there was one! – attending a lecture about the findings of one of the all too few monitoring studies, the same authors write: "Sheldon was greatly disturbed by the ineffectiveness . . . which the study revealed. But he goes on to say: 'I was much more worried (and still am) by the complacent smiles of colleagues all around me.' He characterizes the typical response among social workers to demonstrations of their ineffectiveness as: 'let's pretend nothing of importance has happened'" (1980, p. 184).

Rather than reiterate the same painful and purely negative moral, it is perhaps better to proceed to a smore general and constructive point. It is that those who are in truth both sincerely and single-mindedly devoted to the doing of some subset of all the enormously various goods, which the ever-proliferating institutions of the Welfare State are supposedly established and maintained to do, should have little difficulty in meeting the challenge which the newly established Social Affairs Unit has begun to put to the personnel of these institutions. The SAU is arguing that the burden of proof should be on the professionals, and on the controlling bureaucracies, themselves to show that the goods actually being done are commensurate both in number and in nature with the expenditures currently devoted to their doing (Anderson, 1981a, pp. 29–31). For, for those professionally interested parties, it is all too easy to obstruct any independent investigations which may succeed in getting started; or, failing that, at least to seem thoroughly to discredit the findings of such independent investigations (Anderson, 1980, ch. 1).

Genuinely devoted professionals should have no difficulty in meeting this challenge: both because they are the insiders; and because it is a presupposition of the genuineness of their devotion that they will already have been monitoring the success or failure of their own work. If all our social workers really were as keen to benefit their clients as the British Association of Social Workers assures us that they are, then we should hear far fewer complaints than we do about failures either to make reports or to keep records (Brewer and Lait, 1980, pp. 65–6 and passim).

The second hint comes from what calls itself "The community

mental health movement in the United States". This 'movement' consists in all who 'person' programmes launched under the Community Mental Health Centers Act of 1963. This was passed in response to a Message to the Congress on 'Mental Health and Mental Retardation', dated 5 February 1963. President Kennedy made it absolutely clear what good results were desired. Demanding "a bold new approach" he emphasized that "prevention is far more desirable for all concerned" than cure. Without himself specifying any illustrative examples, he called for "selective specific programs directed at known causes".

Fifteen or more years later a collective of contributors published what was announced as the first of a series of *Annual Reviews of Community Mental Health*. All concerned are members of this 'movement'; and therefore have, it must be added, strong and obvious personal stakes in the continuation and extension of these programmes. Judging by the contents, and still more by what it does not contain, no one expected it to be studied by any critical outsider. For with this book – as with Sherlock Holmes and the dog barking during the night – the most remarkable thing is what does not happen. Nowhere from beginning to end does there occur one single reference, whether direct or indirect, to any evidence that any of these programmes has actually succeeded in reducing the incidence of mental retardation or mental illness; or even in holding it down below the higher level to which it might perhaps otherwise have been expected to rise.

Had there in fact been any such demonstrated successes, we can be sure that this book would have been full of allusions to them. And, furthermore, everyone who had joined and was remaining in 'the movement' with the prime intention of helping to prevent or cure such manifestly evil afflictions would now be rejoicing in the successes already achieved; while anyone proposing fresh initiatives towards similar ends would have been eager to learn and to apply the lessons to be drawn from those past achievements.

The unlovely truth is, however, quite otherwise. These proud "prevention professsionals", professing carers and compassionists though they be, do not, it seems, feel constrained even to pretend to have fulfilled any part of the beneficent (do-gooding) mandate with which they were charged. Yet they are no whit disturbed by what, for all that they themselves have to say to the contrary, appears to have been their expensive and total failure actually to prevent any specifiable and determinate evils.

Instead – with some sideswipes against certain notoriously callous and uncaring Conservatives, suspected of contemplating what to all these people would be cruel cuts in both their programme and, indirectly, their individual budgets – some of them now propose, with no awkward self-questioning about past failures, so to reinterpret the expressions 'mental disease', 'mental disorder', and 'mental retardation', as to facilitate demands for (yet more) further funding and extra staff. This and this alone, they suggest, will enable another and more ambitious kind of good to be done; albeit with equally little reason offered for believing that they will have any more success in attaining these different though no doubt equally worthy objectives (Price and others, 1980, p. 286, also chs. 1 and 10 passim; and compare Flew, 1982c).

In the perspective of the present chapter the most revealing as well as the most scandalous feature of the entire *Annual* is the form taken by a solitary statement of the need for some systematic monitoring of success and failure. Except for this rare moment of illumination all the contributors, like most other members of this and similar 'movements' both there and here, are inclined blindly to identify (their) stated intentions with (their) actual achievements. Because, they argue, our intentions were and are disinterested and beneficent, therefore our actual achievements must inevitably and necessarily be all and only those goods which (we say) we intended; while anyone who questions those actual achievements, or challenges our demands for yet further public funding to secure more of the same, is, upon that ground alone, to be utterly condemned.

Nowhere in this *Annual* is there so much as a hint that some monitoring of actual success or failure is essential to the doing of a decent and progressively improving job. Instead the sole reference to this task points in a quite different direction. A trio of contributors makes what has so far proved to be, from the standpoint of the "community mental health movement in the United States", a quite unwarrantably pessimistic statement: ". . . it is our strong conviction that prevention proponents will lose the political battle for funding without good data – capable of documenting the effectiveness and social utility of prevention programs" (pp. 7 and 288).

2 Radical bad faith, academic and political

One nasty kind of works presented as contributions to the social sciences demands a whole section to itself, however short. For twenty years or more several specimens of this genre have been advertised in successive lists from the major publishers, while the same stuff must be being taught as the latest fashionable gospel in innumerable departments in universities, polytechnics and colleges of education. Yet reviewers rarely treat such material with the harshness it deserves, and almost never challenge the academic and political good faith of the authors. Almost never that is to say, do the reviewers raise and press doubts as to whether these authors are sincerely pursuing truth, and whether their actual political objectives are those to which they themselves pretend to be devoted. (By the way: perhaps the first person to put such charges into print was a lifelong, old-time Social-Democrat, driven from his native Hungary by the Leninists: see Halmos, 1974 and 1976. But they were more fully developed by Gould, who was in consequence much abused by those whom the cap of accusation fitted. Gould was even summoned before the Executive of the British Sociological Association. It seems that they wished: not to determine whether he could prove his charges; but to reproach him for daring to criticize fellow professionals – who were, apparently, to be presumed or even assumed innocent whether or not they had been proved guilty!)

Correctly to appreciate the burden of these accusations we need to develop a contrast between present and earlier generations. Up till World War II and for a decade or two thereafter there was in Britain, as in most similar countries, only one significant organization of the extreme left, the Communist Party (Muscovite). When then members or fellow-travellers of that party maintained that some actual or alleged evil was due to capitalism, they normally accepted the responsibility of labouring to show that in the USSR, under socialism, it either had already disappeared or at least was disappearing. When too they advocated Marxist-Leninist policies as the only answer, they also accepted the corresponding responsibility, to show that the implementation of these policies was in fact delivering the goods, exactly as promised. Whether they did or could succeed in showing what they had to show, is, of course, another story. Here the crucial point is that, to the credit of their sincerity, both academic and political, they tried.

The effluxion of time has, however, made it enormously more difficult to defend the actual results of the recommended revolutionary transformations; while simultaneously giving birth to many other correspondingly converted societies. Perhaps it is for these very reasons that today the usual form is to concentrate exclusively upon 'Western', or 'capitalist', or 'late capitalist' societies; to say or to suggest that everything picked out for condemnation is peculiar to such societies, a product of their distinctive and damnable social system; but then stubbornly to eschew all relevant questions about contemporary socialist societies – or, as is often said, under pressure and for no sufficient reason given, contemporary 'so-called socialist societies'. This is intolerable. It most certainly will not be tolerated by anyone who genuinely wants to know whether these causal claims are true or false.

In a parallel way, no one who has diagnosed 'alienation' as the corrosive endemic evil of a supposedly sick society, and who is sincere in advocating socialism as the only possible remedy, will rest for a moment until he has been able to construct a viable index of alienation, and has discovered the results of applying this first to the workers of a privately owned firm and then to those of a public corporation. One seemingly very fair test would be to apply the test battery first in one of the Fiat Motor Company's Italian plants, and then in the physically identical plant erected by them for the Soviet state in the USSR. If, however, those who go on about alienation in late capitalist society show no concern to discover whether socialism really is an effective cure; then we have no alternative but to conclude that, for them, the appeal of socialism is altogether other.

Some examples are required notwithstanding that, in deference to the British law of libel, we cannot be particular. What, for instance, are we realistically to think either of the scientific integrity or of the humane involvements of those Radical criminologists who say or suggest that delinquency and its mistreatment are the characteristic and ineradicable consequences of a private and pluralist form of economic organization, and that the panacea lies in a total and absolute collectivism; yet all the time without attending for one moment to the experience of the now numerous more or less fully socialist countries? We might perhaps ask how these people continue never to hear of Solzhenitsyn's *The Gulag Archipelago*; were it not for the nasty but not arbitrary suspicion that it is precisely their awareness of the nightmare realities which makes them thus careful to reject the Method of Agreement and Difference (Mill, 1843, bk III, ch. viii, pt 4). In the words of another great Victorian social scientist: "Surely even the weakest-minded must see that our theories of crime … must explain roguery and vagabondage *all over the world …*" (Mayhew, 1861, p. 383).

Again, what score should we give for commitment to either sociological inquiry or human welfare to those who, insolently arrogating to themselves the label 'critical' as a codeword for 'Radical' or 'Marxist', proceed to review the failures of the British welfare state and their putative causes, prescribing socialist revolution as the only cure; and yet remain wholly silent about corresponding phenomena, or the lack of them, in the countries of the Socialist Bloc (Halmos, 1974 and 1976).

Next, as an epitome of all that the present section 2 has been abominating, contemplate the following fine finding: "Social control is a social process occurring continuously within capitalist society, and is a product of the class antagonisms of that society." What more can be said except 'Soviet and East German papers please copy'?

Finally, in order to leave a clean taste in the mouth, let us savour the words of a leading historian of the Netherlands, who was also a great Dutch patriot with a brave record of active wartime Resistance. All this, he said, writing of a far lesser outrage, "not only revolts the scholar in me", and "rouses me to protest" at "the pretence of an empirical investigation"; it also stirs "an irrepressible urge to testify against this false witness and indeed to criticise and oppose a system productive of such pernicious counsels" (Geyl, 1955, pp. 157, 159 and 163).

3 Incentives for the bad, disincentives for the good

Andreski's *Social Sciences as Sorcery* is a rich and worthwhile book, notwithstanding that its abundant materials are neither arranged according to a visible system nor put to the constructive work of showing how things might be improved. Indeed this book itself, like others by the same author, contains several tiresome minor faults which surely would have been removed had the typescript ben read carefully before publication by some sympathetic and well-informed critic. For instance: it is very much to the point to emphasize that a lot of the most important work in the social sciences has been motivated by concerns either for the relief of man's estate and/or that the human condition should not be made worse by misguided attempts to implement counter-productive projects. But it was simply wrong to assert that "Malthus ... began his epoch-making work in order to demonstate the impossibility of James Mill's plans for a perfect society" (Andreski, 1971, p. 144). In fact James Mill, the father of John Stuart Mill, had not published anything substantial before the appearance of the *First Essay*; the full title of which animaadverts to *The Speculations of Mr Godwin, M. Condorcet, and other Writers,* unnamed.

In the first chapter of *Social Sciences as Sorcery* Andreski remarks that this appears to be an area "where anybody can get away with anything". Later chapters do much to sustain this contention. They present case after case of wretched work by people who have nevertheless been able to attain and maintain high rank and status within the sociological profession. These horrid examples of time-serving, of fashion-following, of pretentious pseudo-explanation, of familiar facts deeply disguised as profound fresh discoveries, and so on, constitute a treasury of object-lessons in how not to do social science. The ready availability of this academic Black Museum makes it unnecessary to burden the present volume with anything like so large a collection of illustrations.

The remark quoted in the previous paragraph comes at the end of a discussion of professionalism: "Looking at the matter realistically ... one can find few grounds for assuming that all the professions inherently gravitate towards honest service ... In reality it all depends on what kind of behaviour leads to wealth and status (or, to put it in another way, on the link between true merit and reward) ... Seen from this angle, the social sciences appear as an activity without any intrinsic mechanisms of retribution: where anybody can get away with anything" (1971, p. 16).

Without succumbing to starry-eyed illusions about the existence of areas of human activity in which everything always is what it ideally ought to be, Andreski contrasts this unhappy situation with that in the hard natural sciences. He sees the crucial difference as being that professing social scientists can so much more easily discount apparent falsifications of their hypotheses (p. 38). He puts little or no emphasis upon another difference of which, as was argued earlier, much more should be made. It is that, "whereas most of us have few strong desires to believe this or that about positrons or iguanas or any other elements in the subject-matter of the natural sciences, all of us would very much like to believe, and/or would very much like others to believe, all manner of different things about social affairs and social policies".

If professional promotions and research grants tend to go to people arriving at conclusions congenial to members of the promotions and awards committees, rather than to those single-mindedly dedicated to the pursuit of truth, letting the chips fall where they may; then this is bound to constitute a strong distracting temptation to the ambitious, encouraging them to produce whatever in fact tends to be so rewarded.

Much more insidious and, surely, much more effective are the internal temptations somehow to find our own ways to conclusions which we ourselves are independently inclined to welcome. Certainly we would be doing a power of good if we were able to ensure that the links between merit and reward became as generally satisfactory in the social sciences as they are in the natural. But very few of us are in any position directly to promote that most desirable consummation. What and all that we can do is to force ourselves and others to recognize the necessary marks and preconditions of sincerity of truth-seeking purpose.

Here we have to see, to force others to see, and never to allow ourselves or anyone else to fail to remember, that a general obscurity in assertion and, in particular, evasiveness about what would or would not constitute falsifications of assertions made, are clear signs of insincerity in the search for scientific truth. Popper has famously insisted that the proper criterion for distinguishing scientific from non-scientific utterance is falsifiability (Popper, 1963, ch. 1). If we do not know what would have to occur or to have occurred to show that our utterance expressed a false proposition, then we do not know what if anything we proposed in that utterance. Any kind of indeterminateness in meaning is always bound, and often intended, to disable potential critics. Yet to stubborn dissidents preferring their statements to be true criticism cannot but be welcome. To tolerate either unfalsifiability or any other kind of obscurity is, therefore, to reveal an indifference to truth.

All these salutary points can be rammed home again with a complementary couple of quotations from two very different great Victorians. The first comes from the biologist T. H. Huxley, via his novelist grandson Aldous: "Be clear though you may be convicted of error. If you are clearly wrong you may run up against a fact sometime and get set right. If you shuffle with your subject and study to use language which will give a loophole of escape either way, there is no hope for you" (quoted in Huxley, 1963, p. 63; and compare Orwell, 1970, vol. IV, items 38 and 45).

The second quotation is from a letter of Marx to Engels, dated 15 August 1857. It should be called in evidence during any discussion of the claim made by Engels, in his funeral oration, that Marx as a social scientist was a match for Darwin in biology: "I took the risk of prognosticating in this way, as I was compelled to substitute for you as a correspondent at the *Tribune* ... It is possible I may be discredited. But in that case it will still be possible to pull through with a bit of dialectics. It goes without saying that I phrased my forecasts in such a way that I would prove to be right also in the opposite case" (Flew, 1984, ch. III, sec. 3).

Certainly we need to be ever alert to the possibility that desires to believe and vested interests in believing may, not only in others but also in ourselves, overwhelm what is often the rather weak want to know and to tell the truth regardless. It is, however, much too easy and much too common: either to give an assent so wholehearted that you are misled to infer the absolute impossibility of discovering the truth, the whole truth and nothing but the truth about anything; or else to concur in word only, while in practice never suspecting distortions of interest or desire in some arbitrarily and peculiarly privileged persons – above all yourself.

Since we are all, being human, bound to have some interests in believing this and some desires to believe that, it becomes imperative to insist that, whenever anyone's intersts and desires are mentioned, everyone's must be. If the cards are to be put on the table, then it has to be all the cards, and everyone's. What will not do is what is all too often done; namely, to restrict the revelations to those presenting findings unwelcome to the writer.

Thus in recent years it seems to have become almost established editorial policy for the *Times Educational Supplement* to put down work published by the Centre for Policy Studies or the National Council for Educational Standards as done by people who are committed Conservatives or otherwise 'right-wing'; while preferring not to mention that some of the authors of more congenial findings are members of the Radical Statistics Group or the like. The British Educational Research Association has issued similar statements, again without thinking it appropriate simultaneously to confess the presumably opposite political allegiances of its own members. *New Society* even printed, without Editorial comment or – one trusts – approval, one reader's letter urging that everything coming from the Institute of Economic Affairs ought to be rejected unexamined; for no other or better reason than that that organization is in part financed by gifts from private corporations (21 October 1982). Correspondingly questionable examples could, no doubt, be found at the other end of the political spectrum. But the *TES, New Society* and BERA all have a special importance thanks to the privileged semi-monopoly position which they enjoy in their respective fields.

Once all the cards of interest and allegiance are properly on the table, these cancel out. All parties must have *some* interests and *some* allegiances. Indeed, if the mere facts of having interests in believing or desires to believe had to be accepted as always a decisive disqualification, then no one at all could contribute to the growth of the social sciences. It is, of course, a very different matter to dismiss particular candidate contributors on the given grounds that past experience has exposed them as grossly incompetent, sheerly dishonest, or just unwilling to recognize and to try to counter their own several and peculiar distorting interests and desires.

Andreski, much more than most, has something to say about various sorts of inhibition in the area of the social sciences: both those arising directly from the sensibilities of the potential subject-matter; and those internal to the persons who might initiate investigations. Thus he is, rightly, scathing about "the common tendency to foster international studies not for the sake of finding the truth but for the purpose of cultivating the foreigners' goodwill by writing nice things about them". Also, and equally rightly, he notices the very widespread reluctance to recognize the extremely "important part" played by "corrupt practices ... in social causation", especially in the poorer countries (Andreski, 1971, pp. 56 and 124). It is almost impossible to overstate the effects of these various inhibitions: both, positively, in distorting the pictures which we do get; and, negatively, in ensuring that little or no good work is done in certain areas of practical and/or theoretical importance.

On the positive side, we must never forget that both some institutions in all countries and many whole countries impose various restrictions upon independent investigation; various restrictions up to, and often amounting to, total embargoes. In consequence much more is said and known about the faults of institutions which have exposed themselves generously than about the faults of those which have not. The temptation is to assume, or at least to act as if it was assumed, that the more secretive institutions are superior. But, of course, the always defeasible presumption ought to be that they are the more secretive precisely and only because they have more to hide!

Wherever facilities for research are granted to some but not to others there is danger that those receiving or hoping to receive these privileges will be in some way pressured not to say or to write anything which might offend the relevant authorities. Such privileged researchers need, therefore, to be scrupulous about succumbing to pressures; while all consumers of the resulting reports should be even more than normally critical and suspicious.

The richest source of recent materials on the extent and effectiveness of such pressures, materials which also show a shocking shortage of critical suspicion, is the work of visiting investigators – mainly North Americans – on life in the People's Republic of China during and after the 'Great Leap Forward' and the 'Cultural Revolution'. For it has now become common knowledge that many of these privileged visitors were, on the most charitable view, massively self-deceived.

There has also been at least one case – a case described by the *Wall Street Journal* as "fishy", and by *Time* as "murky" – of a promising visiting scholar whose academic career was aborted. This was, it seems, done: not because his work was anything but excellent and altogether honest – no one outside China denied this; but because, presumably just because his investigations had been so uninhibited and so penetrating, he had fallen foul of the Chinese authorities. Failure to penalize him would result in refusals to grant research privileges in the future (London and Lee, 1984; and compare Hollander, 1981, ch. 7).

On the negative side, we have to notice the many radical inquiries which are either not launched at all or else, if launched, not pressed home, because the most likely investigators are in some way involved in and with the operations about which these radical questions ought to be being asked. Sometimes this is a matter of a very direct, very material interest in not discovering, and/or not making public, what are feared or known to be the true answers. Take, for example, the general question of the effectiveness of social work, and the more particular question of the effectiveness of the courses of training now required of those hoping to secure such employment.

By far the most likely people to undertake research in anything to do with social work, and in one obvious way the best qualified, are the members of the university and polytechnic departments established or expanded in order to run these allegedly essential training courses. With appropriate alterations the same applies to Departments of Education, and to research into any aspect of the educational system; as well as to many other academic sectors, and to their respective objects. University teachers are, after all, hired on the understanding that they will devote roughly half their working hours to teaching and roughly half to research, presumably in some area not too remote from that of their teaching.

Suppose now, what is in fact the case, that there are excellent reasons to suspect that the established courses are, as training for social work, at best useless and at worst counter-productive (Brewer and Lait, 1980, ch. 2 and passim). Then we shall scarcely expect to detect enthusiasm for penetrating investigations among those who make their livings from Departments of Social Work: few people are willing to risk researching themselves out of a job. We ought to be similarly uneasy when we find, as we so often do, that most of those either appointed to the official committees or selected by the media to offer expert opinion are similarly interested. Those who, not without reason, protest against police inquiries into alleged police misdemeanours should be urged to extend the application of the same principle more widely.

Much more important, probably, than the inhibitions and the distortions arising from very direct, very material individual interests are those which spring from a more venial yet equally damaging reluctance to offend colleagues by rocking the boat. It has in recent years been very often remarked in the USA that agencies established to regulate industries tend to become servants of those they were set to regulate, rather than of a more public interest. Specialist journalists exemplify the same phenomenon: Labour Correspondents, for instance, even if they were not originally chosen for these sympathies, tend to side with the union barons; while Education Correspondents defer to all the supply side interest groups, at the expense of the parental and child consumers. It is, after all, hard to do or to say, day after day, things which antagonize people with whom you are, just as regularly, meeting and socializing.

To conclude both section 3 and the entire book let us consider how, and ask ourselves why, a great research opportunity was recently wasted. The London borough of Tower Hamlets had been – as North Americans say – struck by its 275 rank-and-file social workers. They stayed out for ten months. Unlike most, this strike seems not greatly to have inconvenienced anyone. Certainly there were no TV news flashes of desperate clients fighting their way through howling picket lines to secure the services of whatever social workers – 'Scabs! Blacklegs!' – were still social working. At the end of the day the Department of Health and Social Security directed the London Region Social Work Service to produce *The Effect on Clients of Industrial Action in the London Borough of Tower Hamlets: An Investigation.*

The whole affair provided a rare and splendid research opportunity. Clients neglected during the ten months of the strike constituted a perfect group to set against an experimental control group of those not so neglected in some subsequent ten months. It would not be callous researchers who were proposing to deprive the 'clients' of what might or might not be valuable services; but, instead, those 'caring' social workers who had already done so. The wasting of this research opportunity deserves to become – and is hereby becoming – a textbook example.

The report, apparently accepted without any protest either from the Minister himself or from the concerned Department, should leave the critical reader in no doubts about the general quality of the investigation. One single feature is, however, alone totally discrediting. For the two appointed to investigate – who "individualize and personalize" themselves by adding their signatures in facsimile at the end – were asked to find out the effects on *the clients.* Believe it or not, they do not claim to have asked for the views of even one (Lait, 1980, pp. 63–8). So who truly wants to know?

References

This list is intended to include all, but only, those works mentioned in the text. For an obvious reason, works by authors who died before 1900 (and, exceptionally, for works by Lenin), the date given in the text is the date of original publication. Where page numbers are given, however, these refer to the more accessible editions detailed in the reference list. Both dates are given in the reference list, the date of original publication in square brackets and the date of the edition used in round parentheses.

Anderson, D. (ed.) (1980) *The Ignorance of Social Intervention* (London: Croom Helm).

Anderson, D. (ed.) (1981a) *Breaking the Spell of the Welfare State* (London: Social Affairs Unit).

Anderson, D. (ed.) (1981b) *The Pied Pipers of Education* (London: Social Affairs Unit).

Andreski, S. (1972) *Social Sciences as Sorcery* (London: Deutsch).

Andreski, S. (ed.) (1975) *Reflections on Inequality* (London: Croom Helm).

Arblaster, A. (1974) *Academic Freedom* (Harmondsworth: Penguin).

Aristotle (1) (1950) *The Constitution of Athens*, translated by K. von Fritz and E. Kapp (New York: Hafner).

Aristotle (2) (1963) *On Interpretation*, in *Aristotle's Categories and de Interpretatione*, translated by J. L. Ackrill (Oxford: Clarendon).

Aristotle (3) (1926) *Nicomachean Ethics*, translated by H. Rackham (London: Heinemann and New York: Putnam).

Aristotle (4) (1948) *The Politics of Aristotle*, translated by E. Barker (Oxford: Clarendon).

Aubert, V. (1964) 'Law courts and the class structure', in *Sociology of Law* (Oslo: Institute for Social Research).

Austin, J. L. (1961) *Philosophical Papers*, edited by J. O. Urmson and G. J. Warnock (Oxford: Clarendon).

Austin, J. L. (1962) *Sense and Sensibilia,* reconstructed from manuscript notes by G. J. Warnock (Oxford: Clarendon).

Axelrod, R. (1984) *The Evolution of Cooperation* (New York: Basic).

Bacon, F. (1889) *Novum Organum* (Oxford: Clarendon).

Barnes, B. (1974) *Scientific Knowledge and Sociological Theory* (London: Routledge and Kegan Paul).

Bauer, P. (1976) *Dissent on Development* (Cambridge, Mass.: Harvard UP, Revised Edition).

Bauer, P. (1981) *Equality, the Third World and Economic Delusion* (London: Weidenfeld and Nicolson).

Berger, P. L. and Luckmann, T. (1971) *The Social Construction of Reality* (Harmondsworth: Penguin).

Berkeley, G. [1710] (1901) *A Treatise concerning the Principles of Human Knowledge,* in the *Works,* edited by A. C. Fraser (Oxford: Clarendon).

Blackburn, R. (ed.) (1972) *Ideology in Social Science* (London: Collins/Fontana).

Block, W. (1976) *Defending the Undefendable* (New York: Fleet Press).

Bloor, D. (1974) 'Popper's mystification of objective knowledge', *Science Studies,* IV, pp. 65–76.

Bloor, D. (1976) *Knowledge and Social Imagery* (London: Routledge and Kegan Paul).

Bodmer, F. (1943) *The Loom of Language* (London: Allen and Unwin).

Booth, C. (1892–7) *Life and Labour of the People in London* (London: Macmillan).

Borger, R. and Cioffi, F. (eds) (1970) *Explanation in the Behavioural Sciences* (Cambridge: CUP).

Bosanquet, N. and Townsend, P. (eds) (1980) *Labour and Equality* (London: Heinemann).

Bottomore, T. (1984) *Sociology and Socialism* (Brighton: Wheatsheaf).

Boudon, R. (1969) *The Logic of Sociological Explanation* (Harmondsworth: Penguin).

Boudon, R. (1974) *Education, Opportunity and Social Inequality* (New York: Wiley).

Brewer, C. and Lait, J. (1980) *Can Social Work Survive?* (London: Temple Smith).

Broadway, F. (1976) *Upper Clyde Shipbuilders* (London: Centre for Policy Studies).

Bruce-Gardyne, J. (1978) *Meriden: Odyssey of a Lame Duck* (London: Centre for Policy Studies).

Buckle, H. T. (1903) *History of Civilization in England* (London and New York: Longmans Green).

Burnet, J. (Lord Monboddo) (1774) *The Origin and Progress of Language* (Edinburgh).

Burton, J. (1978) 'Private property rights or the spoliation of nature', in S. N. S. Cheung (ed.), *The Myth of Social Cost* (London: Institute of Economic Affairs).

Burton, J. (1979) *The Job Support Machine* (London: Centre for Policy Studies).

Carr, E. H. (1961) *What is History?* (London: Macmillan).

Caton, H. (1984) 'Margaret Mead and Samoa', *Quadrant* (Sydney), March, pp. 28–31.

Coard, B. (1971) *How the West Indian Child is made educationally subnormal in the British School System* (London: New Beacon).

Cockburn, A. and Blackburn, R. (1969) *Student Power* (Harmondsworth: Penguin).

Cohen, G. A. (1972) 'Karl Marx and the withering away of social science', *Philosophy and Public Affairs*, I, 2 (Winter).

Cohen, S. (1972) *Folk Devils and Moral Panics* (London: MacGibbon and Kee).

Comte, Auguste (1830) *Course de Philosophie Positive* (Paris: Bachelier).

Conquest, R. (1967) *The Politics of Ideas in the USSR* (New York: Praeger).

Cox, C. and Marks, J. (1980) *Real Concern* (London: Centre for Policy Studies).

Cox, C. and Marks, J. (1982) 'Cause for concern: research on progress in secondary schools', in C. Cox and J. Marks (eds), *The Right to Learn* (London: Centre for Policy Studies).

Cox, C and Scruton, R. (1984) *Peace Studies: A Critical Survey* (London: Institute for European Defence and Strategic Studies).

Crosland, C. A. R. (1976) *Socialism Now* (London: Cape).

Darwin, C. [1859] (1968) *The Origin of Species*, edited by J. B. Burrow (Harmondsworth: Penguin).

Davie, R., Butler, N. and Goldstein, H. (1972) *From Birth to Seven* (London: Longman).

Dawson, G. (1981) 'Unfitting teachers to teach: sociology in the training of teachers', in D. Anderson (ed.), *The Pied Pipers of Education* (London: Social Affairs Unit).

Descartes, R. [1637] (1931) *A Discourse on the Method*, in *The Philosophical Works of Descartes,* translated by E. S. Haldane and G. R. T. Ross (Cambridge: CUP, Revised Edition).

Diels, Hermann (1906–10) *Die Fragmente der Vorsokratiker* (Berlin: Weidmannische Buchhandlung).

Dilthey, W. (1961) *Meaning in History* (London: Allen and Unwin).

Djilas, M. (1958) *The New Class* (London: Thames and Hudson).

Dray, W. (1957) *Laws and Explanation in History* (London: OUP).

Durkheim, E. [1895] (1964) *The Rules of Sociological Method*, translated by S. A. Soloway and J. H. Mueller and edited by G. E. Catlin (Glencoe, Illinois: Free Press).

Durkheim, E. [1897] (1967) *Le Suicide: étude de sociologie* (Paris: Presses Universitaires de France).

Durkheim, E. [1918] (1965) *Montesquieu and Rousseau: Forerunners of Sociology*, translated by R. Mannheim (Ann Arbor: Michigan UP).

Engels, F. [1844] (1967) *Outlines of a Critique of Political Economy*, in W. O. Henderson (ed.), *Engels: Selected Writings* (Harmondsworth: Penguin).

Engels, F. [1845] (1971) *The Condition of the Working Class in England*, translated and edited by W. O. Henderson and W. H. Challoner (Oxford: Blackwell).

Engels, F. [1878] (1934) *Herr Eugen Dühring's Revolution in Science*, alias *Anti-Dühring*, translated by E. Burns and edited by C. P. Dutt (London: Lawrence and Wishart). Engels drew on three chapters from this book to compose what has probably been the most widely circulated of all Marxist works, *Socialism: Utopian and Scientific*.

Engels, F. [1884] (1940) *The Origin of the Family, Private Property and the State*, translated by A. West and D. Torr (London: Lawrence and Wishart).

Engels, F. [1888] (1934) *Ludwig Feuerbach and the Outcome of German Classical Philosophy*, no translator named, edited by C. P. Dutt (London: Martin Lawrence).

Farrington, B. (1965) *Science and Politics in the Ancient World* (London: Allen and Unwin, Second Edition).

Ferguson, A. [1767] (1966) *An Essay on the History of Civil Society*, edited by D. Forbes (Edinburgh: Edinburgh UP).

Ferguson, A. (1792) *Principles of Moral and Political Science* (London and Edinburgh).

Festinger, L., Riecken, H. W. and Schachter (1956) *When Prophecy Fails* (Minneapolis: Minnesota UP).

Flew, A. G. N. (1956) 'Theology and falsification', in A. Flew and A. C. MacIntyre, *New Essays in Philosophical Theology* (London: SCM Press).

Flew, A. G. N. (1961) *Hume's Philosophy of Belief* (London: Routledge and Kegan Paul).

Flew, A. G. N. (ed.) (1964) *Body, Mind and Death* (New York and London: Collier-Macmillan).

Flew, A. G. N. (1971) *An Introduction to Western Philosophy* (London: Thames and Hudson).

Flew, A. G. N. (1973) *Crime or Disease?* (London: Macmillan).

Flew, A. G. N. (1975) *Thinking about Thinking* (London: Fontana/ Collins, 1975. Also as *Thinking Straight* (Buffalo, NY: Prometheus).

Flew, A. G. N. (1976a) *Sociology, Equality and Education* (London: Macmillan).

Flew, A. G. N. (1976b) 'Ideology and "a new machine of war"', *Philosophy*, XLV.

Flew, A. G. N. (1976c) 'A substitute for sociology', in *Question Nine* (London: Pemberton). This is a Critical Notice of Rockwell.

Flew, A. G. N. (1978) *A Rational Animal* (Oxford: Clarendon).

Flew, A. G. N. (1981) *The Politics of Procrustes* (London: Temple Smith).

Flew, A. G. N. (1982a) 'Another idea of necessary connection', *Philosophy*, LVII.

Flew, A. G. N. (1982b) 'A strong programme for the sociology of belief', *Inquiry* (Oslo), XXV.

Flew, A. G. N. (1982c) 'The spending cure', in *Policy Review* (Washington, D.C.), Winter, pp. 178–84.

Flew, A. G. N. (1983a) 'Good Samaritans become Procrusteans', in K. Jones and J. Stevenson (eds), *The Yearbook of Social Policy in Britain 1982* (London and Henley: Routledge and Kegan Paul).

Flew, A. G. N. (1983b) *Education, Race and Revolution* (London: Centre for Policy Studies).

Flew, A. G. N. (1984) *Darwinian Evolution* (London: Granada/Paladin).

Flew, A. G. N. (1985) 'Prophecy or philosophy, historicism or history', in C. Wilson (ed.), *Marx Refuted* (Oxford: Pergamon).

Freeman, D. (1983a) *Margaret Mead and Samoa* (Cambridge, Mass.: Harvard UP).

Freeman, D. (1983b) 'Inductivism and the test of truth: a rejoinder to Lowell D. Holmes and others', *Canberra Anthropology*, VI (October), pp. 101–92.

Freeman, D. (1984) '"O Rose thou art sick!"', *American Anthropologist*, LXXXVI (June), pp. 400–5.

Friedman, M. and R. (1980) *Free to Choose* (London: Secker and Warburg).

Gardiner, P. L. (1952) *The Nature of Historical Explanation* (London: OUP).

Gellner, E. A. (1959) *Words and Things*. Also in paperback (Harmondsworth: Penguin, 1968).

Gellner, E. A. (1973) *Cause and Meaning in the Social Sciences* (London: Routledge and Kegan Paul).

Geyl, P. (1955) *Debates with Historians* (London: Batsford).

Ginsberg, M. (1956) *The Diversity of Morals* (London: Heinemann).

Gould, J. and others (1977) *The Attack on Higher Education* (London: Institute for the Study of Conflict).

Grigg, J. (1980) *1943: The Victory that Never Was* (London: Hill and Wang).

Grimble, A. (1952) *A Pattern of Islands* (London: Murray).

Halévy, E. (1928) *The Growth of Philosophical Radicalism*, translated by Mary Morris (London: Faber and Faber).

Hall, S. (1976) 'Violence and the media', in N. Tutt (ed.), *Violence* (London: DHSS).

Halmos, P. (1974) 'The moral ambiguity of critical sociology', in R. Fletcher (ed.), *The Science of Society and the Unity of Mankind* (London: Heinemann).

Halmos, P. (1976) Review article on the 'Ideology of welfare', *Times Higher Education Supplement*, 18 June 1976.

Hardin, G. (1977) 'The tragedy of the Commons', in G. Hardin and J. Baden (eds), *Managing the Commons* (San Francisco: W. H. Freeman).

Hayek, F. A. (1944) *The Road to Serfdom* (London: Routledge and Kegan Paul).

Hayek, F. A. (1948) *Individualism and Economic Order* (Chicago: Chicago UP, 1948).

Hayek, F. A. [1952] (1979) *The Counter-Revolution of Science* (Indianapolis: Liberty).

Hayek, F. A. (ed.) (1954) *Capitalism and the Historians* (Chicago: Chicago UP).

Hayek, F. A. (1967) *Studies in Philosophy, Politics and Economics* (London: Routledge and Kegan Paul).

Hayek, F. A. (1978) *New Studies in Philosophy, Politics, Economics and the History of Ideas* (London: Routledge and Kegan Paul).

Herodotus (1910) *The History of Herodotus*, translated by G. Rawlinson (London: Dent and New York: Dutton).

Hollander, P. (1981) *Political Pilgrims* (Oxford: OUP).

Hollis, M. and Lukes, S. (eds) (1982) *Rationality and Relativism* (Oxford: Blackwell).

Hollis, N. and Nell, E. (1975) *Rational Economic Man* (Cambridge: CUP).

Honey, J. (1983) *The Language Trap* (London: National Council for Educational Standards).

Hook, S. (1943) *The Hero in History* (New York: John Day).

Hook, S. (1975) *Revolution, Reform and Social Justice* (Oxford: Blackwell).

Housman, A. E. (1931) *Juvenalis Saturae* (Cambridge: CUP, Revised Edition).

Hudson, W.D. (ed.) (1969) *The Is/Ought Question* (London: Macmillan).

Hume, D. [1739–40] (1974) *A Treatise of Human Nature*, edited by L. A. Selby-Bigge with revisions by P. Nidditch (Oxford: Clarendon).

Hume, D. [1748] (1975) *An Enquiry concerning Human Understanding*, in *Hume's Enquiries*, edited by L. A. Selby-Bigge with revisions by P. Nidditch (Oxford: Clarendon).

Hume, D. [1779] (1947) *Dialogues concerning Natural Religion*, edited by N. Kemp Smith (Edinburgh: Nelson).

Huxley, A. (1936) *The Olive Tree* (London: Chatto and Windus).

Jacka, K., Cox, C. and Marks, J. (1975) *The Rape of Reason* (London: Churchill).

James, R. (1980) *Return to Reason: Popper's Thought in Public Life* (Shepton Mallet, Somerset: Open Books).

Jarvie, I.C. (1973) *Functionalism* (Minneapolis: Burgess).

Jefferson, J. M. (1974) 'Industrialization and poverty: in fact and fiction', in N. Gash (ed.), *The Long Debate on Poverty* (London: Institute of Economic Affairs).

Jefferson, J.M. (1975) 'The concern with inequality in Victorian fiction', in A. Jones (ed.), *Economics and Equality* (Deddington, Oxon: Philip Allan).

Jencks, C. and others (1973) *Inequality: A Reassessment of the Effect of Family and Schooling in America* (London: Allen Lane).

Jones, C. (1977) *The £200,000 Job* (London: Centre for Policy Studies).

Kafka, F. (1961) *Metamorphosis, and other stories*, translated by W. and E. Muir (Harmondsworth: Penguin).

Kant, I. [1790] (1917) *A Critique of Aesthetic Judgement*, translated by J. G. Meredith (Oxford: Clarendon).

Kautsky, K. (1964) *The Dictatorship of the Proletariat*, translated by H. J. Stenning (Ann Arbor: Michigan UP).

Keynes, J. M. (1904) *The Scope and Method of Political Economy* (London: Macmillan).

Kuhn, T. (1962) *The Structure of Scientific Revolutions* (Chicago: Chicago UP).

Lakatos, I. and Musgrave, A. (eds) (1970) *Criticism and the Growth of Knowledge* (Cambridge: CUP).

Lait, J. (1980) 'Central Government's ineptitude in monitoring local welfare', in A. Seldon (ed.), *Town Hall Power or Whitehall Pawn* (London: Institute for Economic Affairs).

Laurenson, D. (ed.) (1978) *The Sociology of Literature: Applied Studies* (Keele, Staffs: Keele UP).

Leach, E. (1970) *Lévi-Strauss* (London: Fontana/Collins).

Lenin, V. I. [1902] (1970) *What is to be Done?*, translated by S. V. and P. Utechin (London: Panther).

Lenin, V. I. [1908] (1952) *Materialism and Empirio-Criticism*, no translator named (London: Lawrence and Wishart).

Lenin, V. I. [1917] (1939) *State and Revolution*, no translator named (London: Lawrence and Wishart).

Lenin, V. I. [1918] (1934) *The Proletarian Revolution and the Renegade Kautsky*, no translator named (New York: International).

Lenin, V. I. [1922] (1947) 'Our Revolution', in *The Essentials of Lenin*, no translator named (London: Lawrence and Wishart).

Lessnoff, M. (1974) *The Structure of Social Science* (London: Allen and Unwin).

Lévi-Strauss, C. (1955) *Tristes Tropiques* (Paris: Librairie Plon).

Lewis, M. (1980) *The Culture of Inequality* (New York: New American Library and London: New English Library).

Locke, J. [1690] (1975) *An Essay concerning Human Understanding*, edited by P. Nidditch (Oxford: Clarendon).

London, M. and Lee, T. (1984) 'Broken faith: Steven Mosher, Stanford and China', *American Spectator*, February, pp. 15–17.

Lukács, G. (1960) *The Historical Novel* (London: Merlin). The original Russian publication was in 1937.

Lukes, S. (1974) 'Relativism: cognitive and moral', *Proceedings of the Aristotelian Society*, supp. vol. XLVIII.

Lundberg, G. (1963) 'The postulates of science and their implications for sociology', in M. Natanson (ed.), *Philosophy of the Social Sciences* (New York: Random House).

MacIntyre, A. C. (1970) *Marcuse* (London: Fontana/Collins).

Malinowski, B. (1922) *Argonauts of the Western Pacific* (London: Routledge).

Malinowski, B. [1944] (1960) *A Scientific Theory of Culture* (New York: OUP).

Malthus, T. R. [1798] (1970) *An Essay on the Principle of Population*, edited by A. Flew (Harmondsworth: Penguin) – The *First Essay*.

Malthus, T. R. [1802] *An Essay on the Principle of Population* (London: Sixth Edition, 1826) – the *Second Essay*.

Malthus, T. R. (1817) *1817 Appendix*. This is an appendix to what is presented as the Fifth Edition of Malthus [1798]. It is reprinted in the Sixth, the last to be revised by the author. This was in truth the Fifth Edition of Malthus, 1802.

Malthus, T. R. [1824] (1953) 'A summary view of the principle of population', in D. V. Glass (ed.), *An Introduction to Malthus* (London: Watts).

Mandeville, B. de [1723] (1970) *The Fable of the Bees,* edited by P. Harth (Harmondsworth: Penguin).

Marcuse, H. (1961) *Soviet Marxism* (London: Routledge and Kegan Paul).

Marcuse, H. (1964) *One Dimensional Man* (London: Routledge and Kegan Paul).

Marx, K. [1843] (1975) 'A contribution to the critique of Hegel's Philosophy of Law: Introduction', in K. Marx and F. Engels, *Collected Works* vol. III (London: Lawrence and Wishart).

Marx, K. [1844] (1964) *The Economic and Philosophical Manuscripts of 1844,* translated by M. Milligan and edited by D. J. Struik (New York: International).

Marx, K. [1847] (1936) *The Poverty of Philosophy*, no translator named (London: Lawrence and Wishart).

Marx, K. [1852] (1934) *The Eighteenth Brumaire of Louis Bonaparte,* no translator named (Moscow: Progress).

Marx, K. [1859] (1970) *A Contribution to the Critique of Political Economy*, translated by S. W. Ryazanskaya and edited by M. Dobb (Moscow: Progress).

Marx, K. [1867] (1961–2) *Capital,* translated by S. Moore and E. Aveling (London: Lawrence and Wishart).

Marx, K. and Engels, F. [1845] (1975—) *The Holy Family,* translated by R. Dixon and C. Dutt, in K. Marx and F. Engels, *Collected Works* (London: Lawrence and Wishart), vol. IV, pp. 5–211.

Marx, K. and Engels, F. [1846] (1964) *The German Ideology,* edited by S. Ryazanskaya, no translator named (Moscow: Progress). Although this work was finished in 1846 it was first published, in the original German, in 1932.

Marx, K. and Engels, F. [1848] (1967) *The Communist Manifesto,* translated by Samuel Moore and edited by A. J. P. Taylor (Harmondsworth: Penguin).

Mayhew, H. (1861) *London Labour and the London Poor* (London: Griffin).

Mayhew, H. (1862) *The Criminal Prisons of London* (London: Griffin).

Mead, M. (1943) *Coming of Age in Samoa* (Harmondsworth: Penguin).

Meek, R. L. (1953) *Marx and Engels on Malthus* (London: Lawrence and Wishart).

Merton, R. K. (1963) *Social Theory and Social Structure* (New York: Free Press).

Michels, R. (1959) *Political Parties,* translated by E. and C. Paul (New York: Dover).

Mill, J. S. (1843) *A System of Logic, Ratiocinative and Inductive* (London: Longmans Green). Also Sixth Edition 1865.

Mille, R. de (1976) *Castaneda's Journey: The Power and the Allegory* (Santa Barbara: Capra).

Mille, R. de (ed.) (1980) *The Don Juan Papers: Further Castaneda Controversies* (Santa Barbara: Ross Erikson).

Moore, G. E. (1903) *Principia Ethica* (Cambridge: CUP).

Morgan, P. (1978) *Delinquent Fantasies* (London: Temple Smith).

Nagel, E. (1961) *The Structure of Science* (London: Routledge and Kegan Paul).

Namier, L. B. (1952) *Avenues of History* (London: Hamilton).

Newton. I. [1687] (1962) *Principia Mathematica Philosophiae Naturalis*, translated by A. Motte, revised and edited by F. Cajori (Berkeley and Los Angeles: California UP).

Newton, I. [1704] (1952) *Opticks*, edited by I. B. Cohen (New York: Dover).

Oakeshott, M. (1966) 'Historical continuity and causal analysis', in W. Dray (ed.), *Philosophical Analysis and History* (New York: Harper and Row).

O'Neill, J. (ed.) (1973) *Modes of Individualism and Collectivism* (London: Heinemann).

Orwell, G. (1945) *Animal Farm* (London: Secker and Warburg).

Orwell, G. (1950) *Nineteen Eighty-Four* (London: Secker and Warburg).

Orwell, G. (1970) *Collected Essays* (Harmondsworth: Penguin).

Papineau, D. (1978) *For Science in the Social Sciences* (London: Macmillan).

Parkinson, C. N. (1981) *The Law* (Harmondsworth: Penguin).

Parsons, T. (1968) *The Structure of Social Action* (New York: Free Press).

Pateman, T. (ed.) (1972) *Counter Course: A Handbook for Course Criticism* (Harmondsworth: Penguin, 1972).

Plato (1) (1963) *The Republic*, translated by P. Shorey (London: Heinemann and Cambridge, Mass.: Harvard UP).

Plato (2) (1952) *The Laws*, translated by R. B. Bury (London: Heinemann and Cambridge, Mass.: Harvard UP).

Polanyi, G. and P. (1976) *Failing the Nation: The Record of the Nationalized Industries* (London: Fraser Ansbacker).

Popkin, R. H. (1960) *The History of Scepticism from Erasmus to Descartes* (Assen: van Gorcum).

Popper, K. R. (1934) *The Logic of Scientific Discovery* (London: Hutchinson, 1959).

Popper, K. R. [1945] (1956) *The Open Society and its Enemies* (London: Routledge and Kegan Paul).

Popper, K. R. (1957) *The Poverty of Historicism* (London: Routledge and Kegan Paul).

Popper, K. R. (1963) *Conjectures and Refutations* (London: Routledge and Kegan Paul).

Popper, K. R. (1979) *Objective Knowledge* (Oxford: Clarendon).

Popper, K. R. (1982) *The Open Universe; An Argument for Indeterminism* (London: Hutchinson).

Pratt, V. (1978) *The Philosophy of the Social Sciences* (London: Methuen).

Price, R. H., Ketterer, R. F., Bader, B. C. and Monahan, H. (eds) (1980) *Prevention in Mental Health: Research, Policy and Practice* (Beverley Hills and London: Sage).

Pryke, R. (1981) *The Nationalized Industries: Policies and Performance since 1968* (Oxford: Martin Robertson).

Quinney, R. (1970) *The Social Realities of Crime* (Boston: Little, Brown).

Randi, J. (1982) *Flim-Flam!* (Buffalo: Prometheus).

Rawls, J. (1971) *A Theory of Justice* (Cambridge, Mass.: Harvard UP and Oxford: Clarendon).

Redwood, J. (1980) *Public Enterprise in Crisis* (Oxford: Blackwell).

Richardson, K. and Spears, D. (eds) (1972) *Race, Culture and Intelligence* (Harmondsworth: Penguin).

Robertson, W. (1890) *The Works of William Robertson* (Edinburgh).

Robbins, L. (1949) *An Essay on the Nature and Significance of Economic Science* (London: Macmillan).

Rockwell, J. (1974) *Fact in Fiction* (London: Routledge and Kegan Paul).

Rottenberg, S. (ed.) (1973) *The Economics of Crime and Punishment* (Washington: American Enterprise Institute).

Routh, J. and Wolff, J. (eds) (1978) *The Sociology of Literature: Theoretical Approaches* (Keele, Staffs.: Keele UP).

Rowntree, B. S. (1901) *Poverty, a Study of Town Life* (London: Macmillan).

Rubinstein, D. and Stoneman, C. (eds) (1972) *Education for Democracy* (Harmondsworth: Penguin).

Rubner, A. (1979) *The Price of a Free Lunch* (London: Wildwood House).

Runciman, W. G. (ed.) (1978) *Weber: Selections in Translation*, translated by E. Matthews (Cambridge: CUP).

Runyon, D. (1950) *Runyon on Broadway* (London: Constable).

Ruskin, J. (1876) Various letters in vol. XXVIII of *The Works of John Ruskin* (London: G. Allen and New York: Longmans Green, 1903–12).

Ruskin, J. (1899) *Unto this Last* (London: G. Allen).

Ryan, A. (1970) *The Philosophy of the Social Sciences* (London: Macmillan).

Sarup, M. (1982) *Education, State and Crisis: A Marxist Perspective* (London and Henley: Routledge and Kegan Paul).

Schelling, T. (1978) *Micromotives and Macrobehaviour* (New York: Norton).

Schwartzschild, L. (1948) *The Red Prussian* (London: Hamish Hamilton).

Seldon, A. (ed.) (1978) *The Economics of Politics* (London: Institute of Economic Affairs).

Seligman, E. R. A. (1907) *The Economic Interpretation of History* (New York: Columbia UP).

Senior, W. N. (1829) *Two Lectures on Population*, with the correspondence between the author and T. R. Malthus (London: Saunders etc.).

Sextus Empiricus (1955) *Works*, translated by R. G. Bury (London: Heinemann and Cambridge, Mass.: Harvard UP).

Shaw, B. (1983) *Comprehensive Schooling: The Impossible Dream?* (Oxford: Blackwell).

Skinner, A. S. and Wilson, T. (eds) (1976) *Essays on Adam Smith* (Oxford: Clarendon).

Skinner, B. F. (1938) *The Behavior of Organisms* (New York: Appleton-Century-Crofts).

Skinner, B. F. (1971) *Beyond Freedom and Dignity* (New York: Knopf and London: Cape).

Smith, A. [1776] (1979) *An Inquiry into the Nature and Causes of the Wealth of Nations*, edited by R. H. Campbell and A. S. Skinner (Indianapolis: Liberty).

Smith, K. (1951) *The Malthusian Controversy* (London: Routledge and Kegan Paul).

Solzhenitsyn, A. (1974–8) *The Gulag Archipelago*, translated by T. P. Whitney and H. T. Willets (London: Fontana/Collins).

Sowell, T. (1975) *Race and Economics* (New York and London: Longman).

Sowell, T. (1980) *Knowledge and Decisions* (New York: Basic).

Sowell, T. (1981a) *Ethnic America: A History* (New York: Basic).

Sowell, T. (1981b) *Markets and Minorities* (New York: Basic).

Sowell, T. (1981c) *Pink and Brown People* (Stanford: Hoover).

Sowell, T. (1983) *The Economics and Politics of Race* (New York: William Morrow).

Speake, J. (1984) *A Dictionary of Philosophy* (London: Macmillan and Pan).

Sumner, W. G. (1940) *Folkways* (Boston: Ginn).

Thouless, R. H. (1930) *Straight and Crooked Thinking* (London: Hodder and Stoughton).

Thurrow, L. (1969) *Poverty and Discrimination* (Washington, D.C.: Brookings Institution).

Toulmin, S. E. (1953) *The Philosophy of Science* (London: Hutchinson).

Townsend, P. (1979) *Poverty in the United Kingdom* (Harmondsworth: Penguin).

Trevor-Roper, H. R. (1957) *Historical Essays* (London: Macmillan).

Trudgill, P. (1975) *Accent, Dialect and the School* (London: Edward Arnold).

Veblen, T. (1899) *The Theory of the Leisure Class* (London and New York: Macmillan).

Weber, M. (1904) ' "Objectivity" in social science and social policy', in *The Methodology of the Social Sciences,* translated by E. A. Shils and H. A. Finch and edited by E. A. Shils (Glencoe, Ill.: Free Press, 1949).

Weber, M. (1917) 'The meaning of "value-freedom" in sociology and economics', in *The Methodology of the Social Sciences,* as above.

Wendt, A. (1983) 'Three Faces of Samoa: Mead's, Freeman's and Wendt's', *Pacific Islands Monthly,* April, pp. 10–13, 69.

West, E. G. (1975) *Education and the Industrial Revolution* (London: Batsford).

Whately, R. [1832] (1855) *Lectures on Political Economy* (Oxford: Parker).

Wiles, P. (1974) 'Explaining violence and Social Work Practice', in *The Lawbreakers* (London: BBC).

Wilson, B. (ed.) (1970) *Rationality* (Oxford: Blackwell).

Wilson, J. Q. (1977) *Thinking about Crime* (New York: Vintage).

Winch, P. (1958) *The Idea of a Social Science* (London: Routledge and Kegan Paul).

Wittfogel, K. A. (1981) *Oriental Despotism: A Comparative Study of Total Power* (New York: Random House, Vintage Edition with a new Foreword by the author).

Wittgenstein, L. (1922) *Tractatus Logico-Philosophicus,* translated by C. K. Ogden (London: Kegan Paul, Trench, Trubner). As well as this Authorized Version there is also a Revised – more accurate but inferior as literature.

Young, M. F. D. (ed.) (1971) *Knowledge and Control* (London: Collier-Macmillan).

Index of Names

Index of Notions